Node.js 6.x Blueprints

Create stunning web applications and Restful APIs
from start to finish with Express, Loopback, MongoDB,
and MySQL using this definitive guide

Fernando Monteiro

[PACKT] open source*
PUBLISHING   community experience distilled

BIRMINGHAM - MUMBAI

Node.js 6.x Blueprints

First published: August 2016

Production reference: 1220816

Published by Packt Publishing Ltd.
Livery Place
35 Livery Street
Birmingham
B3 2PB, UK.
ISBN 978-1-78588-843-4

www.packtpub.com

Credits

Author

Fernando Monteiro

Reviewer

Magesh Kuppan

Commissioning Editor

Amarabha Banerjee

Acquisition Editor

Manish Nainani

Content Development Editor

Mayur Pawanikar

Technical Editor

Karan Thakkar

Copy Editors

Vikrant Phadke
Safis Editing

Project Coordinator

Nidhi Joshi

Proofreader

Safis Editing

Indexer

Mariammal Chettiyar

Production Coordinator

Nilesh Mohite

About the Author

Fernando Monteiro is a full-stack engineer, speaker, and open source contributor. He has built and made some of his personal projects open source, such as Responsive Boilerplate, Frontend Boilerplate, Angm-Generator, and TrelloMetrics, written in AngularJS, Node.js, Less, and SASS.

With around 16 years of experience in information technology, his current focus is on web and mobile JavaScript applications. He has a strong understanding and experience with all phases of the software engineering life cycle, including source control, design, build/release, and automated testing.

He has worked as a manager of e-commerce, and a UX designer for various companies and products, including mobile applications.

When not programming, Fernando enjoys riding Harley Davidson bikes, making his own beer, and watching movies with his family.

You can find him on LinkedIn at
`https://br.linkedin.com/in/fernando-monteiro-69881b28/en`.

The following are his previous books with Packt Publishing:

Instant HTML5 Responsive Table Design How-to in April 2013 :

`http://www.amazon.com/Instant-HTML5-Responsive-Table-Design/dp/1849697264/ref=sr_1_3?s=books&ie=UTF8&qid=1454389499&sr=1-3&keywords=Fernando+Monteiro`.

Learning Single Page Web Application Development in December 2014:

`http://www.amazon.com/Learning-Single-Page-Application-Development/dp/1783552093/ref=sr_1_6?s=books&ie=UTF8&qid=1454389499&sr=1-6&keywords=Fernando+Monteiro`.

AngularJS Directives Cookbook in November 2015 :
`http://www.amazon.com/AngularJS-Directives-Cookbook-Fernando-Monteiro/dp/1784395897/ref=sr_1_1?s=books&ie=UTF8&qid=1454389499&sr=1-1&keywords=Fernando+Monteiro`.

I would like to say thank you to all my family, who supported me in this journey–especially my mother, Paschoalina Patrizzi – for their strength and perseverance in life. And to all of the Packt Publishing crew who helped me with one more book.

About the Reviewer

Magesh Kuppanis a freelance consultant and trainer on web technologies with over 17 years of experience. Everything about technology excites him.

> *I am grateful to my parents, without whom I would not be what I am today. I am also thankful to my wife for she has been instrumental in all my efforts. Thanks to my little son who brings bliss to my life.*

www.PacktPub.com

eBooks, discount offers, and more

Did you know that Packt offers eBook versions of every book published, with PDF and ePub files available? You can upgrade to the eBook version at `www.PacktPub.com` and as a print book customer, you are entitled to a discount on the eBook copy. Get in touch with us at `customercare@packtpub.com` for more details.

At `www.PacktPub.com`, you can also read a collection of free technical articles, sign up for a range of free newsletters and receive exclusive discounts and offers on Packt books and eBooks.

`https://www2.packtpub.com/books/subscription/packtlib`

Do you need instant solutions to your IT questions? PacktLib is Packt's online digital book library. Here, you can search, access, and read Packt's entire library of books.

Why subscribe?

- Fully searchable across every book published by Packt
- Copy and paste, print, and bookmark content
- On demand and accessible via a web browser

Table of Contents

Preface

Web applications with Node.js are increasingly popular and accessible to all developers. Today, with the growing evolution of Node.js, we can see numerous companies using this technology for the development of their applications. Among them, we can mention Netflix, Paypal, and many others who use Node.js in production environments.

The hosting companies also made a breakthrough by supporting Node.js on their platforms. Plus, many building tools, such as task runners, generators and dependence managers, emerged using the Node.js engine, such as Grunt, Gulp, Bower, and more.

Throughout the book, we will show you how to build and deploy Node.js applications from scratch by using all the resources available on the Node.js ecosystem and exploring cloud services for testing, image manipulation, and deployment.

Dealing with all these tools and getting the best out of them all is a very interesting and motivating task.

We will also introduce the concept of Docker containers and continuous integration using different tools and services.

Over the course of our book, we will see how to get the best out of this development method using the latest and greatest technologies to build ten applications from start to end.

Enjoy!

What this book covers

Throughout this book, we'll explore different ways to build Node.js Applications and understand what elements make up a basic blog page using MVC design patterns. We will learn how to deal with different types of view templates such as EJS and SWIG and more complex stuff using command-line tools to deploy and run applications.

We will cover fundamental concepts of the Restful API architecture and client-side communication using jQuery, React.js and Angular.js.

Although some points are advanced, you'll be prepared to understand the core concepts of Node.js applications, and how to deal with different types of database's such as MongoDB, MySQL, and the Express and Loopback frameworks.

Chapter 1, *Building a Twitter-Like Application Using MVC Design Patterns,* shows the main concepts of the MVC pattern applied to Node.js applications using the Express framework, mongoose ODM middleware, and MongoDB database. We see how to deal with user sessions and authentication using Passport middleware.

Chapter 2, *Building a Basic Website Using MySQL Database,* is a real dive into a Node.js application using a relational database. We see how to use the Sequelize (ORM) middleware with Mysql database, how to create database relationships, and how to use migration files.

Chapter 3, *Building a Multimedia Application,* teaches you how to deal with file storage and upload multimedia files such as images and videos. We also see how to save filenames on MongoDB and how to retrieve the files and show them on user interface. Then we learn how to deal with write and read using the Node.js streams API.

Chapter 4, *Don't Take a Photograph, Make It – An App for Photographers,* covers an application to upload, store, and manipulate images using the Cloudnary cloud services, and interacting with MongoDB. Also, we will see how to implement the Materialize.css framework for the user interface, and introduce the use of dot files to load configuration variable.

Chapter 5, *Creating a Store Locator Application with MongoDB Geospatial Query,* explains the core concepts of geospatial data and geolocation using MongoDB, and one of the most useful features to support GEOJSON data format, the 2dspheres indexes. You will understand how to integrate Google Maps API with a Node.js application.

Chapter 6, *Building a Customer Feedback App with Restful API and Loopback.io,* explores the loopback.io framework to build a Restful API. We will see the fundamentals of the Loopback CLI in order to create an entire application using the command line. You'll learn how to deal with the relationship between models using MongoDB and how to use React.js on the client side to communicate with the API.

Chapter 7, *Building a Real-Time Chat Application with Socket.io,* shows the fundamentals of Socket.io events to build a chat application using Express and jQuery for the user interface. It covers the basic concept of task managers and how to use Gulp and livereload plugin.

Chapter 8, *Creating a Blog with Keystone CMS,* discusses the use of a CMS made entirely with Node.js, called Keystone. It's a deep dive into the Keystone application structure and how to extend the framework in order to create new models and views. Also, we will see how to customize and create new Keystone themes.

Chapter 9, *Building a Frontend Process with Node.js and NPM*, is especially interesting because we will create a Restful application using the loopback.io framework and AngularJS for the user interface. Also, we will use different building tools to concatenate, minify, and optimize images using the command line and Node Package Manager (NPM). And we will see how to use the Heroku toolbelt CLI to create and deploy the application.

Chapter 10, *Creating and Deploying Using Continuous Integration and Docker,* explores the continuous delivery development process with Node.js applications. You will learn how to integrate tools such as Github, Codeship, and Heroku into your development environment to deal with unit tests and automated deployment. This chpater also teaches you how to set up environment variables to protect your database credentials and how to create a full application using the concept of Docker containers.

What you need for this book

All the examples in the book use open source solutions and can be downloaded for free from the links provided in each chapter.

The book's examples use many Node.js modules and some JavaScript libraries, such as jQuery, React.js, and AngularJS. The most current versions when writing this book are Node.js 5.6 and 6.1.

In chapter 1, *Building a Twitter-Like Application Using the MVC Design Pattern*, you can follow the step-by-step guide to install Node and Node Package Manager (NPM).

You can use your preferred HTML editor.

A modern browser will be very helpful too. We've used Chrome, but feel free to use your preference. We recommend one of these: Safari, Firefox, Chrome, IE, or Opera, all in their latest versions.

Who this book is for

You must have basic to intermediate knowledge of JavaScript, HTML, and CSS to follow the examples in the book, but slightly more advanced knowledge in web development/Restful APIs and Node.js modules/middleware may be required in some chapters. Do not worry about it; with the examples, we will detail all of the code and give you a lot of links to interesting stuff.

Conventions

In this book, you will find a number of styles of text that distinguish between different kinds of information. Here are some examples of these styles, and an explanation of their meaning.

Code words in text are shown as follows:

Before we proceed, let's change the welcome message from: routes/index.js file to the following highlighted code.

A block of code is set as follows:

```
/* GET home page. */
router.get('/', function(req, res, next) {
    res.render('index', { title: 'Express from server folder' });
});
```

When we wish to draw your attention to a particular part of a code block, the relevant lines or items are set in bold:

```
/* GET home page. */
router.get('/', function(req, res, next) {
    res.render('index', { title: 'Express from server folder' });
});
```

New terms and important words are shown in bold. Words that you see on the screen, in menus or dialog boxes for example, appear in the text like this: "clicking on the Next button moves you to the next screen".

Warnings or important notes appear in a box like this.

Tips and tricks appear like this.

Warnings or important notes appear in a box like this.

Tips and tricks appear like this.

Reader feedback

Feedback from our readers is always welcome. Let us know what you think about this book-what you liked or disliked. Reader feedback is important for us as it helps us develop titles that you will really get the most out of. To send us general feedback, simply e-mail feedback@packtpub.com, and mention the book's title in the subject of your message. If there is a topic that you have expertise in and you are interested in either writing or contributing to a book, see our author guide at www.packtpub.com/authors.

Customer support

Now that you are the proud owner of a Packt book, we have a number of things to help you to get the most from your purchase.

Downloading the example code

You can download the example code files for this book from your account at http://www.packtpub.com. If you purchased this book elsewhere, you can visit http://www.packtpub.com/support and register to have the files e-mailed directly to you.

You can download the code files by following these steps:

1. Log in or register to our website using your e-mail address and password.
2. Hover the mouse pointer on the **SUPPORT** tab at the top.
3. Click on **Code Downloads & Errata**.
4. Enter the name of the book in the **Search** box.
5. Select the book for which you're looking to download the code files.
6. Choose from the drop-down menu where you purchased this book from.
7. Click on **Code Download**.

Once the file is downloaded, please make sure that you unzip or extract the folder using the latest version of:

- WinRAR / 7-Zip for Windows
- Zipeg / iZip / UnRarX for Mac
- 7-Zip / PeaZip for Linux

The code bundle for the book is also hosted on GitHub at `https://github.com/PacktPubl ishing/Node.JS-6.x-Blueprints`. We also have other code bundles from our rich catalog of books and videos available at `https://github.com/PacktPublishing/`. Check them out!

Errata

Although we have taken every care to ensure the accuracy of our content, mistakes do happen. If you find a mistake in one of our books-maybe a mistake in the text or the code-we would be grateful if you could report this to us. By doing so, you can save other readers from frustration and help us improve subsequent versions of this book. If you find any errata, please report them by visiting `http://www.packtpub.com/submit-errata`, selecting your book, clicking on the **Errata Submission Form** link, and entering the details of your errata. Once your errata are verified, your submission will be accepted and the errata will be uploaded to our website or added to any list of existing errata under the Errata section of that title.

To view the previously submitted errata, go to `https://www.packtpub.com/books/conten t/support` and enter the name of the book in the search field. The required information will appear under the **Errata** section.

Piracy

Piracy of copyrighted material on the Internet is an ongoing problem across all media. At Packt, we take the protection of our copyright and licenses very seriously. If you come across any illegal copies of our works in any form on the Internet, please provide us with the location address or website name immediately so that we can pursue a remedy.

Please contact us at `copyright@packtpub.com` with a link to the suspected pirated material.

We appreciate your help in protecting our authors and our ability to bring you valuable content.

Questions

If you have a problem with any aspect of this book, you can contact us at `questions@packtpub.com`, and we will do our best to address the problem.

1
Building a Twitter-Like Application Using the MVC Design Pattern

The **Model View Controller** (**MVC**) design pattern was very popular in the eighties in the software industry. This pattern helped so many engineers and companies to build better software for a while and is still useful nowadays with the rise of Node.js and some Node frameworks as **Express.js** (more information about Express.js and its API can be found at `ht tp://expressjs.com/`).

 As the Express.js website says, it is "*Fast, unopinionated, minimalist web framework for Node.js.*"

Express.js is the most popular Node framework and many companies across the globe have adopted it. So in our first application, let's see how to apply the MVC pattern to create an application using only JavaScript at the backend.

In this chapter, we will cover these topics:

- Installing the Node and Express framework
- MVC design pattern
- Dealing with Yeoman generator
- How to use Express generator
- How to deal with Express template engine
- User authentication
- MongoDB connection with Mongoose Schema

Installing Node.js

First off, we need to install the most up-to-date Node.js version. At the time of writing this book, Node.js's latest update is *v6.3.0*. You can go to the Node.js website at `https://nodejs.org/en/` and choose your platform. For this book, we are using Mac OS X, but the examples can be followed on any platform.

To check the Node and **Node Package Manager** (**NPM**) version, open your terminal/shell and type these:

- `node -v`

- `npm -v`

The book uses Node version *6.3.0* and NPM version *3.10.3*

Installing Yeoman

Throughout this book, we will use some tools that accelerate our development process. One of them is called **Yeoman** (more information can be found at `http://yeoman.io/`), a powerful web application generator.

Now let's install the generator. Open your terminal/shell and type the following code:

```
npm install -g yo
```

Installing Express generator

For our first application, let's use the official Express generator. The generator helps us in creating the initial code of our application and we can modify it to fit into our application.

Simply type the following command in your terminal or shell:

```
npm install -g express
```

Note that the -g flag means installing globally on your machine so that you can use it on any project.

Express is a powerful micro framework for Node.js; with it, it's possible to build web applications with ease.

Building the baseline

The project that will start now will be a fully server-side application. We will not use any interface framework such as AngularJS, Ember.js, and others; let's just concentrate on the express framework.

The purpose of this application is to use all the express resources and middleware to create an application following the MVC design pattern.

Middleware is basically functions that are activated by the routing layer of express. The name refers to when a route is activated until its return (from start to end). Middleware is in the middle as the name suggests. It is important to remember that the functions are executed in the order in which they were added.

In the code examples, we will be using middleware including `cookie-parser`, `body-parser`, and many others.

 You can download the code used in this book directly from the book page present at Packt Publishing Website and you can also download this chapter and all others directly from GitHub at:

`https://github.com/newaeonweb/node-6-blueprints.git`.

Each application is given the name of the relevant chapter, so let's dive into our code now.

First off, create a new folder called `chapter-01` on your machine. From now on, we will call this folder the root project folder. Before we move on and execute the command to start our project, we will see a few lines about the flags that we use with the `express` command.

The command we use is `express --ejs --css sass -git`, where:

- `express` is the default command used to create an application
- `--ejs` means to use the embedded JavaScript template engine, instead of **Jade** (default)
- `--css sass` means use **SASS** instead of plain **CSS** (default)
- `--git`: means to add a `.gitignore` file to the project

As I'm using git for version control, it will be useful to use the express option to add a `.gitignore` file to my application. But I'll skip all git commands in the book.

To check all the options available from the `express` framework, you can type this into your terminal/shell:

```
express -h
```

And the framework gives us all the commands available to start a project:

```
Usage: express [options] [dir]
  Options:
    -h, --help            output usage information
    -V, --version         output the version number
    -e, --ejs             add ejs engine support (defaults to jade)
        --hbs             add handlebars engine support
    -H, --hogan           add hogan.js engine support
    -c, --css <engine>    add stylesheet <engine> support
                          (less|stylus|compass|sass) (defaults to plain css)
        --git             add .gitignore
    -f, --force           force on non-empty directory
```

Now, open your terminal/shell and type the following command:

```
express --ejs --css sass -git
```

The output in the terminal/shell will be as follows:

```
create :
  create : ./package.json
  create : ./app.js
  create : ./.gitignore
  create : ./public
  create : ./public/javascripts
  create : ./public/images
  create : ./public/stylesheets
  create : ./public/stylesheets/style.sass
  create : ./routes
  create : ./routes/index.js
  create : ./routes/users.js
  create : ./views
  create : ./views/index.ejs
  create : ./views/error.ejs
  create : ./bin
  create : ./bin/www
  install dependencies:
    $ cd . && npm install
  run the app:
    $ DEBUG=chapter-01:* npm start
```

As you can see in the following screenshot, the generator is very flexible and only creates the minimum necessary structure to start a project:

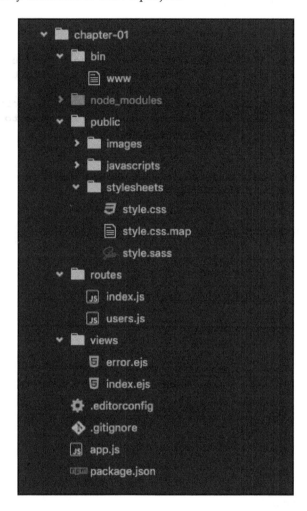

However, we will make some changes before we proceed.

Adding changes to the package.json file

Open `package.json` in the root project folder and add the following highlighted lines of code:

```
{
    "name": "chapter-01",
    "description": "Build a Twitter Like app using the MVC design pattern",
    "license": "MIT",
    "author": {
        "name": "Fernando Monteiro",
        "url": "https://github.com/newaeonweb/node-6-blueprints"
    },
    "repository": {
        "type": "git",
        "url": "https://github.com/newaeonweb/node-6-blueprints.git"
    },
    "keywords": [
        "MVC",
        "Express Application",
        "Expressjs"
    ],
    "version": "0.0.1",
    "private": true,
    "scripts": {
        "start": "node ./bin/www"
    },
    "dependencies": {
        "body-parser": "~1.13.2",
        "cookie-parser": "~1.3.5",
        "debug": "~2.2.0",
        "ejs": "~2.3.3",
        "express": "~4.13.1",
        "morgan": "~1.6.1",
        "node-sass-middleware": "0.8.0",
        "serve-favicon": "~2.3.0"
    }
}
```

Even though it is not a high-priority alteration, it is considered a good practice to add this information to your project.

Now we are ready to run the project; let's install the necessary dependencies that are already listed in the `package.json` file.

On the terminal/shell, type the following command:

```
npm install
```

At the end, we are ready to go!

Running the application

To run the project and see the application in the browser, type the following command in your terminal/shell:

```
DEBUG=chapter-01:* npm start
```

The output in your terminal/shell will be as follows:

```
chapter-01:server Listening on port 3000 +0ms
```

You can run just `npm start`, but you won't see the previous output with the port name; later in this chapter, we will fix it.

Now, just check out `http://localhost:3000`. You'll see the welcome message from express.

Changing the application's structure

Let's make some changes to the structure of directories in our application and prepare it to follow the Model-View-Controller design pattern.

I will list the necessary steps for this refactoring:

1. Inside the `root` project folder:
    - Create a new folder called `server`
2. Inside the `server` folder:
    - Create a new folder called `config`
    - Create a new folder called `routes`
    - Create a new folder called `views`.
3. Do not worry about the `config` folder at this point; we will insert its contents later.

4. Now we need to move the `error.js` and `index.js` files from the `chapter-01/views` folder to the `chapter-01/server/views` folder.

5. Move the `index.js` and `user.js` files from the `chapter-01/routes` folder to the `chapter-01/server/routes` folder.

6. A very simple change here, but during the development process, it will be very useful to better organize all the files of our application.

We still need to change the path to this folder in the main application file, `app.js`. Open the `app.js` file from the project root folder and change the following highlighted lines:

```
...
var routes = require('./server/routes/index');
var users = require('./server/routes/users');

var app = express();

// view engine setup
app.set('views', path.join(__dirname, 'server/views'));
app.set('view engine', 'ejs');
...
```

Before we proceed, let's change the welcome message from the `routes/index.js` file to the following highlighted code:

```
/* GET home page. */
router.get('/', function(req, res, next) {
    res.render('index', { title: 'Express from server folder' });
});
```

To run the project and see the application in your browser, follow these steps:

1. Type the following command in your terminal/shell:

   ```
   DEBUG=chapter-01:* npm start
   ```

2. Open your browser at `http://localhost:3000`.

3. The output in your browser will be as follows:

Express from server folder

Welcome to Express from server folder

Application home screen

Now we can delete the folders and files from:

- `chapter-01/routes:`
    - `index.js`
    - `user.js`
- `chapter-01/views:`
    - `error.js`
    - `index.js`

Changing the default behavior to start the application

As mentioned earlier, we will change the default initialization process of our application. To do this task, we will edit the `app.js` file and add a few lines of code:

1. Open `app.js` and add the following code after the `app.use('/users',
users);` function:

```
// catch 404 and forward to error handler
app.use(function(req, res, next) {
    var err = new Error('Not Found');
    err.status = 404;
    next(err);
});
```

It's a simple `middleware` to intercept 404 errors.

2. Now add the following code after the `module.exports = app;` function:

```
app.set('port', process.env.PORT || 3000);
var server = app.listen(app.get('port'), function() {
    console.log('Express server listening on port ' +
    serer.address().port);
});
```

3. Open the `package.js` file at the root project folder and change the following code:

```
. . .
"scripts": {
    "start": "node app.js"
},
. . .
```

 The debug command is still available if necessary: `DEBUG=chapter-01:*` `npm start`.

4. The `package.json` file is a file of extreme importance in Node.js applications. It is possible to store all kinds of information for the project, such as dependencies, project description, authors, version, and many more.

5. Furthermore, it is possible to set up scripts to minify, concatenate, test, build and deploy an application easily. We'll see more on how to create scripts in `Chapter 9`, *Building a Frontend Process with Node.js and NPM*.

6. Let's test the result; open your terminal/shell and type the following command:

   npm start

7. We will see the same output on the console:

   > node app.js

   Express server listening on port 3000!

Restructuring the views folder using partials

Now we will make a major change to the structure of directories in the `views` folder: we will add an important **Embedded JavaScript(EJS)** resource for the creation of reusable files in our templates.

They are known as partial files and will be included in our application using the `<% = include %>` tag.

> You can find more information about **EJS** on the official project page at:
> `http://ejs.co/`

Inside the `views` folder, we will create two more folders, called `partials` and `pages`:

1. The `pages` folder will be as follows at this point:
2. Now let's move the files that were in the `views` folder to the `pages` folder.
3. Create a `pages` folder inside the `views` folder.
4. Create a `partials` folder inside the `views` folder.
    - `server/`
    - `pages/`
    - `index.ejs`
    - `error.ejs`
    - `partials/`
5. Now we need to create the files that will be included in all templates. Note that we have just two templates: `index.js` and `error.js`.
6. Create a file called `stylesheet.ejs` and add the following code:

```
<!-- CSS Files -->
<link rel='stylesheet' href='https://cdnjs.cloudflare.com/
  ajax/libs/twitter-bootstrap/4.0.0-alpha/css/bootstrap.min.css'>
<link rel='stylesheet' href='/stylesheets/style.css' />
```

> We will use the latest version of the **Twitter Bootstrap** UI framework, which at the time this book is being written is in version *4.0.0-alpha*.

7. We are using a **Content Delivery Network (CDN)** for *CSS* and *JS* files.

8. Create a file called `javascript.ejs` and add the following code to it:

```
<!-- JS Scripts -->
<script src='https://cdnjs.cloudflare.com/ajax/libs
   /jquery/2.2.1/jquery.min.js'></script>
<script src='https://cdnjs.cloudflare.com/ajax/libs/
 twitter-bootstrap/4.0.0-alpha/js/bootstrap.min.js'></script>
</body>
</html>
```

9. Then create a file called `header.ejs` and add the following code:

```
<!-- Fixed navbar -->
<div class="pos-f-t">
    <div class="collapse" id="navbar-header">
        <div class="container bg-inverse p-a-1">
           <h3>Collapsed content</h3>
            <p>Toggle able via the navbar brand.</p>
        </div>
    </div>
    <nav class="navbar navbar-light navbar-static-top">
        <div class="container">
          <button class="navbar-toggler hidden-sm-up" type=
            "button"data-toggle="collapse" data-target=
             "#exCollapsingNavbar2">
            Menu
          </button>
        <div class="collapse navbar-toggleable-xs"
          id="exCollapsingNavbar2">
            <a class="navbar-brand" href="/">MVC App</a>
            <ul class="nav navbar-nav navbar-right">
                <li class="nav-item">
                    <a class="nav-link" href="/login">
                     Sign in
                    </a>
                </li>
                <li class="nav-item">
                    <a class="nav-link" href="/signup">
                     Sign up
                    </a>
                </li>
                <li class="nav-item">
                    <a class="nav-link" href="/profile">
                        Profile</a>
                </li>
                <li class="nav-item">
```

```
                        <a class="nav-link" href="/comments">
                           Comments</a>
                    </li>
                  </ul>
                </div>
              </div>
            </nav>
          </div>
          <!-- Fixed navbar -->
```

10. Create a file called `footer.ejs` and add this code:

```
<footer class="footer">
    <div class="container">
        <span>&copy 2016. Node-Express-MVC-App</span>
    </div>
</footer>
```

11. Let's adjust the path for the view templates in our `app.js` file; add the following lines of code:

```
// view engine setup
app.set('views', path.join(__dirname, 'server/views/pages'));
app.set('view engine', 'ejs');
```

Note that we only added the `pages` folder path that already existed.

12. Now we will replace the code in `pages/index.ejs` with the following code:

```
<!DOCTYPE html>
<html>
<head>
  <title><%= title %></title>
    <% include ../partials/stylesheet %>
</head>
<body>
      <% include ../partials/header %>
      <div class="container">
        <div class="page-header m-t-1">
          <h1><%= title %></h1>
        </div>
        <p class="lead">Welcome to <%= title %></p>
      </div>
      <% include ../partials/footer %>
```

```
        <% include ../partials/javascript %>
    </body>
    </html>
```

13. Let's do the same for the error view file at `pages/error.ejs`:

```
<!DOCTYPE html>
<html>
<head>
    <title>Wohp's Error</title>
    <% include ../partials/stylesheet %>
</head>
<body>
    <% include ../partials/header %>

    <div class="container">
        <div class="page-header m-t-1">
            <h1>Sorry: <%= message %></h1>
            <h2><%= error.status %></h2>
            <pre><%= error.stack %></pre>
        </div>

    </div>
    <% include ../partials/footer %>
    <% include ../partials/javascript %>
</body>
</html>
```

We currently have the following structure in our `server` folder:

- `server/`
- `pages/`
- `index.ejs`
- `error.ejs`
- `partials/`
- `footer.ejs`
- `header.ejs`
- `javascript.ejs`
- `stylesheet.ejs2`

Adding templates for login, sign-up, and profile

Now we have a solid basis to move forward with the project. At this time, we will add some template files for login, sign-up, and profile screens.

The expected result for these pages will be as shown in the following screenshot:

Login screen

Sign-up screen

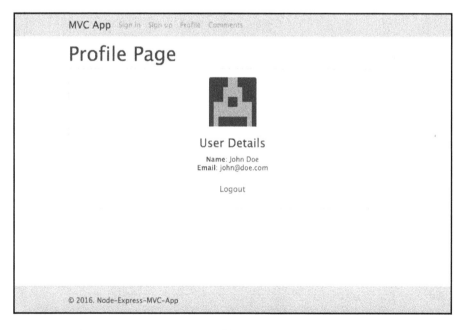

Profile screen

1. Now let's create the login template. Create a new file called `login.ejs` in the `views` folder and place the following code:

```
<!DOCTYPE html>
<html>
<head>
    <title><%= title %></title>
    <% include ../partials/stylesheet %>
</head>
<body>
  <% include ../partials/header %>
  <div class="container">
      <% if (message.length > 0) { %>
          <div class="alert alert-warning alert-dismissible
              fade in" role="alert">
            <button type="button" class="close" data-dismiss=
                "alert" aria-label="Close">
              <span aria-hidden="true">&times;</span>
            </button>
            <strong>Ohps!</strong> <%= message %>.
          </div>
       <% } %>
      <form class="form-signin" action="/login" method="post">
      <h2 class="form-signin-heading">Welcome sign in</h2>
      <label for="inputEmail" class="sr-only">Email address</label>
      <input type="email" id="email" name="email" class="form-
        control" placeholder="Email address" required="">
      <label for="inputPassword" class="sr-only">Password</label>
      <input type="password" id="password" name="password"
       class="form-control" placeholder="Password" required="">
      <button class="btn btn-lg btn-primary btn-block"
         type="submit">Sign in</button>
      <br>
      <p>Don't have an account? <a href="/signup">Signup</a>
         ,it's free.</p>
    </form>
  </div>

  <% include ../partials/footer %>
  <% include ../partials/javascript %>
</body>
</html>
```

2. Add the login route to `routes/index.js` after the index route:

```
/* GET login page. */
router.get('/login', function(req, res, next) {
```

```
    res.render('login', { title: 'Login Page', message:
    req.flash('loginMessage') });
});
```

 In the template, we are making use of the `connect-flash` middleware to display error messages. Later, we will show how to install this component; don't worry right now.

3. Let's add the `signup` template to the `views/pages` folder.
4. Create a new file in `views/pages` and save as `signup.ejs`; then add the following code:

```
<!DOCTYPE html>
<html>
<head>
  <title><%= title %></title>
  <% include ../partials/stylesheet %>
</head>
<body>
  <% include ../partials/header %>
  <div class="container">
    <% if (message.length > 0) { %>
      <div class="alert alert-warning" role="alert">
        <strong>Warning!</strong> <%= message %>.
      </div>
    <% } %>
    <form class="form-signin" action="/signup" method="post">
      <h2 class="form-signin-heading">Please signup</h2>
      <label for="inputName" class="sr-only">Name address</label>
      <input type="text" id="name" name="name" class="form-control"
       placeholder="Name" required="">
      <label for="inputEmail" class="sr-only">Email address</label>
      <input type="email" id="email" name="email" class=
        "form-control" placeholder="Email address" required="">
      <label for="inputPassword" class="sr-only">Password</label>
      <input type="password" id="password" name="password"
        class="form-control" placeholder="Password" required="">
      <button class="btn btn-lg btn-primary btn-block"
        type="submit">Sign in</button>
      <br>
      <p>Don't have an account? <a href="/signup">Signup</a>
          ,it's free.</p>
    </form>
  </div>
  <% include ../partials/footer %>
  <% include ../partials/javascript %>
```

```
    </body>
    </html>
```

5. Now we need to add the route for the sign-up view. Open `routes/index.js` and add the following code right after `login route`:

```
/* GET Signup */
router.get('/signup', function(req, res) {
    res.render('signup', { title: 'Signup Page',
        message:req.flash('signupMessage') });
});
```

6. Next, we will add the template to the `profile` page and the route to this page. Create a file called `profile.ejs` inside the `view/pages` folder and add this code:

```
<!DOCTYPE html>
<html>
<head>
    <title><%= title %></title>
    <% include ../partials/stylesheet %>
</head>
<body>
    <% include ../partials/header %>
    <div class="container">
      <h1><%= title %></h1>
      <div class="datails">
        <div class="card text-xs-center">
            <br>
          <img class="card-img-top" src="<%= avatar %>"
            alt="Card image cap">
            <div class="card-block">
                <h4 class="card-title">User Details</h4>
                <p class="card-text">
                    <strong>Name</strong>: <%= user.local.name %><br>
                    <strong>Email</strong>: <%= user.local.email %>
                </p>
                <a href="/logout" class="btn btn-default">Logout</a>
            </div>
        </div>
      </div>
    </div>
    <% include ../partials/footer %>
    <% include ../partials/javascript %>
</body>
</html>
```

7. Now we need to add the route for the profile view; open `routes/index.js` and add the following code right after the `signup` route:

```
/* GET Profile page. */
router.get('/profile',  function(req, res, next) {
    res.render('profile', { title: 'Profile Page', user : req.user,
    avatar: gravatar.url(req.user.email ,  {s: '100', r: 'x', d:
    'retro'}, true) });
});
```

We are using another middleware called `gravatar`; later, we will show how to install it.

Installing additional middleware

As you can see in the previous sections, we used some middleware to display messages and the user icon using the gravatar. In this section, we will see how to install some very important modules for our application.

Since we created templates for the `signin`, `signup`, and `profile` pages, we will need to store the users with login and password.

These are the middleware that we will use for this task, with the definition for each one:

Component	Description	More details
connect-flash	User-friendly messages	https://www.npmjs.com/package/connect-flash
connect-mongo	Drive to connect with MongoDB	https://www.npmjs.com/package/connect-mongo
express-session	Store user sessions in the DB	https://www.npmjs.com/package/express-session
Gravatar	Show a random user picture	https://www.npmjs.com/package/gravatar
Passport	Authentication middleware	https://www.npmjs.com/package/passport
passport-local	Local user/password authentication	https://www.npmjs.com/package/passport-local

Open your terminal/shell and type:

```
npm install connect-flash connect-mongo express-session gravatar
passport passport-local –save
```

 As we can see, we will use MongoDB to store user data; you can find more information about MongoDB at `https://www.mongodb.org/`, and the installation process at `https://docs.mongodb.org/manual/installation/`. We assume that you already have MongoDB installed on your machine and it is running.

Refactoring the app.js file with the new middleware

At this time, we have to do a major restructuring of the `app.js` file to include the new middleware that we will use.

We will show you step by step how to include each middleware and at the end, we will see the complete file:

1. Open `app.js` and add the following lines before `var app = express()`:

```
// ODM With Mongoose
var mongoose = require('mongoose');
// Modules to store session
var session    = require('express-session');
var MongoStore = require('connect-mongo')(session);
// Import Passport and Warning flash modules
var passport = require('passport');
var flash = require('connect-flash');
```

This is a simple import process.

2. Add the following lines after `app.set('view engine', 'ejs')`:

```
// Database configuration
var config = require('./server/config/config.js');
// connect to our database
mongoose.connect(config.url);
// Check if MongoDB is running
mongoose.connection.on('error', function() {
  console.error('MongoDB Connection Error. Make sure MongoDB is
    running.');
```

```
});

// Passport configuration
require('./server/config/passport')(passport);
```

4. Note that we are using a `config.js` file in the first line; later we will create this file.

5. Add the following lines after `app.use(express.static(path.join(__dirname, 'public')))`:

```
// required for passport
// secret for session
app.use(session({
    secret: 'sometextgohere',
    saveUninitialized: true,
    resave: true,
    //store session on MongoDB using express-session +
    connect mongo
    store: new MongoStore({
        url: config.url,
        collection : 'sessions'
    })
}));

// Init passport authentication
app.use(passport.initialize());
// persistent login sessions
app.use(passport.session());
// flash messages
app.use(flash());
```

Adding config and passport files

As mentioned earlier, let's create a `config` file:

1. Inside `server/config`, create a file called `config.js` and place the following code in it:

```
// Database URL
module.exports = {
    // Connect with MongoDB on local machine
    'url' : 'mongodb://localhost/mvc-app'
};
```

2. Create a new file on `server/config` and name it `passport.js`. Add the following content:

```
// load passport module
var LocalStrategy   = require('passport-local').Strategy;
// load up the user model
var User = require('../models/users');

module.exports = function(passport) {
    // passport init setup
    // serialize the user for the session
    passport.serializeUser(function(user, done) {
        done(null, user.id);
    });
    //       deserialize the user
    passport.deserializeUser(function(id, done) {
        User.findById(id, function(err, user) {
            done(err, user);
        });
    });
    // using local strategy
    passport.use('local-login', new LocalStrategy({
        // change default username and password, to email
        //and password
        usernameField : 'email',
        passwordField : 'password',
        passReqToCallback : true
    },
    function(req, email, password, done) {
        if (email)
        // format to lower-case
        email = email.toLowerCase();
        // process asynchronous
        process.nextTick(function() {
            User.findOne({ 'local.email' :  email },
              function(err, user)
            {
              // if errors
              if (err)
                return done(err);
              // check errors and bring the messages
              if (!user)
                return done(null, false, req.flash('loginMessage',
                'No user found.'));
              if (!user.validPassword(password))
                 return done(null, false, req.flash('loginMessage',
                 'Wohh! Wrong password.'));
              // everything ok, get user
```

```
        else
          return done(null, user);
        });
      });
  }));
// Signup local strategy
passport.use('local-signup', new LocalStrategy({
    // change default username and password, to email and
    //  password
    usernameField : 'email',
    passwordField : 'password',
    passReqToCallback : true
},
function(req, email, password, done) {
    if (email)
    // format to lower-case
    email = email.toLowerCase();
    // asynchronous
    process.nextTick(function() {
        // if the user is not already logged in:
        if (!req.user) {
            User.findOne({ 'local.email' :  email },
              function(err,user) {
        // if errors
        if (err)
          return done(err);
        // check email
        if (user) {
          return done(null, false, req.flash('signupMessage',
            'Wohh! the email is already taken.'));
        }
        else {
          // create the user
            var newUser = new User();
            // Get user name from req.body
            newUser.local.name = req.body.name;
            newUser.local.email = email;
            newUser.local.password =
             newUser.generateHash(password);
            // save data
          newUser.save(function(err) {
         if (err)
           throw err;
           return done(null, newUser);
          });
        }
      });
      } else {
```

```
            return done(null, req.user);
        }               });
    }));
};
```

Note that in the fourth line, we are importing a file called `models`; we will create this file using Mongoose.

Creating a models folder and adding a user schema

Create a models folder inside `server/` and add the following code:

```
// Import Mongoose and password Encrypt
var mongoose = require('mongoose');
var bcrypt   = require('bcrypt-nodejs');

// define the schema for User model
var userSchema = mongoose.Schema({
    // Using local for Local Strategy Passport
    local: {
        name: String,
        email: String,
        password: String,
    }

});

// Encrypt Password
userSchema.methods.generateHash = function(password) {
    return bcrypt.hashSync(password, bcrypt.genSaltSync(8), null);
};

// Verify if password is valid
userSchema.methods.validPassword = function(password) {
    return bcrypt.compareSync(password, this.local.password);
};

// create the model for users and expose it to our app
module.exports = mongoose.model('User', userSchema);
```

Protecting routes

At this point, we have enough code to configure secure access to our application. However, we still need to add a few more lines to the login and sign-up forms to make them work properly:

1. Open `server/routes/index.js` and add the following lines after the `login` GET route:

```
/* POST login */
router.post('/login', passport.authenticate('local-login', {
    //Success go to Profile Page / Fail go to login page
    successRedirect : '/profile',
    failureRedirect : '/login',
    failureFlash : true
}));
```

2. Add these lines after the `signup` GET route:

```
/* POST Signup */
router.post('/signup', passport.authenticate('local-signup', {
    //Success go to Profile Page / Fail go to Signup page
    successRedirect : '/profile',
    failureRedirect : '/signup',
    failureFlash : true
}));
```

3. Now let's add a simple function to check whether the user is logged in; at the end of `server/routes/index.js`, add the following code:

```
/* check if user is logged in */
function isLoggedIn(req, res, next) {
    if (req.isAuthenticated())
        return next();
    res.redirect('/login');
}
```

4. Let's add a simple route to a logout function and add the following code after the `isLoggedIn()` function:

```
/* GET Logout Page */
router.get('/logout', function(req, res) {
    req.logout();
    res.redirect('/');
});
```

5. The last change is to add `isloggedin()` as a second parameter to the profile route. Add the following highlighted code:

```
/* GET Profile page. */
router.get('/profile', isLoggedIn, function(req, res, next) {
    res.render('profile', { title: 'Profile Page', user : req.user,
      avatar: gravatar.url(req.user.email ,  {s: '100', r: 'x',
        d:'retro'}, true) });
});
```

The final `index.js` file will look like this:

```
var express = require('express');
var router = express.Router();
var passport = require('passport');
// get gravatar icon from email
var gravatar = require('gravatar');

/* GET home page. */
router.get('/', function(req, res, next) {
    res.render('index', { title: 'Express from server folder' });
});

/* GET login page. */
router.get('/login', function(req, res, next) {
    res.render('login', { title: 'Login Page', message:
req.flash('loginMessage') });
});
/* POST login */
router.post('/login', passport.authenticate('local-login', {
    //Success go to Profile Page / Fail go to login page
    successRedirect : '/profile',
    failureRedirect : '/login',
    failureFlash : true
}));

/* GET Signup */
router.get('/signup', function(req, res) {
    res.render('signup', { title: 'Signup Page', message:
req.flash('signupMessage') });
});
/* POST Signup */
router.post('/signup', passport.authenticate('local-signup', {
    //Success go to Profile Page / Fail go to Signup page
    successRedirect : '/profile',
    failureRedirect : '/signup',
    failureFlash : true
}));
```

```
/* GET Profile page. */
router.get('/profile', isLoggedIn, function(req, res, next) {
    res.render('profile', { title: 'Profile Page', user : req.user, avatar:
gravatar.url(req.user.email ,  {s: '100', r: 'x', d: 'retro'}, true) });
});

/* check if user is logged in */
function isLoggedIn(req, res, next) {
    if (req.isAuthenticated())
        return next();
    res.redirect('/login');
}
/* GET Logout Page */
router.get('/logout', function(req, res) {
    req.logout();
    res.redirect('/');
});

module.exports = router;
```

We have almost everything set to finalize the application, but we still need to create a page for comments.

Creating the controllers folder

Instead of using the `routes` folder to create the route and functions of the comments file, we will use another format and create the `controllers` folder, where we can separate the route and the controller function, thus having a better modularization:

1. Create a folder called `controllers`.
2. Create a file called `comments.js` and add the following code:

```
// get gravatar icon from email
var gravatar = require('gravatar');
// get Comments model
var Comments = require('../models/comments');

// List Comments
exports.list = function(req, res) {
    // List all comments and sort by Date
    Comments.find().sort('-created').populate('user',
        'local.email').exec(function(error, comments) {
            if (error) {
                return res.send(400, {
                    message: error
```

```
            });
        }
        // Render result
        res.render('comments', {
            title: 'Comments Page',
            comments: comments,
            gravatar: gravatar.url(comments.email,
                {s: '80', r: 'x', d: 'retro'}, true)
        });
    });
};
// Create Comments
exports.create = function(req, res) {
    // create a new instance of the Comments model with request body
    var comments = new Comments(req.body);
    // Set current user (id)
    comments.user = req.user;
    // save the data received
    comments.save(function(error) {
        if (error) {
            return res.send(400, {
                message: error
            });
        }
        // Redirect to comments
        res.redirect('/comments');
    });
};
// Comments authorization middleware
exports.hasAuthorization = function(req, res, next) {
    if (req.isAuthenticated())
        return next();
    res.redirect('/login');
};
```

3. Let's import the controllers on the `app.js` file; add the following lines after `var users = require('./server/routes/users')`:

```
// Import comments controller
var comments = require('./server/controllers/comments');
```

4. Now add the comments route after `app.use('/users', users)`:

```
// Setup routes for comments
app.get('/comments', comments.hasAuthorization, comments.list);
app.post('/comments', comments.hasAuthorization, comments.create);
```

5. Create a file called `comments.ejs` at `server/pages` and add the following lines:

```
<!DOCTYPE html>
<html>
<head>
    <title><%= title %></title>
    <% include ../partials/stylesheet %>
</head>
<body>
  <% include ../partials/header %>
  <div class="container">
    <div class="row">
      <div class="col-lg-6">
        <h4 class="text-muted">Comments</h4>
      </div>
      <div class="col-lg-6">
        <button type="button" class="btn btn-secondary pull-right"
         data-toggle="modal" data-target="#createPost">
            Create Comment
        </button>
      </div>
    </div>
    <!-- Modal -->
    <div class="modal fade" id="createPost" tabindex="-1"
     role="dialog" aria-labelledby="myModalLabel"
      aria-hidden="true">
      <div class="modal-dialog" role="document">
        <div class="modal-content">
          <form action="/comments" method="post">
            <div class="modal-header">
              <button type="button" class="close"
               data-dismiss="modal" aria-label="Close">
                 <span aria-hidden="true">&times;</span>
              </button>
              <h4 class="modal-title" id="myModalLabel">
               Create Comment</h4>
            </div>

            <div class="modal-body">
              <fieldset class="form-group">
                <label  for="inputitle">Title</label>
                <input type="text" id="inputitle" name="title"
                  class="form-control" placeholder=
                    "Comment Title" required="">
              </fieldset>
              <fieldset class="form-group">
                <label  for="inputContent">Content</label>
                <textarea id="inputContent" name="content"
```

```
                                rows="8" cols="40" class="form-control"
                                placeholder="Comment Description" required="">
                            </textarea>
                        </fieldset>

                    </div>
                      <div class="modal-footer">
                        <button type="button" class="btn btn-secondary"
                          data-dismiss="modal">Close</button>
                        <button type="submit" class="btn btn-primary">
                          Save changes</button>
                      </div>
                </form>
              </div>
            </div>
          </div>
            <hr>
          <div class="lead">
            <div class="list-group">
              <% comments.forEach(function(comments){ %>
                <a href="#" class="list-group-item">
                  <img src="<%= gravatar %>" alt="" style="float: left;
                    margin-right: 10px">
              <div class="comments">
              <h4 class="list-group-item-heading">
                <%= comments.title %></h4>
                <p class="list-group-item-text">
                  <%= comments.content %></p>
                <small class="text-muted">By:
                   <%= comments.user.local.email %>
                </small>
              </div>
              </a>

          <% }); %>
          </div>
        </div>
      </div>
      <% include ../partials/footer %>
      <% include ../partials/javascript %>
  </body>
  </html>
```

6. Note that we are using a simple Modal component from Twitter-bootstrap for the addition of comments, as shown in the following screenshot:

Model for the create comments screen

7. The last step is to create a model for the comments; let's create a file named `comments.js` at `server/models/` and add the following code:

```
// load the things we need
var mongoose = require('mongoose');
var Schema = mongoose.Schema;

var commentSchema = mongoose.Schema({
    created: {
        type: Date,
        default: Date.now
    },
    title: {
        type: String,
        default: '',
        trim: true,
        required: 'Title cannot be blank'
    },
```

```
    content: {
        type: String,
        default: '',
        trim: true
    },
    user: {
        type: Schema.ObjectId,
        ref: 'User'
    }
});

module.exports = mongoose.model('Comments', commentSchema);
```

Running the application and adding comments

Now it's time to test whethereverything is working properly:

1. Open terminal/shell at the root project folder and type the following command:

   npm start

2. Check your browser at: `http://localhost:3000`.
3. Go to `http://localhost:3000/signup` and create a user called `John Doe` with the e-mail ID as `john@doe.com` and password as `123456`.
4. Go to `http://localhost:3000/comments`, click on the **create comment** button and add the following content:

```
Title: Sample Title
Comments: Lorem ipsum dolor sit amet, consectetur adipiscing elit,
    sed do eiusmod tempor incididunt ut labore et dolore magna aliqua.
    Ut enim ad minim veniam, quis nostrud exercitation ullamco laboris
    nisi ut aliquip ex ea commodo consequat. Duis aute irure dolor in
    reprehenderit in voluptate velit esse cillum dolore eu fugiat nulla
    pariatur. Excepteur sint occaecat cupidatat non proident, sunt in
    culpa qui officia deserunt mollit anim id est laborum.
```

5. The following screenshotillustrates the final result:

Comments screen

Checking the error messages

Now let's check the flash-connect messages. Go to `http://localhost:3000/login` and try to log in as a user; we will use `martin@tech.com` with password `123`.

The following screenshot illustrates the result:

Error message on the login screen

Now we try to sign up with an already registered user. Go to `http://localhost:3/signup` and place the following content:

```
name: John Doe
email: john@doe.com
password: 123456
```

This screenshot illustrates the result:

Error message on signup screen

Summary

In this chapter, we discussed how to create MVC applications using Node.js and the express framework, with an application fully on the server side-something very similar to applications created with the **Rails** or **Django** framework.

We also built safe routes and a very robust authentication with session control, storage of session cookies, and encrypted passwords.

We used MongoDB to store the data of users and comments.

In the next chapter, we will see how to use another database system with express and Node.js.

2

Build a Basic Website Using MySQL Database

In this chapter we will look at some basic concepts of a Node.js application using a relational database, in this case Mysql.

Let's look at some differences between **Object Document Mapper** (**ODM**) from MongoDB and **Object Relational Mapper** (**ORM**) used by **sequelize** and Mysql. For this we will create a simple application and use the resources we have available which is **sequelize,** a powerful middleware for creation of models and mapping database.

We will also use another engine template called Swig and demonstrate how we can add the template engine manually.

In this chapter we will cover:

- How to use the Swig template engine
- Changing default routes from an express generator to the MVC approach
- Installing Squelize-CLI
- How to use ORM with Sequelize Models
- Working with database migrations scripts
- How to dealing with MySQL database relations

What we are building

At the end of this chapter we will create the following sample application. This chapter assumes that you have already installed and are running Mysql database on your machine.

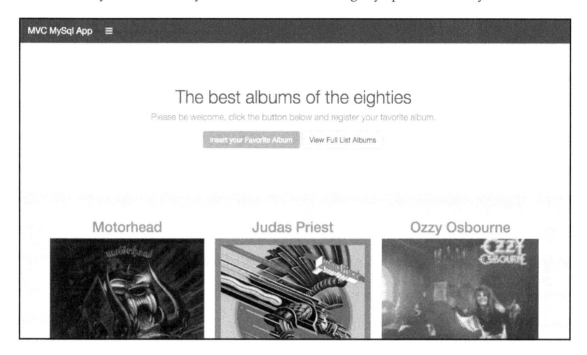

Example application

Creating the baseline applications

The first step is to create another directory, as I keep all the chapters under git control I'll use the same root folder as chapter 1, *Build a Twitter like application using MVC design pattern in Node.js.*

1. Create a folder called chapter-02.
2. Open your terminal/shell on this folder and type the express command:

```
express --git
```

Note that we are using only the `--git` flag this time, we will use another template engine but we will install it manually.

Installing the Swig template engine

The first step to do is to change the default express template engine to use **Swig**, a pretty simple template engine very flexible and stable, also offers us a syntax very similar to AngularJS which denotes expressions just by using double curly brackets `{{ variableName }}`.

> More information about **Swig** can be found on the official website at: `http ://paularmstrong.github.io/swig/docs/`.

1. Open the `package.json` file and replace the `jade` line with the following:

   ```
   "swig": "^1.4.2",
   ```

2. Open terminal/shell in project folder and type:

   ```
   npm install
   ```

3. Before we proceed, let's make some adjustment to `app.js`, we need to add the Swig module. Open `app.js` and add the following code, right after the `var bodyParser = require('body-parser');` line:

   ```
   var swig = require('swig');
   ```

4. Replace the default `jade` template engine line for the following code:

   ```
   var swig = new swig.Swig();
   app.engine('html', swig.renderFile);
   app.set('view engine', 'html');
   ```

Refactoring the views folder

As we did before, let's change the `views` folder to the following new structure:

`views`

- `pages/`
- `partials/`

1. Remove the default `jade` files form `views` folder.
2. Create a file called `layout.html` inside the `pages` folder and place the following code:

```
<!DOCTYPE html>
<html>
<head>
</head>
<body>
    {% block content %}
    {% endblock %}
</body>
</html>
```

3. Create an `index.html` inside the `views/pages` folder and place the following code:

```
{% extends 'layout.html' %}
{% block title %}{% endblock %}
{% block content %}
<h1>{{ title }}</h1>
    Welcome to {{ title }}
{% endblock %}
```

4. Create an `error.html` page inside the `views/pages` folder and place the following code:

```
{% extends 'layout.html' %}
{% block title %}{% endblock %}
{% block content %}
<div class="container">
    <h1>{{ message }}</h1>
    <h2>{{ error.status }}</h2>
    <pre>{{ error.stack }}</pre>
  </div>
{% endblock %}
```

5. We need to adjust the `views` path on `app.js`, and replace the code right after `var app = express();` function with the following code:

```
// view engine setup
app.set('views', path.join(__dirname, 'views/pages'));
```

At this time we have completed the first step of starting our MVC application. In the previous chapter we used pretty much of the original structure created by the express command, but in this example we will use the MVC pattern in its full meaning, Model, View, Controller.

Creating a controllers folder

1. Create a folder called `controllers` inside the root project folder.
2. Create an `index.js` inside the `controllers` folder and place the following code:

```
// Index controller
exports.show = function(req, res) {
// Show index content
    res.render('index', {
        title: 'Express'
    });
};
```

3. Edit the `app.js` file and replace the original `index` route `app.use('/', routes);` with the following code:

```
app.get('/', index.show);
```

4. Add the controller path to the `app.js` file right after `var swig = require('swig');` declaration, replace the original code with the following code:

```
// Inject index controller
var index = require('./controllers/index');
```

5. Now it's time to check if all goes as expected: we'll run the application and check the result. Type in your terminal/shell the following command:

npm start

Check the following URL: `http://localhost:3000`, and you'll see the welcome message of express framework.

Removing the default routes folder

Let's remove the default `routes` folder:

1. Remove the `routes` folder and its contents.
2. Remove the `user route` from the `app.js`, after the index controller line.

Adding partials files for head and footer

Now lets add files for head and footer:

1. Inside the `views/partials` folder create a new file called `head.html` and place the following code:

```
<meta charset="utf-8">
<title>{{ title }}</title>
<link rel='stylesheet' href='https://cdnjs.cloudflare.com/ajax/libs
  /twitter-bootstrap/4.0.0-alpha.2/css/bootstrap.min.css'>
<link rel="stylesheet" href="/stylesheets/style.css">
```

2. Inside the `views/partials` folder create a file called `footer.html` and place the following code:

```
<script src='https://cdnjs.cloudflare.com/ajax/libs/jquery/2.2.1
  /jquery.min.js'></script>
<script src='https://cdnjs.cloudflare.com/ajax/libs/twitter-bootstrap
  /4.0.0-alpha.2/js/bootstrap.min.js'></script>
```

3. Now, its time to add the partials file to the `layout.html` page using the `include` tag. Open `layout.html` and add the following code:

```
<!DOCTYPE html>
<html>
<head>
    {% include "../partials/head.html" %}
</head>
<body>
    {% block content %}
    {% endblock %}
```

```
        {% include "../partials/footer.html" %}
    </body>
    </html>
```

Finally we are ready to continue with our project. This time our directories structure will look like the following screenshot:

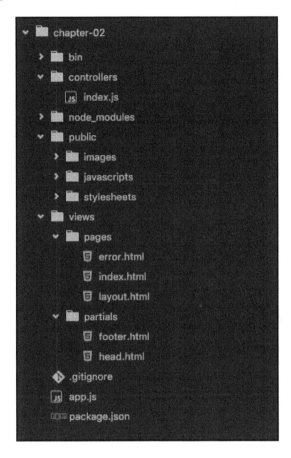

Folder structure

Installing and configuring Sequelize-cli

Sequelize-cli is a very useful command-line interface for creating models, configurations and migration files to databases. It's integrated with Sequelize middleware and operates with many relational databases such as PostgreSQL, MySQL, MSSQL, Sqlite.

You can find more information about Sequelize middleware implementation at: `http://docs.sequelizejs.com/en/latest/` and full documentation of **Sequelize-Cli** at: `https://github.com/sequelize/cli`.

1. Open terminal/shell and type:

```
npm install -g sequelize-cli
```

2. Install `sequelize` with the following command:

```
npm install sequelize -save
```

Remember we always use the `-save` flag to add the module to our `package.json` file.

3. Create a file called `.sequelizerc` on the root folder and place the following code:

```
var path = require('path');
module.exports = {
    'config': path.resolve('./config', 'config.json'),
    'migrations-path': path.resolve('./config', 'migrations'),
    'models-path': path.resolve('./', 'models'),
    'seeders-path': path.resolve('./config', 'seeders')
}
```

4. On terminal/shell, type the following command:

```
sequelize init
```

5. After the `init` command, the terminal will show the following output message:

```
Sequelize [Node: 6.3.0, CLI: 2.3.1, ORM: 3.19.3]

Using gulpfile /usr/local/lib/node_modules/sequelize
-cli/lib/gulpfile.js
Starting 'init:config'...
Created "config/config.json"
Finished 'init:config' after 4.05 ms
Successfully created migrations folder at "/chapter-02/config
/migrations".
Finished 'init:migrations' after 1.42 ms
Successfully created seeders folder at "/chapter-02/config
```

```
/seeders".
Finished 'init:seeders' after 712 μs
Successfully created models folder at "/chapter-02/models".
Loaded configuration file "config/config.json".
Using environment "development".
Finished 'init:models' after 18 msStarting 'init'...
```

This command also creates the models directory to store application schema, a configuration file, and folders to hold seeders and the migrations script. Don't worry about this now, we will look at migrations in the next section.

Editing the config.js file with database credentials

As we can see, the `sequelize` command creates many files, including a database configuration file. This file has a sample configuration for application databases.

1. Open `config/config.json` and edit the `development` tag with our database details, as the following highlighted code:

```
{
  "development": {
  "username": "root",
    "password": "",
    "database": "mvc_mysql_app",
    "host": "127.0.0.1",
    "port": "3306",
    "dialect": "mysql"
  },
  "test": {
    "username": "root",
    "password": null,
    "database": "database_test",
    "host": "127.0.0.1",
    "dialect": "mysql"
  },
  "production": {
    "username": "root",
    "password": null,
    "database": "database_production",
    "host": "127.0.0.1",
    "dialect": "mysql"
  }
}
```

Note that I'm using user root with no password to connect with my database, if you have a different user or are using a different password, replace the previous code with your own credentials.

Creating a User scheme

With the help of `Sequelize-cli` we will create a simple scheme for application users:

Open terminal/shell at the root project folder and type the following command:

```
sequelize model:create --name User --attributes "name:string,
email:string"
```

You will see the following output on your terminal window:

```
Sequelize [Node: 6.3.0, CLI: 2.3.1, ORM: 3.19.3]
Loaded configuration file "config/config.json".
Using environment "development".
Using gulpfile /usr/local/lib/node_modules/sequelize-
cli/lib/gulpfile.js
Starting 'model:create'...
Finished 'model:create' after 13 ms
```

Let's check the user model file present at: `models/User.js`, here add `sequelize` using the `define()` function to create the User scheme:

```
'use strict';
module.exports = function(sequelize, DataTypes) {
  var User = sequelize.define('User', {
    name: DataTypes.STRING,
    email: DataTypes.STRING
  },
  {
    classMethods: {
     associate: function(models) {
        // associations can be defined here
      }
    }
  });
  return User;
};
```

Note that this command created the `User.js` file within the `models` folder and also created a migration file containing a hash and the name of the operation to be performed on the database within the `migrations` folder.

This file contains the boilerplate necessary for creation of the User table in the database.

```
'use strict';
module.exports = {
  up: function(queryInterface, Sequelize) {
    return queryInterface.createTable('Users', {
      id: {
        allowNull: false,
        autoIncrement: true,
        primaryKey: true,
        type: Sequelize.INTEGER
      },
      name: {
          type: Sequelize.STRING
      },
      email: {
        type: Sequelize.STRING
      },
      createdAt: {
        allowNull: false,
        type: Sequelize.DATE
      },
      updatedAt: {
          allowNull: false,
          type: Sequelize.DATE
      }
    });
  },
  down: function(queryInterface, Sequelize) {
      return queryInterface.dropTable('Users');
  }
};
```

Creating Band schema

Let's create the schema that will store in the database the data of each band that the user creates in the system.

1. Open terminal/shell and type the following command:

```
sequelize model:create --name Band --attributes "name:string,
  description:string, album:string, year:string, UserId:integer"
```

2. As in the previous step, two files were created, one for migration of data and another to be used as a Band model, as the following code:

```
'use strict';
module.exports = function(sequelize, DataTypes) {
  var Band = sequelize.define('Band', {
    name: DataTypes.STRING,
    description: DataTypes.STRING,
    album: DataTypes.STRING,
    year: DataTypes.STRING,
    UserId: DataTypes.INTEGER
  }, {
    classMethods: {
      associate: function(models) {
        // associations can be defined here
      }
    }
  });
  return Band;
};
```

Creating associations between Band and User models

As the last step before using the schemes migration script, we will need to create the associations between the User model and the Band model. We will use the following associations:

Model	Association
Band.js	Band.belongsTo(models.User);
User.js	User.hasMany(models.Band);

You can find more about associations at the following link: `http://docs.sequelizejs.com/en/latest/docs/associations/`.

1. Open the `User.js` model and add the following highlighted code:

```
'use strict';
module.exports = function(sequelize, DataTypes) {
  var User = sequelize.define('User', {
    name: DataTypes.STRING,
    email: DataTypes.STRING
  }, {
    classMethods: {
      associate: function(models) {
      // associations can be defined here
        User.hasMany(models.Band);
      }
    }
  });
  return User;
};
```

2. Open the `Band.js` model and add the following highlighted code:

```
'use strict';
module.exports = function(sequelize, DataTypes) {
  var Band = sequelize.define('Band', {
    name: DataTypes.STRING,
    description: DataTypes.STRING,
    album: DataTypes.STRING,
    year: DataTypes.STRING,
    UserId: DataTypes.INTEGER
  }, {
    classMethods: {
      associate: function(models) {
      // associations can be defined here
  Band.belongsTo(models.User);
    }
  }
});
  return Band;
};
```

Creating the database on MySql

Before attempting to access the Mysql console make sure that it is running. To check that:

1. Open terminal/shell and login your Mysql with the following command:

   ```
   mysql -u root
   ```

2. Remember, if you are using a different user or password, using the following command and replace `youruser` and `yourpassword` for your own credentials:

   ```
   mysql -u youruser -p yourpassword
   ```

3. Now let's create our database, type the following command:

   ```
   CREATE DATABASE mvc_mysql_app;
   ```

4. The result after the command will be the following line:

   ```
   Query OK, 1 row affected (0,04 sec)
   ```

This confirms that the operation was successful, and we are ready to go forward.

Using db migrations to insert data on Mysql

Now is the time to do the migration of the schemes to the database. Again we use the `sequelize-cli` for this migration. Before we proceed, we need to install a Mysql module manually.

1. Open terminal/shell and type the following command:

   ```
   npm install
   ```

Note that the `Sequelize` interface depends on the individual modules of each type of database used in the application, in our case we are useing Mysql

2. Open your terminal/shell and type the following command:

```
sequelize db:migrate
```

3. This will be the result of the operation above, the output from your terminal:

```
Sequelize [Node: 6.3.0, CLI: 2.3.1, ORM: 3.19.3, mysql: ^2.10.2]
Loaded configuration file "config/config.json".
Using environment "development".
Using gulpfile /usr/local/lib/node_modules/sequelize-
cli/lib/gulpfile.js
Starting 'db:migrate'...
Finished 'db:migrate' after 438 ms
== 20160319100145-create-user: migrating =======
== 20160319100145-create-user: migrated (0.339s)
== 20160319101806-create-band: migrating =======
== 20160319101806-create-band: migrated (0.148s)
```

Checking database tables

We could use your own Mysql console to see if the tables were created successfully. However I will use another feature with a graphical interface that greatly facilitates the work, as it allows a faster and easier display, and perform operations on the basis of data very quickly.

As I am using Mac OSX I will use an application called **Sequel Pro**, it's a free and lightweight application to manage MySql databases.

> You can find more information about **Sequel Pro** at: http://www.sequelp ro.com/.

The previous command: `sequelize db:migrate` created the tables as we can see on the following figures:

1. This picture shows the Bands table selected on the left side, the right side shows its content with the properties we setup on Band schema:

Band table

2. This picture shows the `SequelizeMeta` table selected on the left side, the right side shows its content with `Sequelize` files generated on the `config/migrations` folder:

Migrations files

3. This picture shows the user table selected on the left side, the right side shows its content with the properties we setup on the User schema:

User table

The `SquelizeMeta` table holds the migration files in the same way that we had on migrations folder.

Now that we have created the necessary files for data insertion in our database, we are ready to move on and create other files for the application.

Creating the application controllers

The next step is to create the controls for the models User and Band:

1. Within the `controllers` folder, create a new file called `User.js` and add the following code:

```
var models = require('../models/index');
var User = require('../models/user');

// Create Users
exports.create = function(req, res) {
    // create a new instance of the Users model with request body
    models.User.create({
      name: req.body.name,
        email: req.body.email
    }).then(function(user) {
        res.json(user);
    });
};
// List Users
exports.list = function(req, res) {
    // List all users
    models.User.findAll({}).then(function(users) {
        res.json(users);
```

```
        });
    };
```

Note that the first line of the file imports the `index` model; this file is the basis for creation of all the controls, it is the `sequelize` that is used to map the other models.

2. Do the same for the Band controller within the `controllers` folder; create a file called `Band.js` and add the following code:

```
var models = require('../models/index');
var Band = require('../models/band');

// Create Band
exports.create = function(req, res) {
    // create a new instance of the Bands model with request body
    models.Band.create(req.body).then(function(band) {
        //res.json(band);
        res.redirect('/bands');
    });
};

// List Bands
exports.list = function(req, res) {
    // List all bands and sort by Date
    models.Band.findAll({
      // Order: lastest created
        order: 'createdAt DESC'
    }).then(function(bands) {
        //res.json(bands);
        // Render result
        res.render('list', {
            title: 'List bands',
            bands: bands
        });
    });
};

// Get by band id
exports.byId = function(req, res) {
    models.Band.find({
        where: {
            id: req.params.id
        }
    }).then(function(band) {
        res.json(band);
```

```
        });
    }
    // Update by id
    exports.update = function (req, res) {
        models.Band.find({
            where: {
                id: req.params.id
            }
        }).then(function(band) {
            if(band){
                band.updateAttributes({
                    name: req.body.name,
                    description: req.body.description,
                    album: req.body.album,
                    year: req.body.year,
                    UserId: req.body.user_id
                }).then(function(band) {
                    res.send(band);
                });
            }
        });
    }

    // Delete by id
    exports.delete = function (req, res) {
        models.Band.destroy({
            where: {
                id: req.params.id
            }
        }).then(function(band) {
            res.json(band);
        });
    }
```

3. Now let's refactor the `index.js` controller and add the following code:

```
    // List Sample Bands
    exports.show = function(req, res) {
        // List all comments and sort by Date
        var topBands = [
            {
                name: 'Motorhead',
                description: 'Rock and Roll Band',
                album: 'http://s2.vagalume.com/motorhead/discografia
                /orgasmatron-W320.jpg', year:'1986',
            },
            {
                name: 'Judas Priest',
```

```
                       description: 'Heavy Metal band',
                       album: 'http://s2.vagalume.com/judas-priest/discografia
                        /screaming-for-vengeance-W320.jpg', year:'1982',
                },
                {
                       name: 'Ozzy Osbourne',
                       description: 'Heavy Metal Band',
                       album: 'http://s2.vagalume.com/ozzy-osbourne/discografia
                        /diary-of-a-madman-W320.jpg', year:'1981',
                }
            ];
            res.render('index', {
                 title: 'The best albums of the eighties',
                 callToAction: 'Please be welcome, click the button below
                 and register your favorite album.', bands: topBands
            });
       };
```

Note that, using the previous code, we just created a simple list to show some albums on the home screen.

Creating the application templates/views

Now let's create the applicationviews:

1. Within the `views/pages` folder, create a new file called `band-list.html` and add the following code:

```
{% extends 'layout.html' %}
{% block title %}{% endblock %}
{% block content %}
<div class="album text-muted">
<div class="container">
<div class="row">
            {% for band in bands %}
<div class="card col-lg-4">
<h2 class="text-lg-center">{{ band.name }}</h2>
                    {% if band.album == null %}
 <img src="https://placehold.it/320x320" alt="{{ band.name }}"
  style="height: 320px; width: 100%; display: block;">
                    {% endif %}
                    {% if band.album %}
 <img src="{{ band.album }}" width="100%" height="320px">
                    {% endif %}
 <p class ="card-text">{{ band.description }}</p>
```

```
    </div>
                {% endfor %}
    </div>
    </div>
    </div>
    {% endblock %}
```

2. Open `views/pages/index.html` and add the following code:

```
{% extends 'layout.html' %}
{% block title %}{% endblock %}
{% block content %}
<section class="jumbotron text-xs-center">
<div class="container">
  <h1 class="jumbotron-heading">{{ title }}</h1>
  <p class="lead text-muted">{{ callToAction }}</p>
  <p>
  <a href="/bands" class="btn btn-secondary">
    View Full List Albums</a>
  </p>
</div>
</section>
<div class="album text-muted">
  <div class="container">
    <div class="row">
            {% for band in bands %}
    <div class="card col-lg-4">
      <h2 class="text-lg-center">{{ band.name }}</h2>
                {% if band.album == null %}
      <img src="https://placehold.it/320x320" alt="{{ band.name }}"
        style="height: 320px; width: 100%; display: block;">
                {% endif %}
                {% if band.album %}
      <img src="{{ band.album }}" width="100%" height="320px">
                {% endif %}
      <p class="card-text">{{ band.description }}</p>
    </div>
            {% endfor %}
    </div>
  </div>
</div>
{% endblock %}
```

3. Open `views/pages/layou.html` and add the followinghighlighted code:

```html
<!DOCTYPE html>
<html>
<head>
    {% include "../partials/head.html" %}
</head>
<body>
<div class="navbar-collapse inverse collapse" id="navbar-header"
 aria-expanded="false" style="height: 0px;">
<div class="container-fluid">
<div class="about">
  <h4>About</h4>
  <p class="text-muted">Add some information about the album below,
     the author, or any other background context. Make it a few
     sentences long so folks can pick up some informative tidbits.
     Then, link them off to some social networking sites or contact
     information.
   </p>
</div>
<div class="social">
<h4>Contact</h4>
<ul class="list-unstyled">
  <li><a href="#">Follow on Twitter</a></li>
  <li><a href="#">Like on Facebook</a></li>
  <li><a href="#">Email me</a></li>
</ul>
</div>
</div>
</div>
<div class="navbar navbar-static-top navbar-dark bg-inverse">
<div class="container-fluid">
  <button class="navbar-toggler collapsed" type="button"
    data-toggle="collapse" data-target="#navbar-header"
    aria-expanded="false">
  </button>
  <a href="/" class="navbar-brand">MVC MySql App</a>
</div>
</div>

        {% block content %}
        {% endblock %}
<footer class="text-muted">
<div class="container">
  <p class="pull-xs-right">
  <a href="#">Back to top</a>
  </p>
  <p>Sample Page using Album example from Â© Bootstrap!</p>
```

```
    <p>New to Bootstrap? <a href="http://v4-alpha.getbootstrap.
        com/getting-started/introduction/">Visit the homepage
    </a>.</p>
</div>
</footer>
    {% include "../partials/footer.html" %}
</body>
</html>
```

Adding style to the application

We'll also add a few lines of CSS in the `public/stylesheet` file to style our example application.

Open `public/stylesheets/style.css` and add the following code:

```css
body {
  min-height: 75rem; /* Can be removed; just added for demo purposes */
}
.navbar {
  margin-bottom: 0;
}
.navbar-collapse .container-fluid {
  padding: 2rem 2.5rem;
  border-bottom: 1px solid #55595c;
}
.navbar-collapse h4 {
  color: #818a91;
}
.navbar-collapse .text-muted {
  color: #818a91;
}
.about {
  float: left;
  max-width: 30rem;
  margin-right: 3rem;
}
.social a {
font-weight: 500;
  color: #eceeef;
}
.social a:hover {
  color: #fff;
}
.jumbotron {
  padding-top: 6rem;
```

```css
    padding-bottom: 6rem;
    margin-bottom: 0;
    background-color: #fff;
}
.jumbotron p:last-child {
    margin-bottom: 0;
}
.jumbotron-heading {
    font-weight: 300;
}
.jumbotron .container {
    max-width: 45rem;
}
.album {
    min-height: 50rem; /* Can be removed; just added for demo purposes */
    padding-top: 3rem;
    padding-bottom: 3rem;
    background-color: #f7f7f7;
}
.card {
    float: left;
    width: 33.333%;
    padding: .75rem;
    margin-bottom: 2rem;
    border: 0;
}
.card > img {
    margin-bottom: .75rem;
}
.card-text {
    font-size: 85%;
}
footer {
    padding-top: 3rem;
    padding-bottom: 3rem;
}
footer p {
    margin-bottom: .25rem;
}
```

Adding routes and a controller to the application

We will edit the app.js file to add routes to the band-list.html view and also their respective controller:

1. Open app.js and add the following lines after the index controller import:

```
// Inject band controller
var bands = require('./controllers/band');
// Inject user controller
var users = require('./controllers/user');
```

2. Add the following code after the index route app.get('/', index.show);:

```
// Defining route to list and post
app.get('/bands', bands.list);
// Get band by ID
app.get('/band/:id', bands.byId);
// Create band
app.post('/bands', bands.create);
// Update
app.put('/band/:id', bands.update);
// Delete by id
app.delete('/band/:id', bands.delete);
// Defining route to list and post users
app.get('/users', users.list);
app.post('/users', users.create);
```

At this moment, we have almost all of the application working; let's check the result on the browser.

3. Open your terminal/shell and type the following command:

npm start

4. Open your browser and go to this URL: http://localhost:3000/

The result will be the followingscreenshot:

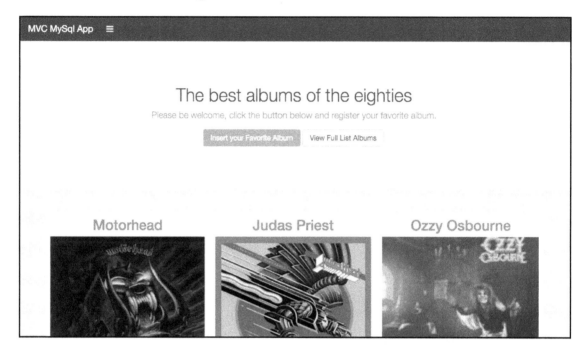

Index template of the home screen

If we check out the Band's route at `http://localhost:3000/bands`, we will see an empty screen, and the same goes for `http://localhost:3000/users`, but here we've found an empty JSON array.

Let's add some content to the Band's routes.

Adding database content

Let's add some content in the database:

1. Create a new file called `mvc_mysql_app.sql` and place the following code:

```
# Dump of table Bands
# ------------------------------------------------------------
DROP TABLE IF EXISTS `Bands`;
CREATE TABLE `Bands` (
  `id` int(11) NOT NULL AUTO_INCREMENT,
```

```
  `name` varchar(255) DEFAULT NULL,
  `description` varchar(255) DEFAULT NULL,
  `album` varchar(255) DEFAULT NULL,
  `year` varchar(255) DEFAULT NULL,
  `UserId` int(11) DEFAULT NULL,
  `createdAt` datetime NOT NULL,
  `updatedAt` datetime NOT NULL,
  PRIMARY KEY (`id`)
) ENGINE=InnoDB DEFAULT CHARSET=utf8;
LOCK TABLES `Bands` WRITE;
/*!40000 ALTER TABLE `Bands` DISABLE KEYS */;
INSERT INTO `Bands` (`id`, `name`, `description`, `album`, `year`,
`UserId`, `createdAt`, `updatedAt`)
VALUES
    (2,'Motorhead','Rock and Roll Band','http://s2.vagalume.com/
    motorhead/discografia/ace-of-spades-W320.jpg','1979',NULL,
    '2016-03-13 21:50:25','2016-03-12 21:50:25'),
    (4,'Black Sabbath','Heavy Metal Band','http://s2.vagalume.com/
    black-sabbath/discografia/heaven-and-hell W320.jpg','1980',
    NULL,'2016-03-12 22:11:00','2016-03-12 23:08:30'),
    (6,'Deep Purple','Heavy Metal band','http://s2.vagalume.com
    /deep-purple/discografia/perfect-strangersW320.jpg',
    '1988',NULL,'2016-03-13 23:09:59','2016-03-12 23:10:29'),
    (7,'White Snake','Heavy Metal band','http://s2.vagalume.com/
    whitesnake/discografia/slip-of-the-tongueW320.jpg','1989',
        NULL,'2016-03-13 01:58:56','2016-03-13 01:58:56'),
    (8,'Iron maiden','Heavy Metal band','http://s2.vagalume.com/
    iron-maiden/discografia/the-number-of-the-beastW320.jpg',
        '1982',NULL,'2016-03-13 02:01:24','2016-03-13 02:01:24'),
    (9,'Queen','Heavy Metal band','http://s2.vagalume.com/queen
    /discografia/greatest-hits-vol-1-W320.jpg','1981',NULL,
        '2016-03-13 02:01:25','2016-03-13 02:01:25');

/*!40000 ALTER TABLE `Bands` ENABLE KEYS */;
UNLOCK TABLES;

/*!40111 SET SQL_NOTES=@OLD_SQL_NOTES */;
/*!40101 SET SQL_MODE=@OLD_SQL_MODE */;
/*!40014 SET FOREIGN_KEY_CHECKS=@OLD_FOREIGN_KEY_CHECKS */;
/*!40101 SET CHARACTER_SET_CLIENT=@OLD_CHARACTER_SET_CLIENT */;
/*!40101 SET CHARACTER_SET_RESULTS=@OLD_CHARACTER_SET_RESULTS */;
/*!40101 SET COLLATION_CONNECTION=@OLD_COLLATION_CONNECTION */;
```

2. Open **Sequel Pro**, click on **File > Import >**, and select the SQL file
   `mvc_mysql_app.sql`.

3. Go back to your browser and refresh the `http://localhost:3000/bands` page; you will see the following result:

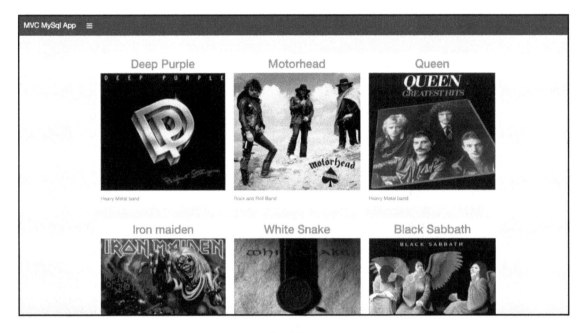

Band-list.html

Creating a Bands form

Now we will create the form for the creation of bands using the modal feature bootstrap:

1. Open the `views/pages/index.html` file and add the following code at the end of the file:

```
<div class="modal fade" id="createBand" tabindex="-1" role="dialog"
   aria-labelledby="myModalLabel" aria-hidden="true">
<div class="modal-dialog" role="document">
<div class="modal-content">
  <form action="/bands" method="post">
    <div class="modal-header">
      <button type="button" class="close" data-dismiss="modal"
      aria-label="Close">
      <span aria-hidden="true">&times;</span>
      </button>
        <h4 class="modal-title" id="myModalLabel">Insert an
```

```
            Album</h4>
      </div>
      <div class="modal-body">
      <fieldset class="form-group">
      <label  for="inputname">Band Name</label>
      <input type="text" id="inputname" name="name"
        class="form-control" placeholder="Band name" required="">
      </fieldset>
      <fieldset class="form-group">
      <label  for="inputdescription">Description</label>
      <textarea id="nputdescription" name="description" rows="8"
        cols="40" class="form-control" placeholder="Description"
        required="">
      </textarea>
      </fieldset>
      <fieldset class="form-group">
      <label  for="inputalbum">Best Album</label>
      <input type="text" id="inputalbum" name="album" rows="8" cols="40"
        class="form-control" placeholder="Link to Album cover">
        </textarea>
      </fieldset>
    <fieldset class="form-group">
      <label  for="inputyear">Release Year</label>
      <input type="text" id="inputyear" name="year" rows="8" cols="40"
        class="form-control" placeholder="Year" required=""></textarea>
    </fieldset>

  </div>
    <div class="modal-footer">
      <button type="button" class="btn btn-secondary"
        data-dismiss="modal">Close</button>
      <button type="submit" class="btn btn-primary">Save
        changes</button>
  </div>
</form>
</div>
</div>
</div>
```

2. Restart the application, open your terminal/shell, and type the following command:

```
npm start
```

3. Click on **Insert an Album** button, and you can see the band form inside the model window, as shown in the following screenshot:

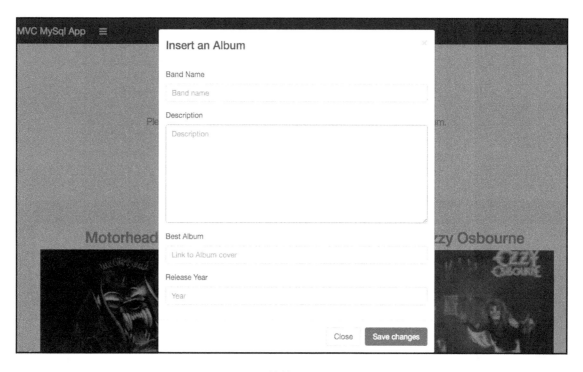

Modal screen

Inserting a new Band

Now let's check the form behavior:

1. Fill in the form with the following data:

- Name: **Sepultura**
- Description: **Brazilian Thrash Metal Band**
- Best album: **https://s2.vagalume.com/sepultura/discografia/roots-W320.jpg**
- Year: **1996**

2. Click on the **save** changes button.

After the form processes, you will be redirected to `band-list.html` with the new record, as the following figure shows:

Band-list.html screen with the new record

The `create()` function on the `Band.js` controller is activated with the form `POST` and the following code from `Band.js` controller is used to save the data and redirect the user:

```
// Create Band
exports.create = function(req, res) {
    // create a new instance of the Bands model with request body
    models.Band.create(req.body).then(function(band) {
        //res.json(band);
        res.redirect('/bands');
    });
};
```

Main difference between ODM (mongoose) and ORM (sequelize)

The main difference between both database mappers is that Sequelize uses promises and Mongoose does not. Promises are easy to handle with asynchronous events. To be more clear, let's see the following code to compare both middlewares:

1. Code block extracted from the `passport.js` file from the previous chapter:

```
User.findOne({ 'local.email' :  email }, function(err, user) {
                // if errors
                if (err)
                return done(err);
                // check email
                if (user) {
                    return done(null, false,
                     req.flash('signupMessage', 'Wohh! the email
                      is already taken.'));
                     } else {
                    // create the user
                    var newUser = new User();
                    // Get user name from req.body
                    newUser.local.name = req.body.name;
                    newUser.local.email = email;
                    newUser.local.password =
                      newUser.generateHash(password);
                    // save data
                    newUser.save(function(err) {
                        if (err)
                        throw err;
                        return done(null, newUser);
                    });
                }
        });
```

2. Now the same code block using the `sequelize` promises function:

```
User.findOne({ where: { localemail: email }})
    .then(function(user) {
  if (user)
      return done(null, false, req.flash('loginMessage', 'That
      email
        is already taken.'));
   if(req.user) {
        var user = req.user;
        user.localemail = email;
        user.localpassword = User.generateHash(password);
        user.save()
            .then (function() {
                done(null, user);
            })
            .catch(function (err) {
                done(null, false, req.flash('loginMessage',
                 err));});
            });
    } else {
        // create the user
        var newUser = User.build ({
            localemail: email,
            localpassword: User.generateHash(password)
        });
        // store the newUser to the database
        newUser.save()
            .then(function() {
                done (null, newUser);
            })
            .catch(function(err) {
                done(null, false, req.flash('loginMessage',
                 err));});
        }
    })
    .catch(function (e) {
        done(null, false, req.flash('loginMessage',e.name + " " +
         e.message));
    })
```

Note the use of the `then()` function is to deal with all returns.

Summary

In this chapter, we explored all the features of the `sequelize-CLI` command line to create a mapping of tables in a relational database. We saw how to create models interactively using the sequelize model feature `create()`, and we also saw how to migrate the schema files to the database.

We started the application with a standard template engine and saw how to refactor the engine templates and use another resource for this, the **Swig** template library.

We learned how to use some SQL commands to connect to the MySQL database and some basic commands for creating tables.

In the next chapter, we will explore the utilization and manipulation of images using Node.js and other important resources.

3
Building a Multimedia Application

One of the most discussed topics in applications with Node.js is undoubtedly the loading and storage of files, whether text, images, audio, or videos. There are also many ways to do it; we will not get into deep technical details, but follow a brief overview of the two most important methods.

One is to save the file in binary format directly in your database, and the other way is to save the file directly on the server (the hard drive of the server), or a simple storage files in the cloud.

In this chapter, we will see a very practical way to make uploading files directly to the hard drive easy and will record the name of the file in our database as a reference. In this way, we can use a scalable storage service in the cloud if necessary.

In this chapter, we will cover these topics:

- How to upload different files to hard disk
- How to use the Stream API to read and write files
- Dealing with multipart form upload
- How to configure the Multer module to store files on a local machine
- How to get the file type and apply simple file validation
- How to use the dynamic user gravatar generator

What we are building?

We will be build an application for uploading images and videos with user authentication using MongoDB and Mongoose; then we can see the images that are going to be the end result of our work.

In this example, we will use another way to begin our project; this time we will start with the `package.json` file.

The following screenshots show what our final application will look like:

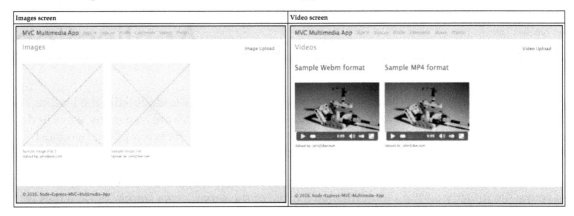

Starting with package.json

As we explained in previous chapters, the `packages.json` file is the heart of the application. The steps to create the necessary file are as follows:

1. Create a folder called `chapter-03`.
2. Create a new file called `package.json` and save it in the `chapter-03` folder with the following code:

```json
{
  "name": "chapter-03",
  "description": "Build a multimedia Application with Node.js",
  "license": "MIT",
  "author": {
    "name": "Fernando Monteiro",
    "url": "https://github.com/newaeonweb/node-6-blueprints"
  },
  "repository": {
    "type": "git",
```

```
    "url": "https://github.com/newaeonweb/node-6-blueprints.git"
  },
  "keywords": [
    "MVC",
    "Express Application",
    "Expressjs",
    "Expressjs images upload",
    "Expressjs video upload"
  ],
  "version": "0.0.1",
  "private": true,
  "scripts": {
    "start": "node app.js"
  },
  "dependencies": {
    "bcrypt-nodejs": "0.0.3",
    "body-parser": "~1.13.2",
    "connect-flash": "^0.1.1",
    "connect-mongo": "^1.1.0",
    "cookie-parser": "~1.3.5",
    "debug": "~2.2.0",
    "ejs": "~2.3.3",
    "express": "~4.13.1",
    "express-session": "^1.13.0",
    "gravatar": "^1.4.0",
    "mongoose": "^4.4.5",
    "morgan": "~1.6.1",
    "multer": "^1.1.0",
    "node-sass-middleware": "0.8.0",
    "passport": "^0.3.2",
    "passport-local": "^1.0.0",
    "serve-favicon": "~2.3.0"
  },
  "devDependencies": {
    "nodemon": "^1.9.1"
  }
}
```

Adding baseline configuration files

Now let's add some of useful files to our project:

1. Create a file called `.editorconfig` and save it in the `chapter-03` folder with the following code:

```
# http://editorconfig.org
root = true

[*]
indent_style = tab
indent_size = 4
charset = utf-8
trim_trailing_whitespace = true
insert_final_newline = true

[*.md]
trim_trailing_whitespace = false
```

2. Create a file called `.gitignore`, save it in `chapter-03`, and include the following code:

```
# Logs
logs
*.log

# Runtime data
pids
*.pid
*.seed
# Directory for instrumented libs generated by jscoverage/JSCover
lib-cov

# Coverage directory used by tools like istanbul
    coverage

# Grunt intermediate
storage (http://gruntjs.com/creating-plugins#storing-task-files)
.grunt

# node-waf configuration
.lock-wscript

# Compiled binary addons (http://nodejs.org/api/addons.html)
build/Release
```

```
# Dependency directory
# https://www.npmjs.org/doc/misc/npm-faq.html#should-i-check-
my-node_modules-folder-into-git-
node_modules

# Debug log from npm
npm-debug.log
```

> Remember, we are using git as source control. Although this file is not necessary to run the application, we strongly recommend that you use a source version control system.

3. Create a file called `app.js`.

Adding server folders

To finish the basic creation of our application, we will now create the directories that store controls, the templates, and other files of the application:

1. Create a folder called `public`, and inside of it, create the following folders:
    - `/images`
    - `/javascripts`
    - `/stylesheets`
    - `/uploads`
    - `/ videos`

2. Create a folder called `server`, and inside of it, create these folders:
    - `/config`
    - `/controllers`
    - `/models`
    - `/views`

3. At this time, our project has all the basic directories and files; let's install the Node modules from `package.json`.

4. Open your terminal/shell at the root project folder and type the following command:

   npm install

The project folder will have the following structure after performing steps 1, 2, and 3:

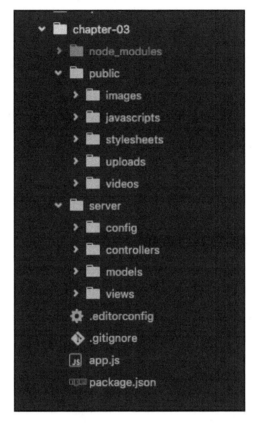

Folder structure

Let's starting creating the `app.js` file content.

Configuring the app.js file

We will, step by step, make the `app.js` file; it will have many similar parts to the application created in `Chapter 01`. However, in this chapter we will be using different modules and a different way to create the application controls.

In, `Node.js` with the Express framework, there are different ways to accomplish the same goals:

1. Open the `app.js` file at the root project folder and add the following modules:

```
// Import basic modules
var express = require('express');
var path = require('path');
var favicon = require('serve-favicon');
var logger = require('morgan');
var cookieParser = require('cookie-parser');
var bodyParser = require('body-parser');

// import multer
var multer  = require('multer');
var upload = multer({ dest:'./public/uploads/', limits: {fileSize:
 1000000, files:1} });
```

Note that we are using the Multer module for handling `multipart/form-data`. You can find more information about `multer` at `https://github.com/expressjs/multer`.

2. Add the following lines right after the `multer` import:

```
// Import home controller
var index = require('./server/controllers/index');
// Import login controller
var auth = require('./server/controllers/auth');
// Import comments controller
var comments = require('./server/controllers/comments');
// Import videos controller
var videos = require('./server/controllers/videos');
// Import images controller
var images = require('./server/controllers/images');
```

Do not worry about these controls files at this time. Later in the book, we will see them one by one. At this point, we will focus on the creation of `app.js`.

3. Add the following lines right after the `controller` importer:

```
// ODM with Mongoose
var mongoose = require('mongoose');
```

```
// Modules to store session
var session = require('express-session');
var MongoStore = require('connect-mongo')(session);
// Import Passport and Warning flash modules
var passport = require('passport');
var flash = require('connect-flash');
// start express application in variable app.
var app = express();
```

The previous code sets the user session with the messaging system and also authentication with Passport.

4. Now let's set the template engine and the connection with the application database. Add the following code right after the express app variable:

```
// view engine setup
app.set('views', path.join(__dirname, 'server/views/pages'));
app.set('view engine', 'ejs');
// Database configuration
var config = require('./server/config/config.js');
// connect to our database
mongoose.connect(config.url);
  // Check if MongoDB is running
mongoose.connection.on('error', function() {
    console.error('MongoDB Connection Error. Make sure MongoDB is
    running.');
});
// Passport configuration
require('./server/config/passport')(passport);
```

The following lines set up some default middlewares and initialize Passport-local and user sessions.

5. Add the following lines right after the previous block of code:

```
app.use(logger('dev'));
app.use(bodyParser.json());
app.use(bodyParser.urlencoded({ extended: false }));
app.use(cookieParser());
app.use(require('node-sass-middleware')({
src: path.join(__dirname, 'public'),
dest: path.join(__dirname, 'public'),
indentedSyntax: true,
sourceMap: true
}));
// Setup public directory
app.use(express.static(path.join(__dirname, 'public')));
```

```
// required for passport
// secret for session
app.use(session({
secret: 'sometextgohere',
saveUninitialized: true,
resave: true,
     //store session on MongoDB using express-session + connect mongo
store: new MongoStore({
url: config.url,
collection : 'sessions'
     })
}));
// Init passport authentication
app.use(passport.initialize());
// persistent login sessions
app.use(passport.session());
// flash messages
app.use(flash());
```

Now let's add all the application routes. We could've used an external file to store all routes, but we will keep it in this file, since we will not have many routes in our application.

6. Add the following code right after `app.use(flash())`:

```
// Application Routes
// Index Route
app.get('/', index.show);
app.get('/login', auth.signin);
app.post('/login', passport.authenticate('local-login', {
   //Success go to Profile Page / Fail go to login page
successRedirect : '/profile',
failureRedirect : '/login',
failureFlash : true
}));
app.get('/signup', auth.signup);
app.post('/signup', passport.authenticate('local-signup', {
    //Success go to Profile Page / Fail go to Signup page
successRedirect : '/profile',
failureRedirect : '/signup',
failureFlash : true
}));
app.get('/profile', auth.isLoggedIn, auth.profile);
// Logout Page
app.get('/logout', function(req, res) {
req.logout();
res.redirect('/');
 });
```

```
// Setup routes for comments
app.get('/comments', comments.hasAuthorization, comments.list);
app.post('/comments', comments.hasAuthorization, comments.create);

// Setup routes for videos
app.get('/videos', videos.hasAuthorization, videos.show);
app.post('/videos', videos.hasAuthorization, upload.single('video'),
videos.uploadVideo);

// Setup routes for images
app.post('/images', images.hasAuthorization, upload.single('image'),
images.uploadImage);
app.get('/images-gallery', images.hasAuthorization, images.show);
```

> Here you can see that we are using the same routes and functions as the sample application in Chapter 01, *Building a Twitter-Like Application Using the MVC Design Pattern*; we kept the routes, authentication and comments, with minor changes.

The last step to be taken is to add the error functions and configure the server port that our application will use.

1. Add the following code after the previous code block:

```
// catch 404 and forward to error handler
app.use(function(req, res, next) {
var err = new Error('Not Found');
err.status = 404;
next(err);
 });
// development error handler
// will print stacktrace
if (app.get('env') === 'development') {
app.use(function(err, req, res, next) {
res.status(err.status || 500);
res.render('error', {
message: err.message,
error: err
         });
    });
}

// production error handler
// no stacktraces leaked to user
app.use(function(err, req, res, next) {
res.status(err.status || 500);
res.render('error', {
```

```
  message: err.message,
error: {}
    });
});

module.exports = app;

app.set('port', process.env.PORT || 3000);

var server = app.listen(app.get('port'), function() {
console.log('Express server listening on port ' +
server.address().port);
});
```

Creating the config.js file

Create a file called config.js inside the config folder at server/config/ and add the following code:

```
// Database URL
module.exports = {
    'url' : 'mongodb://localhost/mvc-app-multimedia'
};
```

Create a file called passport.js inside the config folder at: server/config/.

In this step, we will use the same configuration file for the Passport module used in Chapter 01, *Building a Twitter-Like Application Using the MVC Design Pattern in Node.js*. You can download the sample code from www.packtpub.com or from the official repository of the book from GitHub.

Creating the controller's files

Now let's create the controller's files in server/controllers:

1. Create a file called auth.js and add the following code:

```
// get gravatar icon from email
var gravatar = require('gravatar');
var passport = require('passport');

// Signin GET
exports.signin = function(req, res) {
```

```
        // List all Users and sort by Date
res.render('login', { title: 'Login Page', message:
req.flash('loginMessage') });
};
// Signup GET
exports.signup = function(req, res) {
        // List all Users and sort by Date
res.render('signup', { title: 'Signup Page', message:
req.flash('signupMessage') });

};
// Profile GET
exports.profile = function(req, res) {
        // List all Users and sort by Date
res.render('profile', { title: 'Profile Page', user : req.user,
avatar:gravatar.url(req.user.email ,  {s: '100', r: 'x', d: 'retro'},
true) });
};
// Logout function
exports.logout = function () {
req.logout();
res.redirect('/');
};

// check if user is logged in
exports.isLoggedIn = function(req, res, next) {
if (req.isAuthenticated())
return next();
res.redirect('/login');
};
```

2. Create a file called `comments.js` and add this code:

```
// get gravatar icon from email
var gravatar = require('gravatar');
// get Comments model
var Comments = require('../models/comments');

// List Comments
exports.list = function(req, res) {
   // List all comments and sort by Date
Comments.find().sort('-created').populate('user',
'local.email').exec(function(error, comments) {
 if (error) {
 returnres.send(400, {
 message: error
             });
       }
```

```
        // Render result
    res.render('comments', {
    title: 'Comments Page',
    comments: comments,
    gravatar: gravatar.url(comments.email ,   {s: '80', r: 'x', d:
     'retro'}, true)
            });
    });
};
// Create Comments
exports.create = function(req, res) {
    // create a new instance of the Comments model with request body
var comments = new Comments(req.body);
    // Set current user (id)
comments.user = req.user;
    // save the data received
comments.save(function(error) {
if (error) {
returnres.send(400, {
 message: error
            });
        }
        // Redirect to comments
res.redirect('/comments');
      });
};
// Comments authorization middleware
 exports.hasAuthorization = function(req, res, next) {
    if (req.isAuthenticated())
    return next();
  res.redirect('/login');
};
```

3. Create a file called `index.js` and add the following code:

```
// Show home screen
exports.show = function(req, res) {
    // Render home screen
  res.render('index', {
        title: 'Multimedia Application',
        callToAction: 'An easy way to upload and manipulate files
          with Node.js'
    });
};
```

Now let's create the controllers to handle the uploading of images and videos to our application. We will use the Node.js API stream to read and write our files.

You can find the complete documentation of this API at `https://nodejs.org/api/stream.html`.

1. Create a file called `images.js`.
2. Add the following code:

```
// Import modules
var fs = require('fs');
var mime = require('mime');
// get gravatar icon from email
var gravatar = require('gravatar');
var Images = require('../models/images');
// set image file types
var IMAGE_TYPES = ['image/jpeg','image/jpg', 'image/png'];
```

3. Add the following code right after the `importer` modules:

```
// Show images gallery
exports.show = function (req, res) {

Images.find().sort('-created').populate('user',
'local.email').exec(function(error, images) {
if (error) {
  returnres.status(400).send({
    message: error
    });
}
// Render galley
res.render('images-gallery', {
title: 'Images Gallery',
images: images,
gravatar: gravatar.url(images.email ,  {s: '80', r: 'x', d: 'retro'},
true)
        });
      });
};
```

Now let's add the function that is responsible for saving the file to a temporary directory and transferring it to a directory in the `public` folder.

4. Add the following lines, right after the previous code block:

```
// Image upload
exports.uploadImage = function(req, res) {
var src;
var dest;
var targetPath;
var targetName;
var tempPath = req.file.path;
console.log(req.file);
    //get the mime type of the file
var type = mime.lookup(req.file.mimetype);
   // get file extension
var extension = req.file.path.split(/[. ]+/).pop();
   // check support file types
if (IMAGE_TYPES.indexOf(type) == -1) {
  returnres.status(415).send('Supported image formats: jpeg, jpg,
  jpe, png.');
 }
    // Set new path to images
targetPath = './public/images/' + req.file.originalname;
   // using read stream API to read file
src = fs.createReadStream(tempPath);
   // using a write stream API to write file
dest = fs.createWriteStream(targetPath);
src.pipe(dest);

   // Show error
src.on('error', function(err) {
if (err) {
  returnres.status(500).send({
  message: error
           });
       }
 });
   // Save file process
src.on('end', function() {
       // create a new instance of the Images model with request body
var image = new Images(req.body);
       // Set the image file name
image.imageName = req.file.originalname;
       // Set current user (id)
image.user = req.user;
       // save the data received
image.save(function(error) {
if (error) {
  return res.status(400).send({
  message: error
```

```
                          });
                      }
              });
              // remove from temp folder
      fs.unlink(tempPath, function(err) {
      if (err) {
          return res.status(500).send('Woh, something bad happened here');
              }
              // Redirect to galley's page
          res.redirect('images-gallery');
              });
          });
      };
```

Add the function that checks whether the user is authenticated and authorized to insert an image.

5. Add the following code at the end of the file:

```
// Images authorization middleware
exports.hasAuthorization = function(req, res, next) {
if (req.isAuthenticated())
return next();
res.redirect('/login');
};
```

6. Now let's repeat this procedure for the control of `videos.js`, then create a file called `videos.js`, and add the following code:

```
// Import modules
var fs = require('fs');
var mime = require('mime');
// get gravatar icon from email
var gravatar = require('gravatar');

// get video model
var Videos = require('../models/videos');
// set image file types
var VIDEO_TYPES = ['video/mp4', 'video/webm', 'video/ogg',
  'video/ogv'];

// List Videos
exports.show = function(req, res) {

Videos.find().sort('-created').populate('user',
'local.email').exec(function(error, videos) {
if (error) {
```

```
    return res.status(400).send({
    message: error
            });
        }
        // Render result
console.log(videos);
res.render('videos', {
title: 'Videos Page',
videos: videos,
gravatar: gravatar.url(videos.email ,  {s: '80', r: 'x', d: 'retro'},
true)
        });
    });
};
// Create Videos
exports.uploadVideo = function(req, res) {
var src;
var dest;
var targetPath;
var targetName;
console.log(req);
var tempPath = req.file.path;
    //get the mime type of the file
var type = mime.lookup(req.file.mimetype);
   // get file extenstion
var extension = req.file.path.split(/[. ]+/).pop();
  // check support file types
if (VIDEO_TYPES.indexOf(type) == -1) {
return res.status(415).send('Supported video formats: mp4, webm, ogg,
ogv');
    }
    // Set new path to images
targetPath = './public/videos/' + req.file.originalname;
    // using read stream API to read file
src = fs.createReadStream(tempPath);
  // using a write stream API to write file
dest = fs.createWriteStream(targetPath);
src.pipe(dest);
    // Show error
src.on('error', function(error) {
if (error) {
  return res.status(500).send({
  message: error
            });
        }
    });

    // Save file process
```

```
        src.on('end', function() {
                // create a new instance of the Video model with request body
        var video = new Videos(req.body);
                // Set the video file name
        video.videoName = req.file.originalname;
                // Set current user (id)
        video.user = req.user;
                // save the data received
        video.save(function(error) {
        if (error) {
          return res.status(400).send({
          message: error
                        });
                }
            });
                // remove from temp folder
        fs.unlink(tempPath, function(err) {
        if (err) {
          return res.status(500).send({
          message: error
                        });
                }
                // Redirect to galley's page
        res.redirect('videos');
                });
            });
        };
        // Videos authorization middleware
        exports.hasAuthorization = function(req, res, next) {
        if (req.isAuthenticated())
            return next();
            res.redirect('/login');
        };
```

As you can see, we use the same concept as the image controller to create the video controller.

Due to the stream, the Node.js API can handle any type of file using the
`createReadStream()` and `createWriteStream()` functions.

Creating model files

Now let's create the application's template files. Since we are using the mongoose middleware used in chapter 1, *Building a Twitter-Like Application Using the MVC Design Pattern in Node.js*, we will keep the same type of configuration:

1. Create a file called comments.js inside the models folder at server/models and add the following code:

```
// load the things we need
var mongoose = require('mongoose');
var Schema = mongoose.Schema;

var commentSchema = mongoose.Schema({
created: {
 type: Date,
default: Date.now
    },
title: {
type: String,
default: '',
trim: true,
required: 'Title cannot be blank'
    },
content: {
type: String,
default: '',
trim: true
    },
user: {
type: Schema.ObjectId,
ref: 'User'
   }
});

module.exports = mongoose.model('Comments', commentSchema);
```

2. Create a file called `user.js` inside the models folder at `server/models` and add the following code:

```
// Import Mongoose and password Encrypt
var mongoose = require('mongoose');
var bcrypt   = require('bcrypt-nodejs');

// define the schema for User model
var userSchema = mongoose.Schema({
    // Using local for Local Strategy Passport
local: {
name: String,
email: String,
password: String,
    }

});

// Encrypt Password
userSchema.methods.generateHash = function(password) { return
bcrypt.hashSync(password, bcrypt.genSaltSync(8), null);
};

// Verify if password is valid
userSchema.methods.validPassword = function(password) { return
bcrypt.compareSync(password, this.local.password);
};

// create the model for users and expose it to our app
module.exports = mongoose.model('User', userSchema);
```

3. Then, create a file called `images.js` inside the `models` folder at `server/models` and add this code:

```
// load the things we need
var mongoose = require('mongoose');
var Schema = mongoose.Schema;

var imagesSchema = mongoose.Schema({
created: {
type: Date,
default: Date.now
    },
title: {
type: String,
default: '',
trim: true,
```

```
required: 'Title cannot be blank'
    },
imageName: {
type: String
    },
user: {
type: Schema.ObjectId,
ref: 'User'
    }
});

module.exports = mongoose.model('Images', imagesSchema);
```

4. Next, create a file called `videos.js` inside the `models` folder at `server/models` and add the following code:

```
// load the things we need
var mongoose = require('mongoose');
var Schema = mongoose.Schema;

var videosSchema = mongoose.Schema({
  created: {
    type: Date,
    default: Date.now
  },
  title: {
    type: String,
    default: '',
    trim: true,
    required: 'Title cannot be blank'
  },
  videoName: {
   type: String
  },
  user: {
    type: Schema.ObjectId,
    ref: 'User'
  }
});

module.exports = mongoose.model('Videos', videosSchema);
```

Creating view files

In this section, we will use the same `view` files used in `Chapter 01` for the following files:

- `views / partials / javascripts.ejs`
- `views / partials / stylesheets.ejs`
- `views / pages / login.ejs`
- `views / pages / signup.ejs`
- `views / pages / profile.ejs`
- `views / pages / index.ejs`
- `views / pages / comments.js`
- `views / pages / error.ejs`

As previously commented, you can download these files from the Packt website or the official GitHub repository of the book.

In addition to these files, we will create the `views` files for the photos and videos page, and add these routes to the application menu:

1. Create a file called `footer.ejs` inside the `views/partials` folder and add the following code:

```
<footer class="footer">
<div class="container">
 <span>&copy 2016. Node-Express-MVC-Multimedia-App</span>
</div>
</footer>
```

2. Then create a file called `header.ejs` inside the `views/partials` folder and add this code:

```
<!-- Fixed navbar -->
<div class="pos-f-t">
  <div class="collapse" id="navbar-header">
    <div class="container bg-inverse p-a-1">
      <h3>Collapsed content</h3>
      <p>Toggleable via the navbar brand.</p>
    </div>
  </div>
  <nav class="navbarnavbar-light navbar-static-top">
  <div class="container">
    <button class="navbar-toggler hidden-sm-up" type="button"
    data-toggle="collapse" data-target="#exCollapsingNavbar2">
```

```
    Menu
    </button>
    <div class="collapse navbar-toggleable-xs"
      id="exCollapsingNavbar2">
      <a class="navbar-brand" href="/">MVC Multimedia App</a>
      <ul class="navnavbar-navnavbar-right">
        <li class="nav-item">
          <a class="nav-link" href="/login">Sign in</a>
        </li>
        <li class="nav-item">
          <a class="nav-link" href="/signup">Sign up</a>
        </li>
        <li class="nav-item">
          <a class="nav-link" href="/profile">Profile</a>
        </li>
        <li class="nav-item">
          <a class="nav-link" href="/comments">Comments</a>
        </li>
        <li class="nav-item">
          <a class="nav-link" href="/videos">Videos</a>
        </li>
        <li class="nav-item">
          <a class="nav-link" href="/images-gallery">Photos</a>
        </li>
      </ul>
    </div>
  </div>
  </nav>
</div>
<!-- Fixed navbar -->
```

3. Create a file called `images-gallery.ejs` inside the `views/pages` folder and add the following code:

```
<!DOCTYPE html>
<html>
<head>
  <title><%= title %></title>
  <% include ../partials/stylesheet %>
</head>
<body>
  <% include ../partials/header %>
  <div class="container">
    <div class="row">
      <div class="col-lg-6">
        <h4 class="text-muted">Images</h4>
      </div>
      <div class="col-lg-6">
```

```
      <button type="button" class="btnbtn-secondary pull-right"
      data-toggle="modal" data-target="#createImage">
             Image Upload
      </button>
   </div>
</div>
<!-- Modal -->
<div class="modal fade" id="createImage" tabindex="-1"
 role="dialog" aria-labelledby="myModalLabel"
 aria-hidden="true">
   <div class="modal-dialog" role="document">
     <div class="modal-content">
       <form action="/images" method="post"
         enctype="multipart/formdata">
       <div class="modal-header">
         <button type="button" class="close" data-dismiss="modal"
          aria-label="Close">
           <span aria-hidden="true">&times;</span>
         </button>
         <h4 class="modal-title" id="myModalLabel">
           Upload a imagefile
         </h4>
       </div>

       <div class="modal-body">
         <fieldset class="form-group">
         <label  for="itle">Title</label>
           <input type="text" id="itle" name="title" class="form-
           control" placeholder="Image Title" required="">
         </fieldset>
         <label class="file" style="width: 100%">
           <input type="file" id="image" name="image">
           <span class="file-custom"></span>
         </label>
       </div>
       <div class="modal-footer">
         <button type="button" class="btnbtnsecondary" data
          dismiss="modal">Close
          </button>
         <button type="submit" class="btnbtn-primary">
            Savechanges
         </button>
       </div>
       </form>
     </div>
   </div>
</div>
<hr>
```

```
    <div class="row">
      <% images.forEach(function(images){ %>
      <div class="col-lg-4">
        <figure class="figure">
         <img src="images/<%= images.imageName %>" class="figure-img
          img-fluid img-rounded" alt="<%= images.imageName %>">
         <figcaption class="figure-caption"><%= images.title%>
         </figcaption>
         <small>Upload by: <%= images.user.local.email %></small>
        </figure>
      </div>
      <% }); %>
    </div>
  </div>
  <% include ../partials/footer %>
  <% include ../partials/javascript %>
 </body>
 </html>
```

The previous code sets a form HTML tag to use the
enctype="multipart/form-data type and creates a loop over the image object
to show all the images added to the gallery.

4. Create a file called videos.ejs inside the views/pages folder and add this
   code:

```
<!DOCTYPE html>
<html>
<head>
  <title><%= title %></title>
  <% include ../partials/stylesheet %>
</head>
<body>
<% include ../partials/header %>
<div class="container">
<div class="row">
<div class="col-lg-6">
<h4 class="text-muted">Videos</h4>
</div>
<div class="col-lg-6">
<button type="button" class="btn btn-secondary pull-right"
 data-toggle="modal" data-target="#createVideo">
              Video Upload
 </button>
</div>
</div>
<!-- Modal -->
```

```html
<div class="modal fade" id="createVideo" tabindex="-1" role="dialog"
 aria-labelledby="myModalLabel" aria-hidden="true">
<div class="modal-dialog" role="document">
<div class="modal-content">
<form action="/videos" method="post" enctype="multipart/form-data">
<div class="modal-header">
<button type="button" class="close" data-dismiss="modal"
 aria-label="Close">
<span aria-hidden="true">&times;</span>
</button>
<h4 class="modal-title" id="myModalLabel">Upload a video file</h4>
 </div>

<div class="modal-body">
<fieldset class="form-group">
<label  for="inputitle">Title</label>
<input type="text" id="inputitle" name="title" class="form-control"
 placeholder="Video Title" required="">
</fieldset>
 <label class="file" style="width: 100%"
   onclick="$('input[id=lefile]').click();">
 <input type="file" id="video" name="video">
 <span class="file-custom"></span>
 </label>
 </div>
<div class="modal-footer">
<button type="button" class="btnbtn-secondary"
 data-dismiss="modal">Close</button>
<button type="submit" class="btnbtn-primary">Save changes</button>
</div>
</form>
</div>
</div>
</div>
<hr>
<div class="row">
<% videos.forEach(function(videos){ %>
<div class="col-lg-4">
<h4 class="list-group-item-heading"><%= videos.title %></h4>
<video width="320" height="240" controls preload="auto"
codecs="avc1.42E01E, mp4a.40.2">
<source src="<%= videos.videoName %>" type="video/mp4" />
</video>
<small>Upload by: <%= videos.user.local.email %></small>
 </div>
<% }); %>
</div>
</div>
```

```
<% include ../partials/footer %>
<% include ../partials/javascript %>
</body>
</html>
```

Creating the public folder content

At this stage, we've completed all the necessary steps to create folders and files inside the `server` directory as controllers, models, and views.

Now we need to copy the contents of the `public` folder we created in `Chapter 01`:

1. Copy the following folders and their contents and paste them into the `chapter-03` root project folder:
   - `public/images`
   - `public/javascripts`
     - `bootstrap.min.js`
     - `jquery.min.js`
   - `public/stylesheets`
     - `bootstrap.min.css`
     - `style.css`
     - `style.css.map`
     - `style.sass`

2. Create a folder called `uploads` inside the `public` folder.
3. Then, create a folder called `videos` inside the `public` folder.

Inserting images in the application using the upload form

Now it's time to test the application, noting that for this you should start your MongoDB. Otherwise the application will return a failure error while connecting:

1. Open your terminal/shell at the root project folder and type the following command:

   npm start

2. Go to `http://localhost:3000/signup` and enter the following data:
   - name: **John**
   - email: **john@doe.com**
   - password: **123**

3. Go to `http://localhost:3000/images-gallery` , click on the **Image Upload** button, fill in the form with a title and choose an image (note that we set up the image size limit to *1* MB just for example purposes). You will see a model form, as the following screenshit shows:

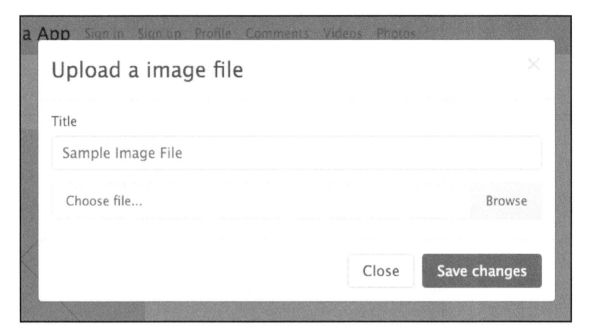

Image upload form

4. After choosing the image, click on the **Save Changes** button, and you're done! You will see the following screenshot at `http://localhost:3000/images-gallery` page:

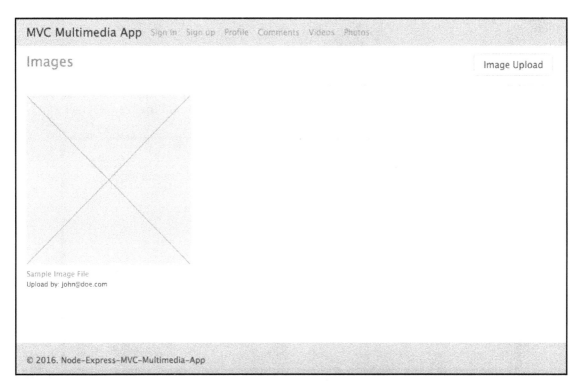

Gallery image screen

Inserting video files into the application using the upload form

As we did to insert an image into our application, let's follow the same procedure to insert a video:

1. Go to `http://localhost:3000/videos`, click on the **Video Upload** button, fill in the form with a title and choose a video file (note that again we set up the image size limit to 1 MB and the video format to *MP4, WEBM* just for example purposes). You will see a modal form, as shown in the following screenshot:

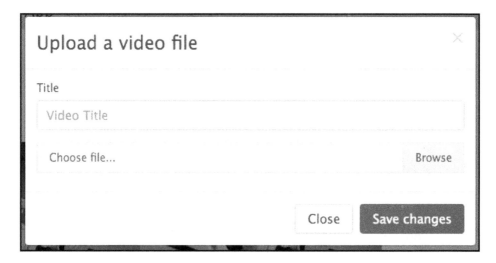

Video upload form

Important notes about image and video upload

Node.js gives us a complete API for handling files (Stream API) such as image, video, pdf, and other formats. There are also several ways to do file uploads to the server or for storage in the cloud, as already noted. Furthermore, the Node.js ecosystem provides us with many modules to deal with the different types of files and to use forms with `enctype = "multipart / form-data"`.

In this chapter, we use the `Multer` module. Multer is a complete middleware for handling files with various methods for upload and file storage.

In this example, we only stored the filename in MongoDB and sent the file directly to a server folder. There is another way to upload, where we send the file in binary format to the database, although it is important to remember that the capacity of MongoDB to store *BSON* file is *16* MB.

If you choose to store the files in the MongoDB database, you can use the GridFS feature of MongoDB and Node.js modules as `GridFS-stream`, as an upload middleware, just like we did with Multer.

In the example for this chapter, we limit the upload size to 1 MB, which we can see in the following highlighted line:

```
var upload = multer({
    dest:'./public/uploads/',
    limits: {fileSize: 1000000, files:1}
});
```

You can find more information about limits in the official documentation for Multer at `https://github.com/expressjs/multer#limits`.

Summary

In this chapter, we built a complete Node MVC application for file upload of images and videos; we also set up a user session with e-mail and password authentication, storing the encrypted password on MongoDB.

In addition, this chapter enabled you to build modular, robust, and scalable MVC applications.

Also, we used very common features across web applications, such as access to the database, sign-in and sign up, and file upload.

In the next chapter, we will see how to manipulate and upload images using a cloud service and store metadata on MongoDB.

4
Don't Take a Photograph, Make It – An App for Photographers

In this chapter, we will discuss a topic much discussed in the Node.js community around the world–image manipulation using the Node.js architecture and cloud.

As we have seen in the previous chapter, we have two ways to store images and files, using a hard disk on our server or directly to the cloud. In Chapter 03, *Building a Multimedia Application*, we used the approach of uploading directly to our server, storing the images on the hard drive.

In this chapter, we will use a server in the cloud to store and manipulate images in our Photobook application.

We will use a service called Cloudinary to store and manipulate the images.

In this chapter, we will cover these topics:

- How to set up an MVC application using generator-express
- How to install the cloudinary npm module
- Implementing the Materialize.css framework
- How to upload images to the cloud and save meta-data on MongoDB
- How to use Global variables with dot files
- Setting up a Cloudinary account and creating folders
- How to upload images using the Cloudinary API
- How to render templates using URL parameters in the Cloudinary API

What we are building

At the end of this chapter, we will have created the following sample application, a robust and scalable photobook:

Home screen of the photobook application

Creating the baseline applications

In this chapter, we will use a slightly modified version of the `express-generator` that we used in previous chapters.

This generator is called `generator-express`; it is heavily based on `express generator`, but with a few more features.

Here are the steps for our installation:

1. Open the terminal/shell and type:

   ```
   npm install -g generator-express
   ```

2. Create a folder called `chapter04`.

3. Open your terminal/shell within the `chapter04` folder and type the following command:

   ```
   yo express
   ```

Now, fill the questions in this order:

- Choose `N`, we already created the project folder in *step 2*
- Choose `MVC` for application type
- Choose `Swig` for template engine
- Choose `None` for CSS preprocessor
- Choose `None` for database (later in the chapter, we will set up the database manually)
- Choose `Gulp` for LiveReload and other stuff

 Don't worry about `Gulp`, if you never heard about it. Later in the book, we will see and explain some building tools.

At the end of the generator, we have the following structure of directories:

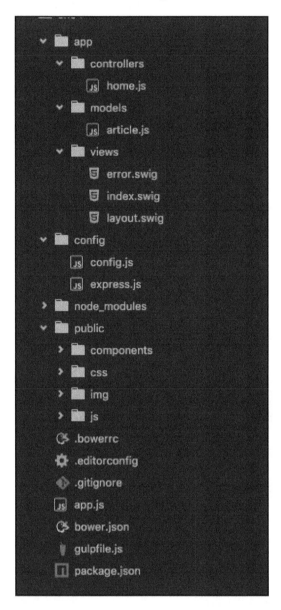

Application folder structure

Changing the application structure

Unlike the example we used in `Chapter 1`, *Building a Twitter-Like Application Using the MVC Design Pattern*, we will not make major changes to the current structure; we will only change the `views` folder.

As the sample application, there will be a book of pictures; we will add a folder named book in the `views` folder:

1. Create a folder called `book` inside the `app/views` folder.
2. Now we will create a configuration file for the Cloudinary service. Later in the chapter, we will discuss all the details about Cloudinary; for now, just create a new file.
3. Create a file called `.env` at the root folder.

Now, we have the necessary basis to move forward.

Adding Node modules to deal with images and the Cloudinary cloud service

Now we will add the necessary modules to our application in the `package.json` file.

1. Add the following highlighted lines of code to the `package.json` file:

```
{
    "name": "chapter-04",
    "description": "Don't take a photograph, make it - An app for
      photographers",
    "license": "MIT",
    "author": {
      "name": "Fernando Monteiro",
      "url": "https://github.com/newaeonweb/node-6-blueprints"
    },
    "repository": {
      "type": "git",
      "url": "https://github.com/newaeonweb/node-6-blueprints.git"
    },
    "keywords": [
      "MVC",
      "Express Application",
      "Expressjs",
      "Expressjs cloud upload",
      "Expressjs cloudinary upload"
```

```
        ],
        "version": "0.0.1",
        "private": true,
      "scripts": {
        "start": "gulp"
      },
      "dependencies": {
        "body-parser": "^1.13.3",
        "cloudinary": "^1.3.1",
        "compression": "^1.5.2",
        "connect-multiparty": "^2.0.0",
        "cookie-parser": "^1.3.3",
        "dotenv": "^2.0.0",
        "express": "^4.13.3",
        "glob": "^6.0.4",
        "jugglingdb": "^2.0.0-rc3",
        "jugglingdb-mongodb": "^0.1.1",
        "method-override": "^2.3.0",
        "morgan": "^1.6.1",
        "serve-favicon": "^2.3.0",
        "swig": "^1.4.2"
      },
      "devDependencies": {
        "gulp": "^3.9.0",
        "gulp-nodemon": "^2.0.2",
        "gulp-livereload": "^3.8.0",
        "gulp-plumber": "^1.0.0"
      }
    }
```

With just a few modules, we can build a very robust and scalable application. Let's describe each one:

Module name	Description	More information
cloudinary	Cloud service to store and pipeline image and video files	https://www.npmjs.com/package/cloudinary
connect-multiparty	Middleware to accept multipart form upload	https://www.npmjs.com/package/connect-multiparty
dotenv	Load environment variables	https://www.npmjs.com/package/dotenv
jugglingdb	Cross–database ORM	https://www.npmjs.com/package/jugglingdb
jugglingdb-mongodb	MongoDB connector	https://www.npmjs.com/package/jugglingdb-mongodb

Creating the book controller

We will follow the same generator code pattern that the generator suggests; one of the advantages of using this generator is that we already have the MVC pattern at our disposal.

> Remember, you can download the example files from the Packpub website, or directly from the GitHub book repository.

1. Create a file called `books.js` inside the `controllers` folder.
2. Add the following code to the `book.js` file:

```
var express = require('express'),
    router = express.Router(),
    schema = require('../models/book'),
    Picture = schema.models.Picture,
    cloudinary = require('cloudinary').v2,
    fs = require('fs'),
    multipart = require('connect-multiparty'),
    multipartMiddleware = multipart();


module.exports = function (app) {
    app.use('/', router);
};
// Get pictures list
router.get('/books', function (req, res, next) {
    Picture.all().then(function (photos) {
        console.log(photos);
    res.render('book/books', {
        title: 'PhotoBook',
        photos: photos,
        cloudinary: cloudinary
    })
    });
});
// Get form upload
router.get('/books/add', function (req, res, next) {
    res.render('book/add-photo', {
    title: 'Upload Picture'
  });
});
// Post to
router.post('/books/add', multipartMiddleware, function (req, res,
 next)
```

```
{
    // Checking the file received
    console.log(req.files);
    // create a new instance using Picture Model
    var photo = new Picture(req.body);
    // Get temp file path
    var imageFile = req.files.image.path;
    // Upload file to Cloudinary
    cloudinary.uploader.upload(imageFile, {
        tags: 'photobook',
        folder: req.body.category + '/',
        public_id: req.files.image.originalFilename
        // eager: {
        //    width: 280, height: 200, crop: "fill", gravity: "face"
        // }
    })
      .then(function (image) {
        console.log('Picture uploaded to Cloudinary');
        // Check the image Json file
        console.dir(image);
        // Added image informations to picture model
        photo.image = image;
        // Save photo with image metadata
        return photo.save();
      })
      .then(function (photo) {
          console.log('Successfully saved');
          // Remove image from local folder
          var filePath = req.files.image.path;
          fs.unlinkSync(filePath);
      })
      .finally(function () {
          // Show the result with image file
          res.render('book/posted-photo', {
              title: 'Upload with Success',
              photo: photo,
              upload: photo.image
          });
      });
});
```

Let's explain some important points about the previous code example:

- In order to use the Cloudinary API inside our views, we need to pass the `cloudinary` variable to our views:

```
res.render('book/books', {
        title: 'PhotoBook',
        photos: photos,
        cloudinary: cloudinary
})
```

- For best practices when using `multipartMiddleware`, we need to clean up each file that we upload to the cloud:

```
.then(function (photo) {
    console.log('Successfully saved');
    // Remove image from local folder
    var filePath = req.files.image.path;
    fs.unlinkSync(filePath);
})
```

Later we will discuss more about the Cloudinary API.

Note that when you use the multipart connect, it by default loads the image to a folder on your hard drive, so you should always delete all the files loaded in your application.

Creating the book model file

The procedure for creating models for this application is very similar to what we have seen in previous chapters; almost every module's **ORM/ODM** has a very similar operation.

Let's see how to create the model for the book object:

1. Create a file called `book.js` inside `app/models` and place the following code:

```
var Schema = require('jugglingdb').Schema;
// Pay attention, we are using MongoDB for this example.
var schema = new Schema('mongodb', {url: 'mongodb://localhost
/photobookapp'});

// Setup Books Schema
var Picture = schema.define('Picture', {
```

```
    title : { type: String, length: 255 },
    description: {type: Schema.Text},
    category: {type: String, length: 255 },
    image : { type: JSON}
});

module.exports = schema;
```

Note that we are using MongoDB to store the book model. Also remember that you must have your local MongoDB up and running before starting the application.

Adding a CSS framework to the application

In all the chapters of this book, we will always use the most up to date technologies, as we have seen in previous chapters with the use of the new Bootstrap (Alpha Release).

In this chapter in particular, we will use a design pattern known as `Material Design`.

You can read more about the design material at `https://www.google.com /design/spec/material-design/introduction.html`.

For this, we'll use a simple `CSS` framework called `Materialize.css`.

You can find more information about Materialize at this link: `http://mate rializecss.com/`.

1. Replace all of the content from the `app/views/layout.swig` file with the following lines of code:

```
<!doctype html>
<html lang="en">
<head>
    <meta charset="UTF-8">
    <meta name="viewport" content="width=device-width">
    <title>{{ title }}</title>
    <!--Let browser know website is optimized for mobile-->
    <meta name="viewport" content="width=device-width, initial-
    scale=1.0"/>
```

```
<!-- Import Google Material font and icons -->
<link href="https://fonts.googleapis.com/icon?family=
Material+Icons" rel="stylesheet">
 <!-- Compiled and minified CSS -->
 <link rel="stylesheet" href="https://cdnjs.cloudflare.com/
 ajax/libs/materialize/0.97.6/css/materialize.min.css">
 <link rel="stylesheet" href="/css/style.css">
</head>
<body>
    <nav class="orange darken-4" role="navigation">
        <div class="nav-wrapper container"><a id="logo-container"
        href="/" class="brand-logo">Logo</a>
            <ul class="right hide-on-med-and-down">
                <li><a href="/books">Books</a></li>
                <li><a href="/books/add">Add Picture</a></li>
            </ul>

            <ul id="nav-mobile" class="side-nav" style="transform:
             translateX(-100%);">
                <li><a href="/books">Books</a></li>
                <li><a href="/books/add">Add Picture</a></li>
            </ul>
            <a href="#" data-activates="nav-mobile" class="button-
            collapse">
            <i class="material-icons">menu</i></a>
        </div>
    </nav>
    {% block content %}{% endblock %}
    <!-- Footer -->
    <footer class="page-footer orange darken-4">
        <div class="container">
            <div class="row">
                <div class="col l6 s12">
                    <h5 class="white-text">Some Text Example</h5>
                    <p class="grey-text text-lighten-4">Lorem ipsum
                    dolor sit amet, consectetur adipiscing elit,
                    sed do eiusmod tempor incididunt ut labore et
                    dolore magnaaliqua. Ut enim ad minim veniam, quis
                    nostrud exercitation ullamco laboris nisi ut
                    aliquip ex ea commodo consequat. Duis aute irure
                    dolor in reprehenderit in voluptate velit esse
                    cillum dolore eu fugiat nulla pariatur.</p>
                </div>
                <div class="col l3 s12">
                    <h5 class="white-text">Sample Links</h5>
                    <ul>
                      <li><a class="white-text" href="#!">Link 1
                        </a></li>
```

```
                            <li><a class="white-text" href="#!">Link 2
                                </a></li>
                            <li><a class="white-text" href="#!">Link 3
                                </a></li>
                            <li><a class="white-text" href="#!">Link 4
                                </a></li>
                        </ul>
                    </div>
                  <div class="col 13 s12">
                      <h5 class="white-text">Sample Links</h5>
                      <ul>
                        <li><a class="white-text" href="#!">Link 1
                            </a></li>
                        <li><a class="white-text" href="#!">Link 2
                            </a></li>
                        <li><a class="white-text" href="#!">Link 3
                            </a></li>
                        <li><a class="white-text" href="#!">Link 4
                            </a></li>
                      </ul>
                  </div>
              </div>
          </div>
            <div class="footer-copyright">
              <div class="container">
                MVC Express App for: <a class="white-text text-darken-2"
                href="#">Node.js 6 Blueprints Book</a>
              </div>
            </div>
        </footer>
        <!-- Place scripts at the bottom page-->
        {% if ENV_DEVELOPMENT %}
        <script src="http://localhost:35729/livereload.js"></script>
        {% endif %}

        <!--Import jQuery before materialize.js-->
        <script type="text/javascript"
          src="https://code.jquery.com/jquery-2.1.1.min.js"></script>
        <!-- Compiled and minified JavaScript -->
        <script src="https://cdnjs.cloudflare.com/
        ajax/libs/materialize/0.97.6/js/materialize.min.js"></script>
        <!-- Init Rsponsive Sidenav Menu  -->
        <script>
        (function($){
            $(function(){
              $('.button-collapse').sideNav();
              $('.materialboxed').materialbox();
            });
```

```
        })(jQuery);
        </script>
</body>
</html>
```

To avoid CSS conflict, clean up your `public/css/style.css` file.

Refactoring the views folder

Now we will make a small change to the `app/views` folder and add some more files:

1. First off, let's edit `app/views/index.js`. Replace the original code with the following code:

```
{% extends 'layout.swig' %}

{% block content %}
<div class="section no-pad-bot" id="index-banner">
  <div class="container">
        <br><br>
        <h1 class="header center orange-text">{{ title }}</h1>
        <div class="row center">
          <h5 class="header col s12 light">Welcome to
              {{ title }}
          </h5>
        </div>
        <div class="row center">
            <a href="books/add" id="download-button" class="btn-large
            waves-effect waves-light orange">Create Your Photo
            Book
            </a>
        </div>
        <br><br>
    </div>
</div>
<div class="container">
    <div class="section">

        <!--   Icon Section   -->
        <div class="row">
          <div class="col s12 m4">
            <div class="icon-block">
```

```
                    <h5 class="center">Animals</h5>
                    <img src="http://lorempixel.com/300/200/animals"/>
                    <p class="light">Lorem ipsum dolor sit amet,
                        consectetur adipiscing elit, sed do eiusmod
                        tempor incididunt ut laboreet dolore magna-
                        aliqua.</p>
                </div>
            </div>
                <div class="col s12 m4">
                    <div class="icon-block">
                        <h5 class="center">Cities</h5>
                        <img src="http://lorempixel.com/300/200/city"/>
                        <p class="light">Lorem ipsum dolor sit amet,
                            consectetur adipiscing elit, sed do eiusmod
                            tempor incididunt ut laboreet dolore magna-
                            aliqua.</p>
                    </div>
                </div>
                <div class="col s12 m4">
                    <div class="icon-block">
                        <h5 class="center">Nature</h5>
                        <img src="http://lorempixel.com/300/200/nature"/>
                        <p class="light">Lorem ipsum dolor sit amet,
                            consectetur adipiscing elit, sed do eiusmod
                            tempor incididunt ut laboreet dolore magna-
                            aliqua..</p>
                    </div>
                </div>
            </div>

        </div>
        <br><br>
        <div class="section">
        </div>
    </div>

{% endblock %}
```

2. Create a file called `add-photo.swig` and add the following code:

```
{% extends '../layout.swig' %}

{% block content %}
<div class="section no-pad-bot" id="index-banner">
    <div class="container">
        <br>
        <br>
        <h1 class="header center orange-text">{{ title }}</h1>
```

```
<div class="row center">
    <h5 class="header col s12 light">Welcome to
      {{ title }}</h5>
</div>

<div class="photo">
  <h2>{{ photo.title }}</h2>
  {% if photo.image.url %}
  <img src="{{ photo.image.url }}" height='200' width='100%'>
  </img>
  <a href="{{ photo.image.url }}" target="_blank">
    {{ cloudinary.image(photo.image.public_id, {width: 150,
    height: 150, quality:80,crop:'fill',format:'png',
    class:'thumbnail inline'})  }}
  </a>
  {% endif %}
</div>
<div class="card">
    <div class="card-content orange-text">
      <form action="/books/add" enctype="multipart/form-data"
        method="POST">
            <div class="input-field">
                <input id="title" name="title" type="text"
                  value="{{ photo.title }}" class="validate">
                <label for="title">Image Title</label>
            </div>
            <div class="file-field input-field">
                <div class="btn orange">
                    <span>Choose File</span>
                    <input type="file" name="image">
                  <input id="photo_image_cache"
                    name="image_cache" type="hidden" />
                </div>
                <div class="file-path-wrapper">
                  <input class="file-path validate"
                    type="text">
                </div>
            </div>
            <div class="input-field col s12">
                <select class="browser-default" id="category"
                  name="category">
                  <option value="" disabled selected>Choose a
                    category</option>
                  <option value="animals">Animals</option>
                  <option value="cities">Cities</option>
                  <option value="nature">Nature</option>
                </select>
            </div>
```

```
                        <div class="input-field">
                            <input id="description" name="description"
                             type="text" value="{{ photo.description }}"
                              class="validate">
                            <label for="description">Image Text
                                Description</label>
                        </div>
                        <br>
                        <br>
                        <div class="row center">
                            <button class="btn orange waves-effect waves
                             light" type="submit" name="action">
                                Submit
                             </button>
                        </div>
                    </form>
                </div>
            </div>
            <br>
            <br>
            <br>
        </div>
    </div>

    {% endblock %}
```

3. Then create a file called books.swig and add this code:

```
{% extends '../layout.swig' %}

{% block content %}
<div class="section no-pad-bot" id="index-banner">
    <div class="container">
        <br><br>
        <h1 class="header center orange-text">{{ title }}</h1>
        <div class="row center">
         < h5 class="header col s12 light">Welcome to {{ title }}
         </h5>
        </div>
        <br><br>

        {% if photos.length == 0 %}
          <div class="row center">
              <div class="card-panel orange lighten-2">No photos yet,
                click add picture to upload</div>
          </div>
          {% endif %}
```

```
                <div class="row">
                {% for item in photos %}
                    <div class="col s12 m4">
                        <div class="icon-block">
                            <h5 class="center">{{ item.title }}</h5>
                                {{ cloudinary.image(item.image.public_id, {
                                    width:280, height: 200, quality:80,
                                    crop:'fill',format:'png', effect:
                                    'brightness:20', radius: 5, class:
                                    'materialboxed' }) | safe }}
                            {#
                                Swig comment tag
                                <img class="materialboxed" src="
                                {{ item.image.url }}" height='200'
                                width='100%' alt="{{ item.title }}"
                                data-caption="{{item.description}}"></img>
                            #}
                            <p class="light">{{ item.description }}</p>
                        </div>
                    </div>
                {% endfor %}
                </div>
            </div>
        </div>
{% endblock %}
```

4. Create a file called `posted-photo.swig` and add the following code:

```
{% extends '../layout.swig' %}

{% block content %}
<div class="section no-pad-bot" id="index-banner">
    <div class="container">
        <br><br>
        <h1 class="header center orange-text">{{ title }}</h1>
        <div class="row center">
            <h5 class="header col s12 light">Welcome to
                {{ title }}
            </h5>
        </div>
        <div class="photo col s12 m12">
          <h2>{{ photo.title }}</h2>
          {% if photo.image.url %}
          <img src="{{ photo.image.url }}" width='100%'></img>
          <a href="{{ photo.image.url }}" target="_blank">
            {{ cloudinary.image(photo.image.public_id, {width: 150,
              height: 150, quality: 80,crop:'fill',format:'png',
              class:'thumbnail inline'})  }}
```

```
            </a>
          {% endif %}
        </div>
        <br>
        <br>
        <br>
      </div>
    </div>
  {% endblock %}
```

Creating the .env.js file

At this point, we will create the env.js file; this file verifies the configurations of the Cloudinary service. Create a file called env.js inside the config folder and place the following code:

```
// get Env variable / cloudinary
module.exports = function(app, configEnv) {

    var dotenv = require('dotenv');
    dotenv.load();
    var cloudinary = require('cloudinary').v2;
    // Log some messages on Terminal
    if ( typeof(process.env.CLOUDINARY_URL) == 'undefined' ){
      console.log('Cloudinary config file is not defined');
      console.log('Setup CLOUDINARY_URL or use dotenv mdule file')
    } else {
      console.log('Cloudinary config, successfully used:');
      console.log(cloudinary.config())
    }
}
```

Now we have a fully configured application; however, we still need to create an account on the Cloudinary service.

Creating and configuring a Cloudinary account

Cloudinary is a cloud service used to store and manipulate images and video files; you can find more information about Cloudinary services at http://cloudinary.com:

1. Go to https://cloudinary.com/users/register/free and register for a free account.

> At the end of the register form, you can set up a name for your cloud. We chose n6b (Node.js 6 Blueprints); choose your own name.

2. Copy the data (Environment variable) from your account right onto your dashboard panel, as shown in the following screenshot:

Account Details   Download: YML, PY

Cloud name:	**n6b**
API Key:	**82499**
API Secret:	************************** Reveal
Environment variable:	CLOUDINARY_URL=cloudinary://82499 :**************************|
Base delivery URL:	http://res.cloudinary.com/n6b ▼
Secure delivery URL:	https://res.cloudinary.com/n6b ▼
API Base URL:	https://api.cloudinary.com/v1_1/n6b ▼

Cloudinary dashboard panel

3. Now update the following code with your own credentials in the .env.js file:

```
PORT=9000
CLOUDINARY_URL=cloudinary://82499XXXXXXXXX:dXXXXXXXXXXX@n6b
```

How Cloudinary works

Besides we storing files on Cloudinary, we can use a powerful API to manipulate and transform images, apply effects, resize, and do a lot more things without using any software on our machine.

Let's go back to the `books.js` controller to check what we used. We extracted the extra code inside the promises function to focus on the highlighted lines of code:

```
cloudinary.uploader.upload(imageFile,
    {
        tags: 'photobook',
        folder: req.body.category + '/',
        public_id: req.files.image.originalFilename
        // eager: {
        //    width: 280, height: 200, crop: "fill", gravity: "face"
        // }
    })
    .then(function (image) {
        ...
    })
    .then(function (photo) {
        ...
    })
    .finally(function () {
        ...
    });
```

Here we set up a folder, `folder: req.body.category`, to store our images, and overwrite the default `public_id: req.files.image.originalFilename` to use the image name. This is a good practice since the API provides us a `public_id` with a random string–nothing wrong but very useful. For example, see a link such as this: `http://res.cloudinary.com/demo/image/upload/mydog.jpg`

Instead of this: `http://res.cloudinary.com/demo/image/upload/8jsb1xofxdqamu2rzwt 9q.jpg`.

The commented `eager` property gives the ability to transform the image and generate a new image with all the eager options. In this case, we can save a transformed image with *280px* of width, *200px* of height, crop with fill content, and if we have some faces in the picture, the thumbnail will be centered on the face. It's a very useful feature to save image profiles.

You can use any transform combination on the upload method; here's an example of the JSON returned by the API:

```
{ title: 'Sample01',
    description: 'Example with Transformation',
    image:
    { public_id: 'cpl6ghhoiqphyagwvbaj',
      version: 1461269043,
      signature: '59cbbf3be205d72fbf7bbea77de8e7391d333363',
```

```
width: 845,
height: 535,
format: 'bmp',
resource_type: 'image',
created_at: '2016-04-21T20:04:03Z',
tags: [ 'photobook' ],
bytes: 1356814,
type: 'upload',
etag: '639c51691528139ae4f1ef00bc995464',
url: 'http://res.cloudinary.com/n6b/image/upload/v146126904
    /cpl6ghhoiqphyagwvbaj.bmp',
secure_url: 'https://res.cloudinary.com/n6b/image/upload
    /v1461269043/cpl6ghhoiqphyagwvbaj.bmp',
  coordinates: { faces: [ [ 40, 215, 116, 158 ] ] },
  original_filename: 'YhCmSuFxm0amW5TFX9FqXt3F',
  eager:[ { transformation: 'c_thumb,g_face,h_100,w_150',
  width: 150, height: 100,url: 'http://res.cloudinary.com
  /n6b/image/upload/c_thumb,g_face,h_100,w_150/v1461269043
  /cpl6ghhoiqphyagwvbaj.bmp', secure_url:
   'https://res.cloudinary.com/n6b/image/upload
    /c_thumb,g_face,h_100,w_150/v1461269043
    /cpl6ghhoiqphyagwvbaj.bmp' } ] }
```

Note the highlighted code with the URL transformation:

```
c_thumb,g_face,h_100,w_150
```

You can find more about the Cloudinary upload API at the following link: http://cloudinary.com/documentation/node_image_upload.

Running the application

Now it's time to execute the application and upload some photos:

1. Open your terminal/shell and type the following command:

```
npm start
```

2. Go to `http://localhost:3000/books` and you will see the following screen:

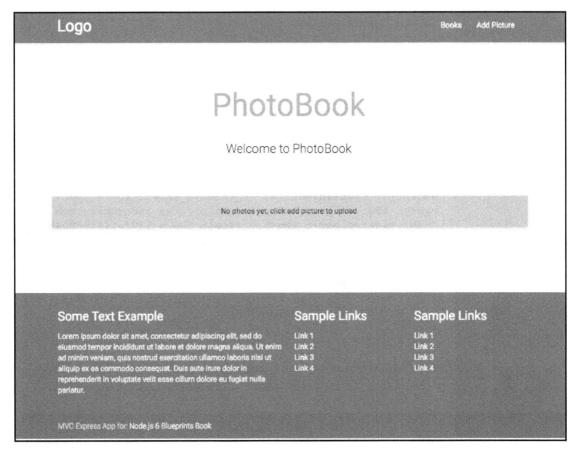

Books screen

Uploading and showing images

Now let's insert some images and check the behavior of our application:

1. Go to `http://localhost:3000/books/add`, and fill in the form:

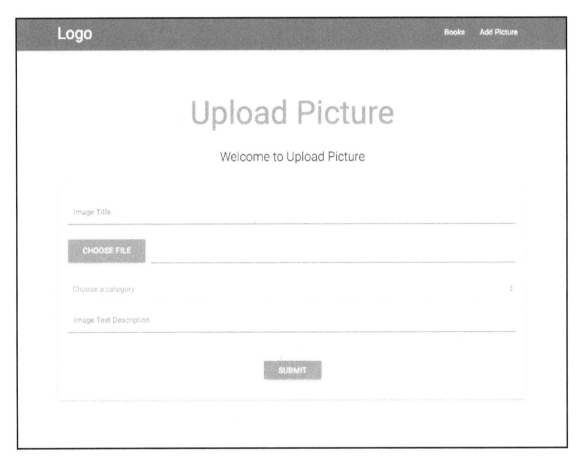

Upload form

Add the following information:

Title: **Image Sample 02**

File: choose the sample02.jpg file.

Category: **cities**

Description: **Lorem ipsum dolor sit amet, consectetur adipiscing elit, sed do eiusmod tempor incididunt ut labore et dolore magna aliqua.**

2. Let's check our MongoDB to see what happens before we go further.
3. Open your RoboMongo and select the first object:

Key	Value	Type
▼ 〔〕 (1) ObjectId("571a4372b94b110008f8f...	{ 5 fields }	Object
⊡ _id	ObjectId("571a4372b94b110008f8f195")	ObjectId
"" title	Image Sample 01	String
"" description	Lorem ipsum dolor sit amet, consectetur adipi...	String
"" category	cities	String
▼ 〔〕 image	{ 15 fields }	Object
"" public_id	cities/sample01.jpg	String
# version	1461338993	Int32
"" signature	2305f19edc4f8532d1711cb65e129aa172333...	String
# width	800	Int32
# height	542	Int32
"" format	jpg	String
"" resource_type	image	String
"" created_at	2016-04-22T15:29:53Z	String
▶ 〔〕 tags	[1 element]	Array
# bytes	494640	Int32
"" type	upload	String
"" etag	c08ea0497acbb619839f6fcbfab3a099	String
"" url	http://res.cloudinary.com/n6b/image/upload/v...	String
"" secure_url	https://res.cloudinary.com/n6b/image/upload/...	String
"" original_filename	3qkBfWgXKZXSvXvsGzv-Kn05	String

Screenshot from MongoDB (RoboMongo)

Note that you must select the right database from the left-hand panel menu.

4. When we upload an image, the API returns a JSON with all information related to that image. We store this JSON as an image property with our books model, inside MongoDB, as we can see in the previous image.

5. Repeat *Step 1* with *Sample02* through *Sample06*.

Checking the MongoDb picture collection

Let's see the picture collection on MongoDB:

1. Open RoboMongo and select the right database form the left panel.
2. Open the `collections` folder and double-click on **Picture collections**.
3. On the top–right of the panel, click on the `view results in table mode` icon.

Now you can see the following screenshot on the **RoboMongo** interface:

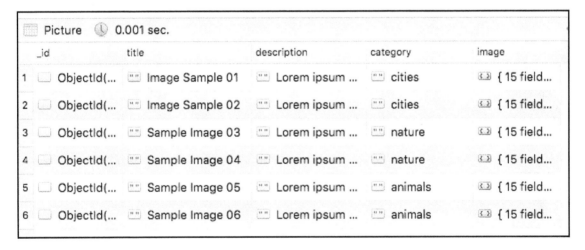

	_id	title	description	category	image
1	ObjectId(...	Image Sample 01	Lorem ipsum ...	cities	{ 15 field...
2	ObjectId(...	Image Sample 02	Lorem ipsum ...	cities	{ 15 field...
3	ObjectId(...	Sample Image 03	Lorem ipsum ...	nature	{ 15 field...
4	ObjectId(...	Sample Image 04	Lorem ipsum ...	nature	{ 15 field...
5	ObjectId(...	Sample Image 05	Lorem ipsum ...	animals	{ 15 field...
6	ObjectId(...	Sample Image 06	Lorem ipsum ...	animals	{ 15 field...

Screenshot from the picture collection

Creating folders in the Cloudinary dashboard

As previously mentioned, we set up folders (`folder: req.body.category`). In this case, the folder name will be the category name. To better organize our images in the cloud, as we did this programmatically, we need to create them directly in Cloudinary dashboard:

1. Log in to your Cloudinary account.
2. Go to `https://cloudinary.com/console/media_library`:

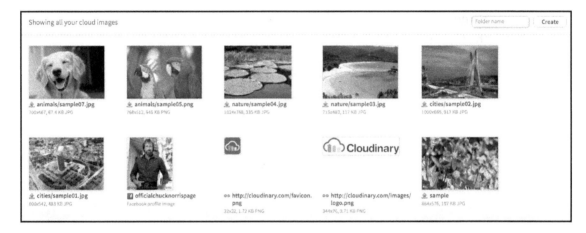

Create folder screenshot

 Don't worry about the other images on the Cloudinary dashboard; they are the default in every account. You can delete them if you want.

3. Click on the input field (folder name) on the right–hand side and create a folder, `animals`.
4. Click on the input field (folder name) on the right–hand side and create a folder, `cities`.
5. Click on the input field (folder name) on the right–hand side and create a folder, `nature`.

You can see all the categories created at the top of the images, as the following screenshot shows:

Categories screenshot

Now when you choose a category, you see only the images belonging to that category, in this case `animals`, as shown in the following image:

Screenshot from the animals folder

This is a more effective way to organize all your photos, and you can create several albums, for example:

```
my-vacations/germany/berlin
road-trip/2015/route-66
```

URL transformation rendering

As part of Cloudinary API, we can manipulate the images just by using the URL parameter settings, as we did on the books page:

1. Go to `http://localhost:3000/books`.

2. Open your web inspector and check the rendered code for the first image; you will see the following code:

```
<img src="http://res.cloudinary.com/n6b/image/upload
/c_fill,e_brightness:20,h_200,q_80,r_5,w_280/v1/cities/sample01.jpg
.png" class="materialboxed initialized" height="200" width="280">
```

The API creates the `img` tag and applies the object properties defined in `app/views/books.swig` as URL parameters, as we can see in the following code:

```
{{ cloudinary.image(item.image.public_id, { width: 280, height: 200,
quality: 80,crop: 'fill',format:'png', effect: 'brightness:20',
radius: 5, class:'materialboxed' }) | safe }}
```

Object property	URL parameter
width: *280*	w_280
height: *200*	h_200
crop: *fill*	c_fill
quality: *80*	q_80
effect:brightness:20	e_brightness:20
Radius: 5	r_5

The curly brackets and safe filter `{{... | safe}}` are tags from the `Swig` template engine for rendering the variable safely on the view.

Also, we can directly use the `img` tag, as you can see in the following code:

```
<img class="materialboxed" src="{{ item.image.url }}" height='200'
width='100%' alt="{{ item.title }}"
data-caption="{{item.description}}">
</img>
```

Adding a direct link to the original image

We can also use the API to generate the original image link without applying any transformation:

1. Open `app/views/books.swig` and add the following highlighted code:

```
<div class="icon-block">
<h5 class="center">{{ item.title }}</h5>
```

```
{{ cloudinary.image(item.image.public_id, { width: 280, height:
  200, quality: 80,crop: 'fill',format:'png', effect:
  'brightness:20', radius:5,class:'materialboxed' }) | safe }}
{#
  Swig comment tag
  <img class="materialboxed" src="{{ item.image.url }}"
   height='200' width='100%' alt="{{ item.title }}"
   data-caption="{{item.description}}">
  </img>
#}
<p class="light">{{ item.description }}</p>
<a href="{{ cloudinary.url(item.image.url) }}" target="_blank">
Link to original image
</a>
</div>
```

2. Now when we click on the link to original image, we can see the full image in another browser window:

Screenshot from the Books page with original image link

It is important to note that we also use a simple `colorbox` from the `Materialize.css` framework, so when we hover the mouse over an image, we can see an icon that shows the image at full size.

Summary

We have arrived at the end of another chapter. With this chapter, we finished a series of four chapters addressing the MVC pattern of software development with Node.js.

In this chapter, we saw how to build an application for uploading and manipulating images using a cloud service, and also show how to apply effects, such as brightness and border radius. In addition, we saw how to build a simple image gallery using a simple interface framework, **Materialize.css**.

We explored a different way to use an ORM module and save all the information about the images directly in MongoDB in JSON format.

In the next chapter, we will see how to build a web application using Node and the Firebase cloud service.

5
Creating a Store Locator Application with MongoDB Geospatial Query

In this chapter, we will build an application to store **Geolocation** data with coordinates (latitude and longitude) and show them on the map by only using resources of the express framework, the **Google Maps API,** and pure JavaScript.

It is very common nowadays to use JavaScript libraries for this purpose, but most of them are used only on the frontend of the application, often consuming an endpoint with data in JSON format and updating the UI using Ajax. But we will use only JavaScript on the backend, building a MVC application.

Also, we will use a very powerful feature from MongoDB which is the ability to generate indexes in coordinates the using operators such as $near, $geometry, and others, to locate certain records in a map that are next to a particular location.

In this chapter we will cover the following topics:

- Creating models/schema to store coordinates in MongoDB
- Creating 2dspheres indexes
- Dealing with the Google Maps API
- Dealing with the HTML5 Geolocation API
- Mixing Swig variables with pure JavaScript inside templates

What we are building

In this chapter, we will be building a store locator application and a simple add store interface. The result will be as shown in the following screenshot:

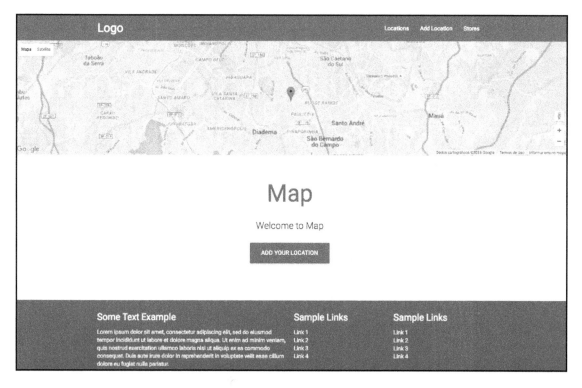

Home Screen

Creating the baseline application

We will use the same version of the `express-generator` that we used in `Chapter 4`, *Don't Take a Photograph, Make it – An App for Photographers*. This time, we do not need any additional modules to complete our task:

1. Create a folder called `chapter05`.

2. Open your terminal/shell within the `chapter05` folder and type the following command:

yo express

Note that we already installed the `generator-express` in `chapter 04`, *Don't Take a Photograph, Make it – An App for Photographers*.

3. Now, fill in the questions in this order:
   - Choose `N`: we have already created a folder
   - Choose `MVC`: for the application type
   - Choose `Swig`: for the template engine
   - Choose `None`: for the CSS preprocessor
   - Choose `MongoDb`: for the database
   - Choose `Gulp`: for LiveReload and other stuff

Don't worry about `Gulp` if you've never heard of it; later in the book we will see and explain some building tools.

Refactoring the default structure

As we know, and as we have done previously, we need to make some adjustments in our application structure to make it more scalable and follow our MVC pattern:

1. Inside the `app/views` folder, create a folder called `pages`.
2. Inside the `app/views` folder, create a folder called `partials`.
3. Move all files at the root of the `views` folder to the `pages` folder.

Creating partial views for footer and head

Now, as a best practice, let's create some partials files for footer and head:

1. Create a file called `footer.html` inside `app/view/partials/`.
2. Create a file called `head.html` inside `app/view/partials/`.

Setting Swig template to use HTML extension

As you can see, we used the `.html` file extension, unlike the previous example where we use the `.swig` file extension. Because of this, we need to change the express `app.engine` configuration file, so that it uses this type of extension:

1. Open the `express.js` file from `app/config/`.
2. Replace the following highlighted lines of code:

```
app.engine('html', swig.renderFile);
if(env == 'development'){
  app.set('view cache', false);
  swig.setDefaults({ cache: false });
}
app.set('views', config.root + '/app/views/pages');
app.set('view engine', 'html');
```

This way we can use the `.html` file extension inside the applications templates.

Creating partial files

Now it's time to create the partials file itself:

1. Open `head.html` from `app/views/partials` and add the following code:

```
<head>
  <meta charset="UTF-8">
  <meta name="viewport" content="width=device-width">
  <title>{{ title }}</title>
  <!--Let browser know website is optimized for mobile-->
  <meta name="viewport" content="width=device-width, initial-scale=
    1.0"/>
  <!-- Import Google Material font and icons -->
  <link href="https://fonts.googleapis.com/icon?family=
    Material+Icons" rel="stylesheet">
  <!-- Compiled and minified CSS -->
  <link rel="stylesheet" href="https://cdnjs.cloudflare.com/ajax
    /libs/materialize/0.97.6/css/materialize.min.css">
  <link rel="stylesheet" href="/css/style.css">
  <!--Import jQuery before materialize.js-->
  <script type="text/javascript" src="https://code.jquery.com/
    jquery-2.1.1.min.js"></script>
  <!-- Compiled and minified JavaScript -->
  <script src="https://cdnjs.cloudflare.com/ajax/libs/materialize
    /0.97.6/js/materialize.min.js"></script>
```

```
<!-- Google Maps API to track location  -->
<scriptsrc="https://maps.googleapis.com/maps/api/js?key=<YOUR
  API KEY GOES HERE>"></script>
</head>
```

Note that we already included a CSS framework called `materialize.css` and the Google maps API link: `<script src="https://maps.googleapis.com/maps/api/js?key=<YOUR API KEY GOES HERE>"></script>`

2. Open `footer.html` from `app/views/partials` and add the following code:

```
<footer class="page-footer teal darken-1">
<div class="container">
  <div class="row">
    <div class="col l6s12">
      <h5 class="white-text">Some Text Example</h5>
      <p class="grey-text text-lighten-4">Lorem ipsum dolor
        sit amet, consecteturadipiscingelit, sed do
        eiusmodtemporincididuntutlabore et dolore magna aliqua.
        Utenim ad minim veniam, quisnostrud
        exercitationullamcolaboris nisi utaliquip ex
        eacommodoconsequat. Duisauteirure dolor in reprehenderit
        in voluptatevelitessecillumdoloreeufugiatnullapariatur.</p>
    </div>
    <div class="col l3s12">
      <h5 class="white-text">Sample Links</h5>
      <ul>
        <li><a class="white-text" href="#!">Link 1</a></li>
        <li><a class="white-text" href="#!">Link 2</a></li>
        <li><a class="white-text" href="#!">Link 3</a></li>
        <li><a class="white-text" href="#!">Link 4</a></li>
      </ul>
    </div>
    <div class="col l3s12">
      <h5 class="white-text">Sample Links</h5>
      <ul>
        <li><a class="white-text" href="#!">Link 1</a></li>
        <li><a class="white-text" href="#!">Link 2</a></li>
        <li><a class="white-text" href="#!">Link 3</a></li>
        <li><a class="white-text" href="#!">Link 4</a></li>
      </ul>
    </div>
  </div>
</div>
<div class="footer-copyright">
```

```
<div class="container">
  MVC Express App for: <a class="white-text text-darken-2"
  href="#">Node.js 6 Blueprints Book</a>
</div>
</div>
</footer>
<!-- Live reload for development -->
  {% if ENV_DEVELOPMENT %}
    <scriptsrc="http://localhost:35729/livereload.js"></script>
  {% endif %}
<!--InitRsponsiveSidenav Menu  -->
<script>
      (function ($) {
        $(function () {
            $('.button-collapse').sideNav();
        });
      })(jQuery);
</script>
```

Creating applications template files

Now we will replace the contents of the template files created by the `generator`:

1. Open `index.html` from `app/views/pages/` and add the following code:

```
{% extends 'layout.html' %}
{% block content %}
<div id="map" style="height: 300px"></div>
  <div class="section">
    <div class="container">
    <br>
      <h1 class="header center teal-text">{{ title }}</h1>
      <div class="row center">
        <h5 class="header col s12 light">Welcome to {{ title }}
        </h5>
      </div>
      <div class="row center">
        <a href="locations/add" id="download-button"
          class="btn-large waves-effect waves-light teal">
          Add your location
      </a>
      </div>
        <br><br>
    </div>
  </div>
    <!-- Tracking current user position -->
```

```
<scriptsrc="/js/getCurrentPosition.js"></script>
{% endblock %}
```

Note the `getCurrentPosition.js` file added to `index.html` template. Later in this chapter we will explain what happens with this file.

2. Open `layout.html` from `app/views/pages/` and add the following code:

```
<!doctype html>
<html lang="en">
{% include "../partials/head.html" %}
<body>
  <nav class="teal" role="navigation">
  <div class="nav-wrapper container"><a id="logo-container"
    href="/" class="brand-logo">Logo</a>
    <ul class="right hide-on-med-and-down">
      <li><a href="/locations">Locations</a></li>
      <li><a href="/locations/add">Add Location</a></li>
      <li><a href="/stores">Stores</a></li>
    </ul>
    <ul id="nav-mobile" class="side-nav" style="transform:
      translateX(-100%);">
      <li><a href="/locations">Locations</a></li>
      <li><a href="/locations/add">Add Location</a></li>
      <li><a href="/stores">Stores</a></li>
    </ul>
    <a href="#" data-activates="nav-mobile" class="button-
      collapse"><i class="material-icons">menu</i></a>
  </div>
</nav>
{% block content %}{% endblock %}
 <!-- Footer -->
 {% include "../partials/footer.html" %}
</body>
</html>
```

3. Open `error.html` from `app/views/pages/` and add the following code:

```
{% extends 'layout.html' %}
{% block content %}
<div class="section">
  <div class="container">
  <br>
    <h1 class="header center teal-text">{{ message }}</h1>
    <div class="row center">
      <h3 class="header col s12 light">{{ error.status }}</h3>
    </div>
    <div class="row center">
      <pre>{{ error.stack }}</pre>
    </div>
    <br><br>
  </div>
</div>
{% endblock %}
```

Now we have the necessary baseline to start the application development, but we need to set up the `getCurrentPosition.js` file.

Using the Geolocation HTML5 API

We can use various resources to get the user's position, so we are using the **HTML5 API** in this example. We will use an external JavaScript file to create a map with the exact location of the user:

1. Create a file called `getCurrentPosition.js` and save it within the `public/js` folder.

2. Place the following code in `getCurrentPosition.js`:

```
function getCurrentPosition() {
    // Check boreswer/navigator support
if (navigator.geolocation) {
var options = {
  enableHighAccuracy : true,
  timeout : Infinity,
  maximumAge : 0
};
  navigator.geolocation.watchPosition(getUserPosition, trackError,
  options);
}
else {
```

```
  alert('Ops; Geolocation is not supported');
}
   // Get user position and place a icon on map
function getUserPosition(position) {
     // Check longitude and latitude
console.log(position.coords.latitude);
console.log(position.coords.longitude);
     // Create the user' coordinates
var googlePos = new google.maps.LatLng(position.coords.latitude,
position.coords.longitude);
var mapOptions = {
  zoom : 12,
  center :googlePos,
  mapTypeId :google.maps.MapTypeId.ROADMAP
};
  // Set a variable to get the HTML div
  var mapObj = document.getElementById('map');
  // Create the map and passing: map div and map options
  var googleMap = new google.maps.Map(mapObj, mapOptions);
  // Setup a marker on map with user' location
  var markerOption = {
    map :googleMap,
    position :googlePos,
    animation :google.maps.Animation.DROP
  };
// Create a instance with marker on map
  var googleMarker = new google.maps.Marker(markerOption);
  // Get the user's complete address information using the Geocoder
  //Google API
  var geocoder = new google.maps.Geocoder();
    geocoder.geocode({
       'latLng' : googlePos
    },
    function(results, status) {
      if (status == google.maps.GeocoderStatus.OK) {
        if (results[1]) {
          var popOpts = {
          content : results[1].formatted_address,
          position :googlePos
          };
          // Setup an info window with user information
          var popup = new google.maps.InfoWindow(popOpts);
          google.maps.event.addListener(googleMarker,
          'click', function() {
            popup.open(googleMap);
          });
        }
        else {
```

```
                alert('No results found');
              }
          }
          else {
           alert('Uhh, failed: ' + status);
          }
        });
      }
      // Setup a error function
      function trackError(error) {
      var err = document.getElementById('map');
       switch(error.code) {
       case error.PERMISSION_DENIED:
       err.innerHTML = "User denied Geolocation.";
       break;
       case error.POSITION_UNAVAILABLE:
       err.innerHTML = "Information is unavailable.";
       break;
       case error.TIMEOUT:
       err.innerHTML = "Location timed out.";
       break;
       case error.UNKNOWN_ERROR:
       err.innerHTML = "An unknown error.";
       break;
       }
      }
    }
    getCurrentPosition();
```

So, when we go to `http://localhost:3000/`, we can see our address pointed out on the map, as in the following screenshot:

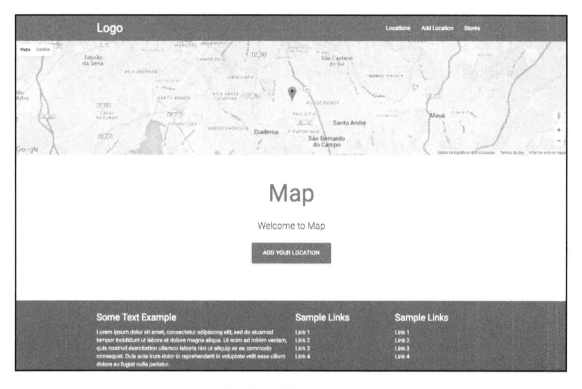

Home Screen with Geolocation activated

Note that your browser will ask permission to track your location

Creating the application controller

Now the next step is to create the application controller's:

1. Create a new file called `locations.js` inside `app/controllers/` and add the following code:

```
var express = require('express'),
    router = express.Router(),
```

```
mongoose = require('mongoose'),
Location = mongoose.model('Location');
module.exports = function (app) {
app.use('/', router);
};
router.get('/locations', function (req, res, next) {
Location.find(function (err, item) {
if (err) return next(err);
  res.render('locations', {
    title: 'Locations',
    location: item,
    lat: -23.54312,
    long: -46.642748
  });
  //res.json(item);
    });
});
router.get('/locations/add', function (req, res, next) {
res.render('add-location', {
title: 'Insert Locations'
    });
});
router.post('/locations', function (req, res, next) {
    // Fill loc object with request body
varloc = {
  title: req.body.title,
  coordinates: [req.body.long, req.body.lat]
};
var locations = new Location(loc);
// save the data received
 locations.save(function(error, item) {
 if (error) {
   returnres.status(400).send({
   message: error
   });
 }
 //res.json({message: 'Success', obj: item});
   res.render('add-location', {
   message: 'Upload with Success',
   obj: item
        });
     });
});
```

Note that we placed a fixed location to center the map and created 3 routes:

- `router.get('/locations',...);` to get all the locations from MongoDB
- `router.get('/locations/add',...);` to render the add location form
- `router.post('/locations',...);` to add the new location to MongoDB

Another important point to mention is the commented code on `get(/locations)`:

`//res.status(200).json(stores);`.

This way we can return a pure JSON object instead to render a template with variables.

Creating models

Now let's create our model to hold the location data:

Inside the `app/models` folder, create a file called `locations.js` and add the following code:

```
// Example model
var mongoose = require('mongoose'),
   Schema = mongoose.Schema;
varLocationSchema = new Schema({
   title: String,
   coordinates: {
     type: [Number],
     index: '2dsphere'
   },
   created: {
     type: Date,
     default: Date.now
   }
});
mongoose.model('Location', LocationSchema);
```

It's important to note the data type of the coordinates property and the index of 2dsphere on the previous code.

> You can read more about 2dsphere in the official documentation of MongoDB at: `https://docs.mongodb.com/manual/core/2dsphere/`.

Creating the views template

Now let's create the `view` file. This file is very important for our application, because that is where we integrate the resources of `Swig` variables with our JavaScript code:

1. Create a file called `locations.html` and save it within the `app/views/pages/` folder.

2. Place the following code inside the `locations.html` file:

```
{% extends 'layout.html' %}
{% block content %}
<div class="section">
  <div class="container">
  <br><br>
    <h1 class="header center teal-text">{{ title }}</h1>
    <div class="row center">
      <h5 class="header col s12 light">Welcome to
        {{ title }}
      </h5>
    </div>
    <div class="row">
      <div class="col s12">
      <form action="/nearme" method="POST">
        <div class="row">
          <div class="col s12" id="map" style="height:600px;
          width: 100%; margin-bottom: 20px"></div>
          <br>
            <h5 class="grey-text center">
                      Find a store near by you
            </h5>
          <br>
          <div class="input-field col s5">
            <input placeholder="Insert Longitude"
             name="longitude" id="longitude" type="text"
             class="validate" value="{{long}}">
            <label for="longitude">Longitude</label>
          </div>
          <div class="input-field col s5">
          <input placeholder="Insert latitude" name="latitude"
            id="latitude" type="text" class="validate"
            value="{{lat}}">
          <label for="latitude">Latitude</label>
          </div>
          <div class="input-field col s2">
            <select class="browser-default" name="distance"
             id="distance">
```

```
                    <option value="" disabled selected>Distance
                    </option>
                    <option value="2">2 Km</option>
                    <option value="3">3 km</option>
                    <option value="9">9 km</option>
                  </select>
                </div>
              </div>
              <div class="row">
              <button class="btn waves-effect waves-light"
                type="submit" name="action">SUBMIT</button>
              </div>
            </form>
            <br>
          </div>
        </div>
      </div>
    </div>
```

The previous code is pretty simple; we just have an empty `map` div:

```
<div class="col s12" id="map" style="height: 600px; width: 100%;
  margin-bottom: 20px"></div>
```

We also have a simple form with a `POST` method to find the nearest location based on latitude and longitude:

```
<form action="/nearme" method="POST">
```

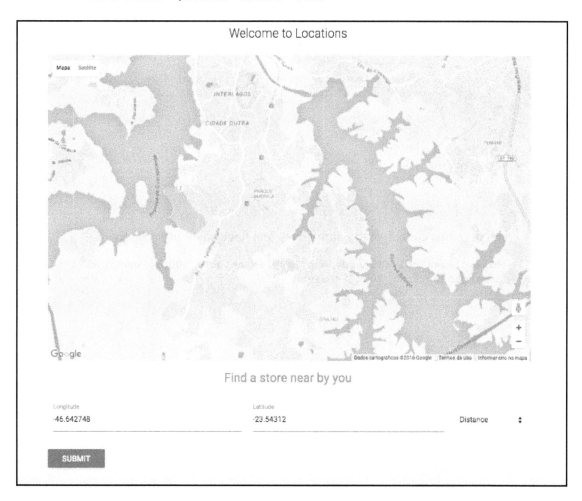

Screenshot of locations.html

The most important code comes next:

1. Add the following code at the end of the `locations.html` file:

```
<script type="text/javascript">
var loadMap = function() {
    // Center map with current lat and long (Simulated with fixed
```

```
      point for this example)
    var googlePos = new google.maps.LatLng({{ lat }} , {{ long }});
     // Setup map options
    var mapOptions = {
      zoom : 12,
      center :googlePos,
      mapTypeId :google.maps.MapTypeId.ROADMAP
    };
  // Set a variable to get the HTML div
  var mapObj = document.getElementById('map');
  var googleMap = new google.maps.Map(mapObj, mapOptions);
   // Create markers array to hold all markers on map
  var markers = [];
  // Using the Swig loop to get all data from location variable
  {% for item in location %}
      // Setup a lat long object
    var latLng = new google.maps.LatLng({{ item.coordinates[1] }},
     {{ item.coordinates[0] }});
      // Create a marker
    var marker = new google.maps.Marker({
      map :googleMap,
      position: latLng,
      animation :google.maps.Animation.DROP
    });
    markers.push(marker);
      // Setup the info window
    varinfowindow = new google.maps.InfoWindow();
      // Add an event listener to click on each marker and show
        an info window
    google.maps.event.addListener(marker, 'click', function () {
    // using the tittle from the Swig looping
      infowindow.setContent('<p>' + " {{ item.title }} " + '</p>');
      infowindow.open(googleMap, this);
    });
    {% endfor %}
  };
// load the map function
window.onload = loadMap;
</script>
{% endblock %}
```

This code snippet does many things, including creating a new object map:

```
varmapObj = document.getElementById('map');
vargoogleMap = new google.maps.Map(mapObj, mapOptions);
```

And it adds the marks or points that came from MongoDB and are inside the loop of location the object:

```
{% for item in location %}
    . . .
{% endfor %}
```

You can see that each line of the previous code has a comment; in this way it is very easy to understand what is happening to each line.

2. Let's create a new file. Create a file called `add-location.html` and save it within the `app/views/pages/` folder.

3. Place the following code in the `add-location.html` file:

```html
{% extends 'layout.html' %}
{% block content %}
<div class="section">
  <div class="container">
  <br><br>
    <h1 class="header center teal-text">{{ title }}</h1>
    <div class="row center">
      <h5 class="header col s12 light">Welcome to
        {{ title }}
      </h5>
    </div>
    <div class="row">
      <div class="col s12">
          {% if message %}
            <h4 class="center teal-text">
                 {{ message }}
            </h4>
          {% endif %}
          <h5 class="grey-text">
              Insert a new location
          </h5>
          <br>
          <form action="/locations" method="POST">
            <div class="row">
            <div class="input-field col s4">
              <input placeholder="Insert Location Title"
               name="title" id="title" type="text" class="validate">
              <label for="title">Title</label>
              </div>
              <div class="input-field col s4">
                <input placeholder="Insert Longitude"
                 name="long" id="long" type="text" class="validate">
                <label for="long">Longitude</label>
```

```
          </div>
          <div class="input-field col s4">
          <input placeholder="Insert lat" name="lat" id="lat"
           type="text" class="validate">
          <label for="lat">Latitude</label>
          </div>
            <br>
            <br>
          <div class="col s12 center">
          <button class="btn waves-effect waves-light"
           type="submit" name="action">SUBMIT</button>
          </div>
        </div>
      </form>
      </div>
    </div>
  </div>
</div>
{% endblock %}
```

This is a simple form to add some locations to MongoDB, and will look like the following screenshot:

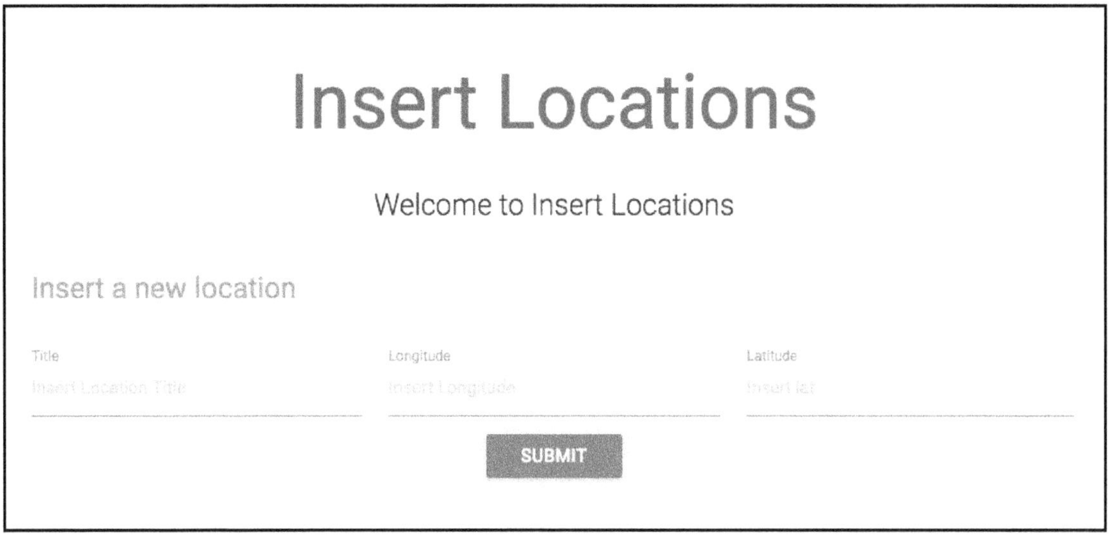

Screenshot of add-location.html

Adding locations to MongoDB

Now is the fun part of our application. We need to insert the records in our application; for didactic purposes, we will use the form (`add-location.html`) to insert the records one by one.

The example shows how to insert a record, and you should do the same for others.

> You can skip this step and load the sample file that populates its database, but we recommend you follow the steps in this book.

At the end of this example, we will explain how to load all records at once using RoboMongo panel.

1. Open terminal/shell at the project root folder and type the following command:

   gulp

> Note that you must have your MongoDB up and running before taking the previous action.

2. Go to `http://localhost:3000/locations/add` and fill in the form with the following information:

> Note you can use your own location, but you need to set up the map center to your own location too, at the `locations.js` controller on latitude and longitude properties:
> ```
> router.get('/locations', function (req, res, next) {
> Location.find(function (err, item) {
> ...
> res.render('locations', {
> ...
> lat: -23.54312,
> long: -46.642748
> });
> });
> });
> ```

Title = **Republica**

Longitude = **-46.642748**

Latitude = **-23.54312**

Press the **SUBMIT** button and you will see a success message above the map.

3. Now we will add the next seven locations using the RoboMongo interface. Copy the following code:

```
db.locations.insert(
[{
    "title": "Mackenzie",
    "coordinates": [-46.651659, -23.54807]
}, {
    "title": "Shopping Maia B",
    "coordinates": [-46.539545, -23.44375]
}, {
    "title": "MorumbiSaraiva",
    "coordinates": [-46.699053, -23.62376]
}, {
    "title": "Shopping Center Norte",
    "coordinates": [-46.617417, -23.51575]
}, {
    "title": "Mooca Plaza Shopping",
    "coordinates": [-46.594408, -23.57983]
}, {
    "title": "Shopping Metro Tucuruvi",
    "coordinates": [-46.602695, -23.47984]
}, {
    "title": "Market Place",
    "coordinates": [-46.696713, -23.61645]
}]
)
```

4. On the RoboMongo interface, select the `maps-api-development` database on the left-hand panel.

5. Paste the code inside the RoboMongo interface:

```
* db.getCollection('locations').find({})

  chapter-01      localhost:27017      maps-api-development

db.locations.insert(
[{
    "title": "Mackenzie",
    "coordinates": [-46.651659, -23.54807]
}, {
    "title": "Shopping Maia B",
    "coordinates": [-46.539545, -23.44375]
}, {
    "title": "Morumbi Saraiva",
    "coordinates": [-46.699053, -23.62376]
}, {
    "title": "Shopping Center Norte",
    "coordinates": [-46.617417, -23.51575]
}, {
    "title": "Mooca Plaza Shopping",
    "coordinates": [-46.594408, -23.57983]
}, {
    "title": "Shopping Metro Tucuruvi",
```

Screenshot of RoboMongo interface terminal

6. Let's check the result: double-click on **locations** collection, on the left-hand menu.
7. On the right-hand side of the RoboMongo view, click **view result in table mode**; you will see the following result:

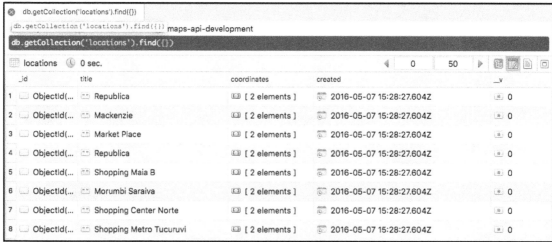

Screenshot of the RoboMongo panel

At this time, we already have all locations inside our map on
`http://localhost:3000/locations`, but the find nearby stores form is still not
working, so we need to set up a MongoDB 2dsphere index.

Understanding Geospatial indexes on MongoDB

Starting from version 2.4 of MongoDB, we have the `Geospatial` search feature using
GeoJSON format.

> You can find more information about GeoJSON at the official link: `http:/`
> `/geojson.org/`.

GeoJSON is an open source specification for formatting shapes in coordinates. It is widely
used and very useful for making applications with geographical data. The format is pretty
simple, and we used this format on the `locations` model, as you can see:

```
var LocationSchema = new Schema({
  title: String,
  coordinates: {
    type: [Number],
    index: '2dsphere'
  },
  created: {
    type: Date,
    default: Date.now
  }
});
```

The highlighted code is the GeoJSON format to store coordinates.

> You can read more about `Geospatial` query on MongoDB here: `https://`
> `docs.mongodb.com/manual/reference/operator/query-geospatial/`,
> and more `geospatial indexes` here: `https://docs.mongodb.com/manu`
> `al/applications/geospatial-indexes/`.

Creating 2dsphere indexes in MongoDB

Let's check our locations collection in MongoDB:

1. Open your RoboMongo and select the **maps-api-development** database on the left panel.
2. Double-click on **locations** collection, and you will see the following data:

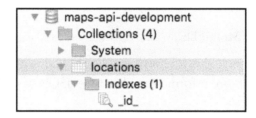

Screenshot of the locations collection before index

You will note that we have just one folder with an id index; this is the default from MongoDB.

3. Copy the following code and place in the RoboMongo interface:

```
db.locations.ensureIndex({ 'coordinates' : '2dsphere'})
```

4. Click on the **play** button in the top-right menu bar.

The result will be like the following screenshot:

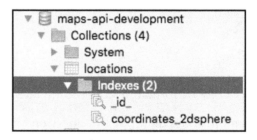

Screenshot after ensure.index()

Note that now we have created the 2dsphere indexes.

Checking the Geolocation application

This is the time to test the application. We have already created eight records in our database, already indexed all positions using the `ensure.index ()` MongoDB, and we can already see all the points rendered in the map, as we can see in the following screenshot:

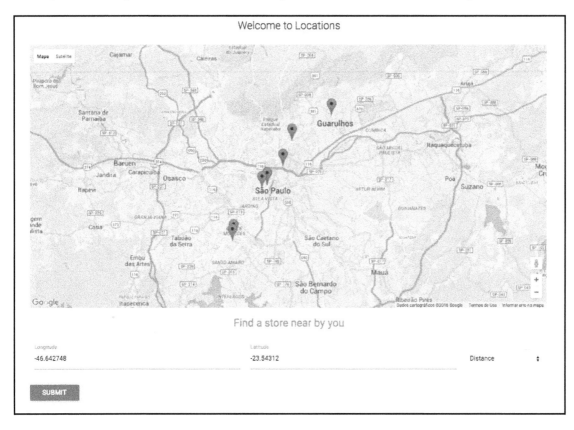

Screenshot from locations.html

In this previous screenshot, you may notice that the points raised in the map are away from each other, which is able to show the difference in the distance of points shown when we change the distance search field.

In this example, we can insert any latitude and longitude in the search field, but we leave this field fixed only to illustrate the geolocation functionality of the application.

When we access the locations route for the first time, we show all records in the database, as we saw in the previous screenshot:

Let's change the distance on the `locations.html` form to check what happens; go to `http://localhost:3000/locations`, select *2km* in the **Distance** field, and press the **SUBMIT** button.

The result of our new query in MongoDB using the `$near` and `$geometry` functions will be as follows:

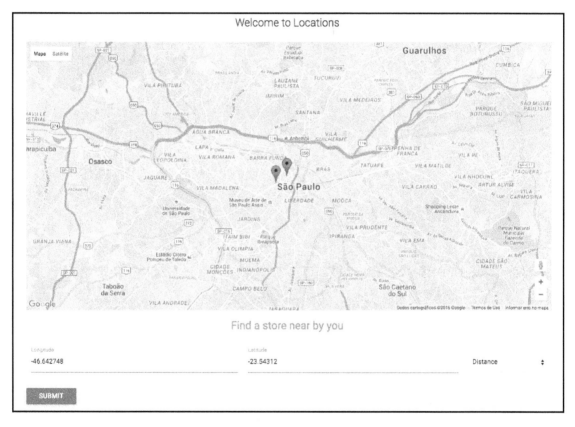

Screenshot of locations page filtered by 2km

This is very useful information for a store locator application, but we cannot see where the nearest point we are seeking is. To facilitate this view, we will add a list of points on the map, on the left-hand side, listed in order from the nearest to the furthest point.

Ordering points by distance

Let's add some code lines to make our search more intuitive:

1. Add the following lines on `app/views/pages/locations.html`, between the highlighted code:

```
<div class="row">
<div class="col s3">
        . . .
</div>
<div class="col s9">
<form action="/nearme" method="POST">
        . . .
</div>
</div>
```

Note that you can download the full code on the Packt Publishing website or on the official GitHub repository of the book.

2. Add the following function, at the end of `locations.html` right after the `{% endfor %}` loop:

```
// get all the pan-to-marker class
var els = document.querySelectorAll(".pan-to-marker");
// looping over all list elements
for (vari = 0, len = els.length; i<len; i++) {
  els[i].addEventListener("click", function(e){
    e.preventDefault();
// Use -1 for index because loop.index from swig starts on 1
var attr = this.getAttribute('data-marker-index') -1;
    // get longitude and latitude of the marker
  var latitude = markers[attr].getPosition().lat();
  var longitude = markers[attr].getPosition().lng();
  console.log(latitude, longitude );
    // Center map and apply zoom
    googleMap.setCenter({lat: latitude, lng: longitude});
    googleMap.setZoom(18);
    });
}
```

Now when we go back to the `locations` page, we can see a list of points on the left-hand side of the map, ordered by distance. See the following screenshot:

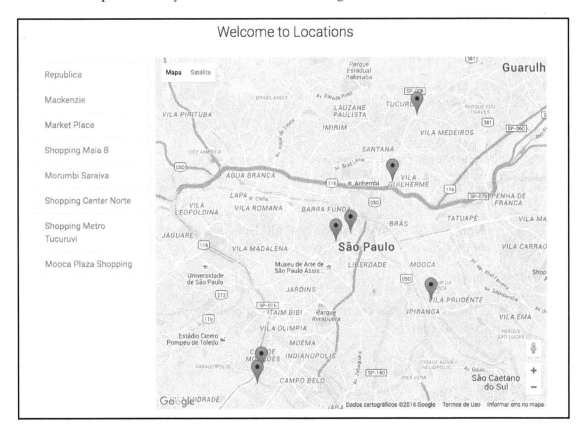

Screenshot of the stores list on the left-hand side

And now we can click on any store on the left-panel. We can also zoom in on the map, as we can see in the following screenshot:

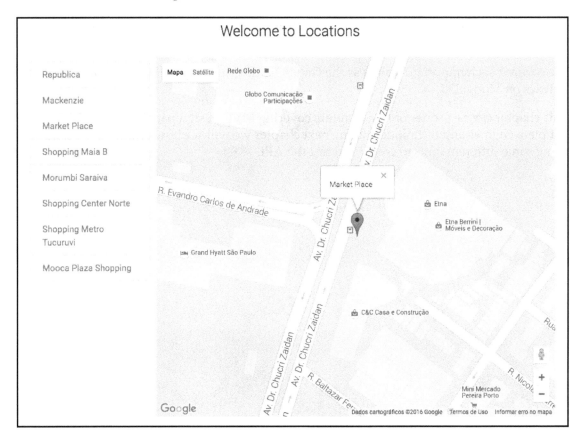

Screenshot of locations.html with a store selected

Summary

In this chapter, we covered a lot of things related to the Google Maps API and the Geospatial query on MongoDB, and built a full store locator application using Node.js and a few default Express modules.

We covered such important points as the GeoJSON file format and how to create geospatial indexes on MongoDB.

This chapter closes a series of five chapters covering MVC design patterns using different template engines and techniques. In the next chapter we will see how to build a Node.js API using some different tools to create and test the API.

6
Building a Customer Feedback App with a Restful API and Loopback.io

As previously commented, the Node.js ecosystem has various frameworks for developing powerful web applications. In previous chapters, we used the most popular of all the Express framework.

In this chapter, we will explore another framework known as `loopback.io`. This framework is heavily based on Express, however, it provides us with some more features to create Restful APIs very quickly.

It has a **Command-line Interface** (**CLI**) where it is possible to create APIs without using code, plus it exposes an interface for manipulation of HTTP verbs, a kind of Restful client embedded in your application, and a few more advantages.

We also see how to consume this API on the frontend of our application using the `React.js` library.

In this chapter we will cover the following topics:

- Installing the LoopBack framework
- The fundamentals of LoopBack CLI
- Creating models using command line
- Dealing with datasource and database relations
- Creating a simple React.js application to consume the API

What we are building

In this chapter we will build an API to store any type of product, in this case a classic model of motorcycle, and store comments/feedback from users of this motorcycle. The result will look like the following screenshot:

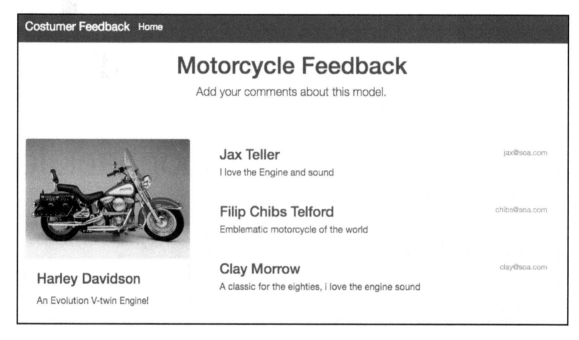

Screenshot of Home page

Creating the baseline structure

First let's install the LoopBack framework:

1. Open your terminal/shell and type the following command:

   ```
   npm install strongloop -g
   ```

2. Open your terminal/shell and type the following command:

   ```
   slc loopback
   ```

3. Enter the name: chapter-06 for the directory option.

4. Choose the `empty-server (An empty LoopBack API, without any`

`configured models or datasources)` option.

Don't worry about the end of the output, we will explain this in the next topic.

The result will be the following structure of folders and files:

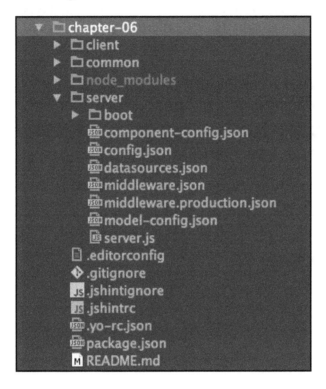

Screenshot of folders and files

The structure is pretty simple; almost all configurations from LoopBack are inside JSON files, as we can see for **component-config.json**, **config.json**, **datasources.json**, and all the other files inside the **server** folder.

You can find out more about the `slc` command line by typing: `slc -help` in your terminal window.

Creating models with command line

At this time, we have the necessary structure to start the development of our API.

We will now use the command line to create the models of our application. We will build two models: one model for the product/motorcycle and another for the user/consumer.

1. Open terminal/shell inside the `chapter-06` folder and type the following command:

   slc loopback:model

2. Fill in the following information for `motorcycle` model, as shown in the following screenshot:

```
? Enter the model name: mortorcycle
? Select model's base class PersistedModel
? Expose mortorcycle via the REST API? Yes
? Custom plural form (used to build REST URL): motorcycles
? Common model or server only? common
```

Screenshot of the terminal output after model motorcycle created

3. Fill in the property name:

```
Property name: image
? Property type: string
? Required? Yes
? Default value[leave blank for none]:
Property name: make
? Property type: string
? Required? Yes
? Default value[leave blank for none]:
Property name: description
? Property type: string
? Required? Yes
? Default value[leave blank for none]:
Property name: model
? Property type: string
? Required? Yes
? Default value[leave blank for none]:
Property name: category
? Property type: string
? Required? Yes
? Default value[leave blank for none]:
Property name: year
```

```
? Property type: string
? Required? Yes
? Default value[leave blank for none]:
```

4. Let's create the `customer` model. Open terminal/shell and type the following command:

   `slc loopback:model`

5. Fill in the information for `review` model, as shown in the following figure:

```
? Enter the model name: review
? Select model's base class PersistedModel
? Expose review via the REST API? Yes
? Custom plural form (used to build REST URL): reviews
? Common model or server only? common
```

Screenshot of the terminal output after model review created

6. Fill in the property name:

```
Property name: name
? Property type: string
? Required? Yes
? Default value[leave blank for none]:
Property name: email
? Property type: string
? Required? Yes
? Default value[leave blank for none]:
Property name: review
? Property type: string
? Required? Yes
? Default value[leave blank for none]:
```

Even using the command line, we can check and edit the model you just created.

 An important point to note here is that the property `common` creates a directory and shares it with the `client` and `server` folders. If you are using the property `server`, the code is stored in the `server` folder and is not shared with the `client` folder.

Editing models after creation with command line

We can edit the models right into the `common/models/` folder. We have two files for each model created.

The first is a JSON file with all the properties, as we can see in the following code for `review.json` file:

```json
{
    "name": "review",
    "base": "PersistedModel",
    "idInjection": true,
    "options": {
      "validateUpsert": true
    },
    "properties": {
      "name": {
      "type": "string",
      "required": true
    },
    "email": {
      "type": "string",
      "required": true
    },
    "review": {
        "type": "string",
        "required": true
    }
  },
    "validations": [],
    "relations": {},
    "acls": [],
    "methods": {}
  }
```

The second is a JavaScript file, as we can see in the following code for `review.js` file:

```
module.exports = function(Review) {
};
```

The JavaScript file is where you can configure the application methods. You may notice that while creating the model, its function is empty; this is due to the fact that the LoopBack framework abstracts the CRUD operations, commonly found in other applications, by using the Express framework as we did in the previous chapter.

Creating a datasource through the command line

We will use a database to store the feedback of our customers, so we will create the datasource using the LoopBack CLI:

1. Open terminal/shell in the root project and type the following command:

   slc loopback:datasource

2. Fill in the options with the following information:

```
? Enter the data-source name: motorcycleDataSource
? Select the connector for motorcycleDataSource: MongoDB (supported by StrongLoop)
Connector-specific configuration:
? host: localhost
? port: 27017
? user:
? password:
? database: motorcycle-feedback
? Install loopback-connector-mongodb@^1.4 Yes
```

Screenshot of the datasource terminal output

Note that the final option is to install the MongoDB connector. So, don't forget to create the database: `motorcycle-feedback` on your MongoDB instance.

 For the book example, we are not using User and Password for the database, but it is strongly recommended that you use a User and a strong Password in a production environment.

The datasource configuration can be found at: `server/datasources.json` file, as we can see in the following code:

```
{
  "motorcycleDataSource": {
    "host": "localhost",
    "port": 27017,
    "database": "motorcycle-feedback",
    "password": "",
    "name": "motorcycleDataSource",
    "user": "",
    "connector": "mongodb"
  }
}
```

The Loopback API offers us the possibility to configure more on a datasource with different databases.

Connecting models to datasources

The next step is to make a relationship between models and datasources, for this we will edit the file manually.

Remember that the command line also offers this feature with `slc loopback:relation`: however, at the time of writing, there is a bug in the generator and we cannot use this feature at the moment. However, this does not prevent us from continuing with our application, since the command-line tool is not mandatory:

Open `server/model-config.json` and add the following highlighted code:

```
{
  "_meta": {
    "sources": [
      "loopback/common/models",
      "loopback/server/models",
      "../common/models",
      "./models"
    ],
    "mixins": [
      "loopback/common/mixins",
      "loopback/server/mixins",
      "../common/mixins",
      "./mixins"
    ]
```

```
    },
    "motorcycle": {
      "dataSource": "motorcycleDataSource",
      "public": true
    },
    "review": {
      "dataSource": "motorcycleDataSource",
      "public": true
    }
  }
```

At this stage, it is very common to use the visual interface known as the ARC tool for building, deploying, and managing our Node APIs, but for the book's examples we will not use it, thus keeping all our attention on the code.

You can find more information about the ARC at this link: https://docs.strongloop.com/display/APIS/Using+Arc.

Using the API Explorer

One of the best features of the LoopBack API Explorer is to generate a localhost API endpoint that allows us to view and test all endpoints generated by our API.

Also, it could be worth as documentation, containing all the necessary instructions as HTTP verbs GET, POST, UPDATE, DELETE, sending token access if necessary, the data type, and JSON format.

1. Open terminal/shell and type the following command:

   npm start

2. Go to `http://localhost:3000/explorer/#/`. The result will be the following screenshot:

Screenshot of the API Explorer

It is possible to see the API base URL and the API version, our project name and the application endpoints.

3. When we click on the **review** model we can see all the endpoints with the HTTP verb, as we can see in the following image:

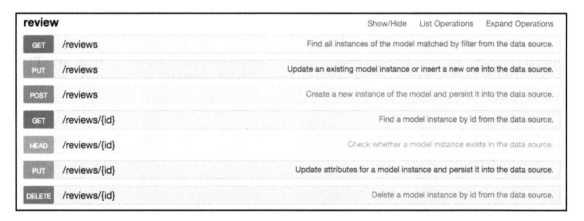

Screenshot of the review endpoint and the HTTP verbs

The endpoints created are the following:

- `http://localhost:3000/api/reviews`
- `http://localhost:3000/api/motorcycles`

And of course, it is possible to access them directly with your browser.

It is important to note that the GET and POST endpoints are the same, the difference is: when we want to retrieve content we use GET method and when we want to insert content we use POST method, and the same goes for PUT and DELETE, where we need to pass the ID at the end of the URL as `http://localhost:3000/api/reviews/23214`.

We can also see that at the right-hand side of each endpoint is a brief description of its purpose.

It also has some additional and very useful endpoints, as shown in the following image:

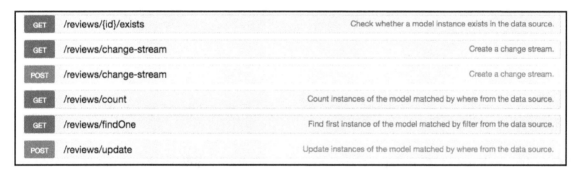

Screenshot of the additional methods from review endpoint

Inserting records using endpoint

Now we will use the API Explorer interface to insert a record in the database. We will insert a product, in our case, a motorcycle:

1. Go to
   `http://localhost:3000/explorer/#!/motorcycle/motorcycle_create`.
2. Place the following content inside the `data value` field and press the **try it out** button:

   ```
   {
       "make": "Harley Davidson",
       "image": "images/heritage.jpg",
   ```

```
            "model": "Heritage Softail",
            "description": "An Evolution V-twin Engine!",
            "category": "Cruiser",
            "year": "1986"
    }
```

The response body will be as shown in the following screenshot:

```
Request URL

    http://localhost:3000/api/motorcycles

Response Body

    {
      "image": "images/heritage.jpg",
      "make": "Harley Davidson",
      "description": "An Evolution V-twin Engine!",
      "model": "Heritage Softail",
      "category": "Cruiser",
      "year": "1986",
      "id": "573791fe8ca46c310ea96eca"
    }

Response Code

    200
```

Screenshot of the success of POST

Note that we have a HTTP status code **200** and an ID for the newly created data.

Retrieving records using endpoint

Now we will use the API Explorer interface to retrieve a record from the database. We will use the motorcycle endpoint:

1. Go to
   `http://localhost:3000/explorer/#!/motorcycle/motorcycle_find`.
2. Click on the **try it out** button, and we have the same as the previous screenshot.

   Note that we are using the API explorer, but we have all the API endpoints exposed through `http://localhost:3000/api/`.

3. Go to `http://localhost:3000/api/motorcycles` and you can see the
   following result on your browser:

```
[
  - {
        image: "images/heritage.jpg",
        make: "Harley Davidson",
        description: "An Evolution V-twin Engine!",
        model: "Heritage Softail",
        category: "Cruiser",
        year: "1986",
        id: "57337088fabe969f2dd4078e"
    }
]
```

Screenshot of the motorcycles endpoint

Note that we are using a Chrome extension called **JSON VIEW** that you
can get here: `https://chrome.google.com/webstore/detail/jsonview/`
`chklaanhfefbnpoihckbnefhakgolnmc.`

It is very useful when dealing with large JSON files.

Adding database relations

Now that we already have our configured endpoints, we need to create the relationship
between the application models.

Our feedback will be inserted into a particular type of product, in this case, our motorcycle
example, then each motorcycle model can receive various feedbacks. Let's see how simple it
is to create the relationship between the models by directly editing the source code:

1. Open `common/models/motorcycle.json` and add the following highlighted
   code:

```
{
    "name": "motorcycle",
    "base": "PersistedModel",
    "idInjection": true,
    "options": {
        "validateUpsert": true
```

```
      },
      "properties": {
        "image": {
          "type": "string",
          "required": true
        },
        "make": {
          "type": "string",
          "required": true
        },
        "description": {
          "type": "string",
          "required": true
        },
        "model": {
          "type": "string",
          "required": true
        },
        "category": {
          "type": "string",
          "required": true
        },
        "year": {
          "type": "string",
          "required": true
        }
      },
      "validations": [],
      "relations": {
          "review": {
            "type": "hasMany",
            "model": "review",
            "foreignKey": "ObjectId"
          }
      },
      "acls": [],
      "methods": {}
}
```

2. Re-launch the application, open terminal window, and type the following command:

```
npm start
```

3. Go to `http://localhost:3000/explorer`.

   We can see that LoopBack has created new endpoints for this relationship, as shown in the following figure:

GET	/motorcycles/{id}/review	Queries review of motorcycle.
POST	/motorcycles/{id}/review	Creates a new instance in review of this model.
DELETE	/motorcycles/{id}/review	Deletes all review of this model.
GET	/motorcycles/{id}/review/{fk}	Find a related item by id for review.
PUT	/motorcycles/{id}/review/{fk}	Update a related item by id for review.
DELETE	/motorcycles/{id}/review/{fk}	Delete a related item by id for review.
GET	/motorcycles/{id}/review/count	Counts review of motorcycle.

Screenshot of the new endpoints created

Now we can get all feedback related to a motorcycle model using:

```
http://localhost:3000/api/motorcycles/<id>/review.
```

We can also get one comment by simply adding the review ID as the following URL:

```
http://localhost:3000/api/motorcycles/<id>/review/<id>.
```

Dealing with LoopBack boot files

Boot files are very important in applications using a LoopBack framework. These files are started when the application is executed, and can perform various kinds of task.

The application already has all the endpoints that it needs. So, let's see how to create a boot file and use another feature from the LoopBack framework to migrate our models to the database.

In this example, we will see how to use the `automigrate` function to insert some content in the database at the time we start the application:

You can read more about the `LoopBack API` at `http://apidocs.strongloop.com/`.

Inside `server/boot,` create a new file called `create-sample-models.js` and place the following content in it:

```
module.exports = function(app) {
    // automigrate for models, every time the app will running,
      db will be replaced with this data.
    app.dataSources.motorcycleDataSource.automigrate('motorcycle',
    function(err) {
    if (err) throw err;
    // Simple function to create content
      app.models.Motorcycle.create(
        [
          {
            "make": "Harley Davidson",
            "image": "images/heritage.jpg",
            "model": "Heritage Softail",
            "description": "An Evolution V-twin Engine!",
            "category": "Cruiser",
            "year": "1986",
            "id": "57337088fabe969f2dd4078e"
          }
      ], function(err, motorcycles) {
          if (err) throw err;
          // Show a success msg on terminal
            console.log('Created Motorcycle Model: \n',
            motorcycles);
          });
      });
    app.dataSources.motorcycleDataSource.automigrate
      ('review', function(err) {
    if (err) throw err;
    // Simple function to create content
    app.models.Review.create(
        [
          {
            "name": "Jax Teller",
            "email": "jax@soa.com",
            "id": "57337b82e630a9152ed6554d",
            "review": "I love the Engine and sound",
            "ObjectId": "57337088fabe969f2dd4078e"
          },
          {
            "name": "Filip Chibs Telford",
            "email": "chibs@soa.com",
            "review": "Emblematic motorcycle of the world",
            "id": "5733845b00f4a48b2edd54cd",
            "ObjectId": "57337088fabe969f2dd4078e"
          },
```

```
        {
          "name": "Clay Morrow",
          "email": "clay@soa.com",
          "review": "A classic for the eighties, i love
            the engine sound",
          "id": "5733845b00f4a48b2edd54ef",
          "ObjectId": "57337088fabe969f2dd4078e"
        }
      ], function(err, reviews) {
      if (err) throw err;
      // Show a success msg on terminal
       console.log('Created Review Model: \n', reviews);
      });
    });
  };
```

The previous code is pretty simple; we just created objects using the objects properties from models. Now, every time the application starts, we send one motorcycle record and three motorcycle feedbacks to the database.

This step completes our API. Despite being a very trivial example, we explored several powerful features of the LoopBack framework.

Also, we can use the ARC editor. As mentioned, it is possible to create models and migrations using only the graphical interface. It is also very useful for other purposes, such as deploying and other things.

Consuming the API

Now we will explore how to consume this API. We have seen that the API is contained in: `localhost:3000/api/`, and our root path only has some information regarding the API, as we can see by visiting `localhost:3000`:

```
  {
    started: "2016-05-15T15:20:24.779Z",
    uptime: 7.017
  }
```

Let's change the `root.js` and `middleware.json` files and use some client side libraries to interact with the API.

Adding HTML content to client side

1. Change the name of the `root.js` file inside `server/boot` to `_root.js`.
2. Open `middleware.json` from `server/` folder and add the following highlighted code:

```
{
  "initial:before": {
  "loopback#favicon": {}
},
  "initial": {
    ...
    },
    "helmet#xssFilter": {},
    "helmet#frameguard": {
      ...
    },
    "helmet#hsts": {
      ...
    },
    "helmet#hidePoweredBy": {},
    "helmet#ieNoOpen": {},
    "helmet#noSniff": {},
    "helmet#noCache": {
      ...
    }
  },
  "session": {},
  "auth": {},
  "parse": {},
  "routes": {
    ...
    }
  },
  "files": {
    "loopback#static": {
      "params": "$!../client"
    }
  },
  "final": {
    "loopback#urlNotFound": {}
  },
```

```
    "final:after": {
      "loopback#errorHandler": {}
    }
  }
```

3. Create a new file called `index.html` and save it in the `client` folder.

Now we configure the application to map the `client` folder and make it public access. This is very similar to when we set the static route for the Express framework. There are other ways we can set routes to application, but for this example let's keep it that way.

Adding Bootstrap framework and React library

Now let's add the dependencies to our HTML file; we will use Bootstrap and `React.js`.

Note the highlighted files are serving from a **Content Delivery Network (CDN)**, but if you want you can store these files inside the `client` folder or subdirectories for CSS and JavaScript:

1. Open the newly created file `index.html` and add the following code:

```html
<!DOCTYPE html>
<html>
<head><title>Motorcycle Customer feedback</title></head>
<link rel='stylesheet' href='https://cdnjs.cloudflare.com/
 ajax/lib/twitter-bootstrap/4.0.0-alpha/css/bootstrap.min.css'>
<style>
  body {
    padding-top: 5rem;
  }
  .starter-template {
    padding: 3rem 1.5rem;
    text-align: center;
  }
</style>
  <body>
    <nav class="navbar navbar-fixed-top navbar-dark bg-inverse">
    <div class="container">
      <a class="navbar-brand" href="#">Custumer Feedback</a>
      <ul class="nav navbar-nav">
        <li class="nav-item active">
          <a class="nav-link" href="#">Home <span class="sr-only">
          (current)</span></a>
        </li>
      </ul>
```

```
      </div>
    </nav>
    <div class="container">
      <!-- This element's contents will be replaced with
         your component. -->
    <div id="title">
      <div class="starter-template">
        <h1>Motorcycle Feedback</h1>
        <p class="lead">Add your comments about this model.</p>
      </div>
    </div>
    <div class="row">
      <div class="col-lg-4">
        <div id="motorcycle"></div>
      </div>
      <div class="col-lg-8">
        <div id="content"></div>
      </div>
    </div>
  </div>
</div>
    <!-- Scripts at bottom -->
    <script src='https://cdnjs.cloudflare.com/ajax/libs
      /jquery/2.2.1/jquery.min.js'></script>
    <script src='https://cdnjs.cloudflare.com/ajax/libs
      /twitter-bootstrap/4.0.0-alpha/js/bootstrap.min.js'></script>
    <script src="https://cdnjs.cloudflare.com/ajax/libs/
      babel-core/5.8.24/browser.js"></script>
    <script src="https://cdnjs.cloudflare.com/ajax/libs
      /react/15.0.1/react.js"></script>
    <script src="https://cdnjs.cloudflare.com/ajax/libs/react
      /15.0.1/react-dom.js"></script>
    <script type="text/babel" src="js/reviews.js"> </script>
    <script type="text/babel" src="js/motorcycles.js"> </script>
  </body>
</html>
```

As you can see, on the previous code we added two files in a `script text/babel` type. These files will be our application components built with the `React.js` library.

You can find more information about the `React.js` here: `https://facebook.github.io/react/`.

2. Inside the `client` folder, create a new folder called `images`.

You can copy and paste the motorcycle sample image to this folder. Also, you can download all the example code for the book at the Packt Publishing website and at the official GitHub repository of the book.

Creating React components

Similar `jQuery` widget and `AgularJS` directives there is `React.js`, which is very useful library for creating interface components. However, it is not a complete framework like `AngularJS` or `Ember.js`.

The way to think about `React.js` is by thinking about interface components: everything is a component and a component may be composed of one or more components.

See the following figure:

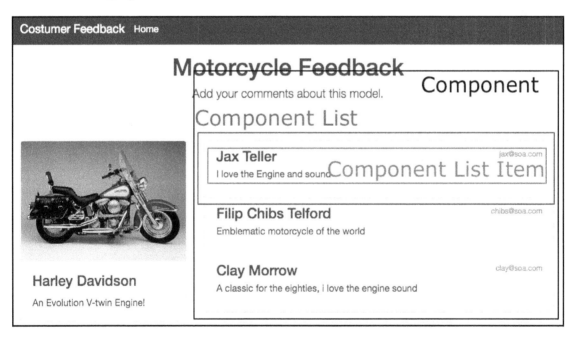

Screenshot simulating React.js components

Let's create the components one by one for a better understanding:

1. Inside the `client` folder, create a new folder called `js`.
2. Inside the `js` folder, create a new file called `review.js` and add the following content:

```
var Review = React.createClass({

        render: function() {
            return (
                <div className="list-group-item">
                  <small className="text-muted pull-right">
                    {this.props.email}
                  </small>
                  <h4 className="list-group-item-heading">
                        {this.props.name}
                  </h4>
                  <p className="list-group-item-text">
                    {this.props.review}
                  </p>
                </div>
            );
        }
    });
```

This is the list-item component.

3. Now let's add the `ReviewBox`. Add the following code right after the previous one:

```
var ReviewBox = React.createClass({
        loadReviewsFromServer: function() {
            $.ajax({
                url: this.props.api,
                type: 'GET',
                dataType: 'json',
                cache: false,
                success: function(data) {
                    console.log(data);
                    this.setState({data: data});
                }.bind(this),
                error: function(xhr, status, err) {
                    console.error(this.props.api, status,
                      err.toString());
                }.bind(this)
            });
        },
```

```
    handleReviewSubmit: function(review) {
        var reviews = this.state.data;
        // Don' use Date.now() on production, this is here
            just for the example.
        review.id = Date.now().toString();
        var newReviews = reviews.concat([review]);
         this.setState({data: newReviews});
        console.log(review);
        $.ajax({
            url: this.props.api,
            dataType: 'json',
            type: 'POST',
           data: review,
            success: function(data) {
                console.log(data);
            }.bind(this),
            error: function(xhr, status, err) {
                this.setState({data: reviews});
                console.error(this.props.api, status,
                    err.toString());
            }.bind(this)
        });
    },
    getInitialState: function() {
        return {
            data: []
        };
    },
    componentDidMount: function() {
        this.loadReviewsFromServer();
    },
    render: function() {
        return (
            <div>
                <ReviewList data={this.state.data} />
                <ReviewForm onReviewSubmit=
                 {this.handleReviewSubmit} />
            </div>
        );
    }
});
```

This is the ReviewBox component and its two received components; one is the ReviewList component, and the second one is the ReviewForm component. Note that we are using the $.get() function from jQuery to get the reviews from the localhost:3000/api/reviews, using the GET method.

Also, we have a function called `handleReviewSubmit()` for dealing with the form submit action to the same endpoint: `localhost:3000/api/reviews`, using the `POST` method.

We have the `getInitialState()` function to set an array of data, which waits for a promise function on a `componentDidMount()` function:

1. Now let's add the `ReviewList` component to `reviews.js`. Add the following code right after the previous one:

```
var ReviewList = React.createClass({
    render: function() {
      var reviewNodes = this.props.data.map(function(review)
      {
        return (
            <Review name={review.name} review={review.review}
              email={review.email} key={review.id}> </Review>
        );
      });
      return (
          <div className="list-group">
                {reviewNodes}
          </div>
      );
    }
});
```

2. Now we add the `ReviewForm` component. Add the following code right after the previous one:

```
var ReviewForm = React.createClass({
    getInitialState: function() {
        return {name: '', email: '', review: '', model: ''};
    },
    handleAuthorChange: function(e) {
        this.setState({name: e.target.value});
    },
    handleEmailChange: function(e) {
        this.setState({email: e.target.value});
    },
    handleTextChange: function(e) {
        this.setState({review: e.target.value});
    },
    handleSubmit: function(e) {
        e.preventDefault();
        var name = this.state.name.trim();
        var email = this.state.email.trim();
        var review = this.state.review.trim();
```

```
        var model = '57337088fabe969f2dd4078e';
         if (!review || !name) {
             return;
         }
         this.props.onReviewSubmit({name: name, email:email,
           model:model, review: review});
         this.setState({name: '', email: '', review: '',
           model: ''});
    },
    render: function() {
        return (
          <div>
            <hr/>
              <form onSubmit={this.handleSubmit}>
                <div className="row">
                  <div className="col-lg-6">
                    <fieldset className="form-group">
                      <label for="InputName">Name</label>
                      <input type="review" className=
                        "form-control" id="InputName"
                         placeholder="Name" value=
                          {this.state.name}
                        onChange={this.handleAuthorChange} />
                    </fieldset>
                  </div>
                  <div className="col-lg-6">
                    <fieldset className="form-group">
                      <label for="InputEmail">Email</label>
                      <input type="review" className="form-control"
                        id="InputEmail" placeholder="Email" value=
                        {this.state.email}
                        onChange={this.handleEmailChange}/>
                    </fieldset>
                  </div>
                </div>
                <fieldset className="form-group">
                <label for="TextareaFeedback">Feedback</label>
                <textarea className="form-control"
                 id="TextareaFeedback" rows="3" value=
                 {this.state.review} onChange=
                 {this.handleTextChange} />
                </fieldset>

                <button type="submit" className=
                  "btn btn-primary" value="Post">
                    Submit
                </button>
              </form>
```

```
            </div>
          );
        }
});
```

3. Finally, we just need to create a React method to render all the contents. Add the following code right after the previous one:

```
ReactDOM.render(
    <ReviewBox api="/api/reviews"/>,
      document.getElementById('content')
);
```

This previous piece of code will render the ReviewBox component inside: <div id="content"></div>; making a brief analogy of CSS classes, we have a component structure like this:

- ReviewBox
- ReviewList
- Review
- ReviewForm

So, the render() method of the ReviewBox component renders two components:

```
render: function() {
  return (
    <div>
      <ReviewList data={this.state.data} />
      <ReviewForm onCommentSubmit={this.handleReviewSubmit} />
    </div>
  );
}
```

Now we do the same for the motorcycle component:

1. Create a new file called motorcycle.js inside the common/js folder and add the following code:

```
// create a interface component for motorcycle item
var Motorcycle = React.createClass({
  render: function() {
    return (
      <div className="card">
        <img className="card-img-top" src={this.props.image}
          alt={this.props.make} width="100%"/>
```

```
      <div className="card-block">
        <h4 className="card-title">{this.props.make}</h4>
        <p className="card-text">{this.props.description}</p>
      </div>
      <ul className="list-group list-group-flush">
        <li className="list-group-item"><strong>Model:
          </strong> {this.props.model}</li>
        <li className="list-group-item"><strong>Category:
          </strong> {this.props.category}</li>
        <li className="list-group-item"><strong>Year:
          </strong> {this.props.year}</li>
      </ul>
    </div>
  );
  }
});
```

2. Let's add the `MotorcycleBox` component. Add the following code right after the previous one:

```
// create a motorcycle box component
var MotorcycleBox = React.createClass({
  loadMotorcyclesFromServer: function() {
    $.ajax({
      url: this.props.api,
      type: 'GET',
      dataType: 'json',
      cache: false,
      success: function(data) {
        console.log(data);
        this.setState({data: data});
      }
      .bind(this),
      error: function(xhr, status, err) {
        console.error(this.props.api, status,
        err.toString());
      }
      .bind(this)
    });
  },
  getInitialState: function() {
    return {
      data: []
    };
  },
  componentDidMount: function() {
    this.loadMotorcyclesFromServer();
  },
```

```
      render: function() {
        return (
          <div>
            <MotorcycleList data={this.state.data} />
          </div>
        );
      }
    });
```

3. Let's create a `motorcycleList` component. Add the following code right after the previous one:

```
// create a motorcycle list component
var MotorcycleList = React.createClass({
  render: function() {
    var motorcycleNodes = this.props.data.map(function(motorcycle)
    {
      console.log(motorcycle);
      return (
        <Motorcycle image={motorcycle.image} make=
          {motorcycle.make} model={motorcycle.model} description=
          {motorcycle.description} category={motorcycle.category}
          year={motorcycle.year} key={motorcycle.id}>
        </Motorcycle>
      );
    });
    return (
      <div className="motorcycles">
        {motorcycleNodes}
      </div>
    );
  }
});
```

Note that we create a list to render all the motorcycle models from our database. This is recommended if you want to add or render more items in this collection. For our example, we have only one.

The last method is the `render()` function to render the `MotorcycleBox` component

4. Add the following line, right after the previous one:

```
ReactDOM.render(
   <MotorcycleBox api="/api/motorcycles"/>,
      document.getElementById('motorcycle')
);
```

This `render` method tells to render the `MotorcycleBox` component inside the HTML motorcycle div tag: `<div id="motorcycle"></div>`.

Creating new feedbacks

Now it is time to create new feedbacks using the application we built:

1. Open terminal/shell and type the following command:

   npm start

2. Go to `http://localhost:3000/` and fill in the form with the following data and press the **submit** button:

   - Name: **John Doe**
   - E-mail: **john@doe.com**
   - Feedback: **Great red and white classic bike!**

The result is shown instantly on the screen, as we can see in the following screenshot.

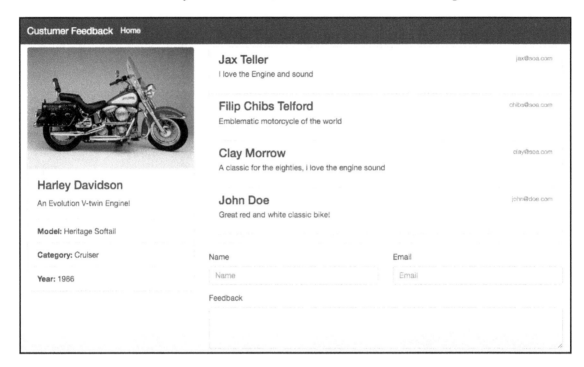

Screenshot of the newly created feedback

Simple checking endpoints

Let's make a simple checking on our API. The preceding image shows four feedbacks for a particular model of motorcycle; we can see that counting the comments appear in the image, but our API has an endpoint that shows this data.

Go to `http://localhost:3000/api/reviews/count` and we can see the following result:

```
{
    count: 4
}
```

Disable remote LoopBack endpoints

By default, LoopBack creates a number of additional endpoints than the traditional CRUD operations. We saw this earlier, including the previous example. But sometimes, we don't need to expose all the endpoints through the API explorer.

Let's see how we can reduce the number of endpoints using just a few lines of code:

1. Open `common/models/review.js` and add the following highlighted lines of code:

```
module.exports = function(Review) {
    // Disable endpoint / methods
    Review.disableRemoteMethod("count", true);
    Review.disableRemoteMethod("exists", true);
    Review.disableRemoteMethod("findOne", true);
    Review.disableRemoteMethod('createChangeStream', true);
    Review.disableRemoteMethod("updateAll", true);
};
```

2. Re-launch the application, open your terminal/shell, and type the following command:

   npm start

3. Go to `http://localhost:3000/explorer/` and click on **review** model.

The result will be as in the following image, with only the CRUD endpoints:

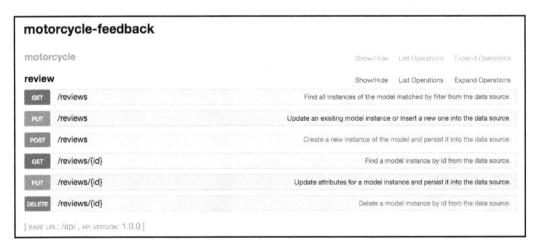

Screenshot of the review endpoints

You can find more information about hiding and showing endpoints at:
`https://docs.strongloop.com/display/public/LB/Exposing+models+ov`
`er+REST#ExposingmodelsoverREST-Hidingendpointsforrelatedmodels`.

Summary

In this chapter we discussed the creation of robust APIs using a LoopBack framework, and approached some very important points regarding the web application as a database, relationships between models, and datasources.

We also saw some similarities between Express and Loopback and learned how to use the web interface of API explorer.

We built an interactive interface using the `React.js` library and approached the main concept of `React.js`, which is the creation of components.

In the next chapter, we will see how to build a real-time application using some very useful resources from Node.js.

7
Building a Real–Time Chat Application with Socket.io

Some time ago, when Node.js applications emerged, we had a boom of new possibilities, using the Node.js resources and things such as `Socket.io` to build real-time applications (as the site says, Socket.io enables event-based bi-directional real-time communication. It works on every platform, device, or browser, focusing equally on reliability and speed).

`Socket.io` allows us to emit events between the client and server, and other possibilities.

In this chapter, we will cover the following topics:

- Installing Socket.io
- The fundamentals of Socket.io events
- Creating an Express chat application
- Dealing with jQuery on the client side
- How to use Gulp.js and the LiveReload plugin on development

What we are building

In this chapter, we will build a real-time chat application with `Node.js`, `Socket.io`, and jQuery:

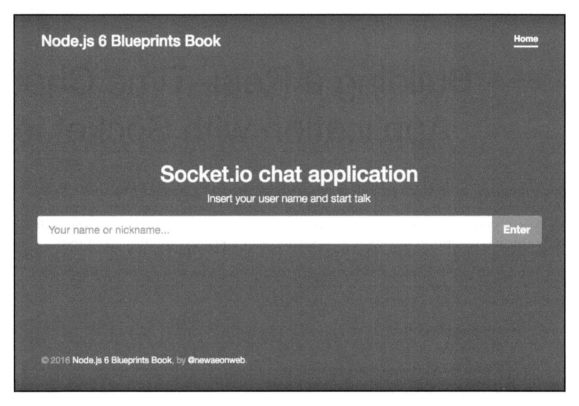

Screenshot of the home screen

Starting with a package.json file

In this chapter we have adopted a different way to start our application; as we have seen in a previous chapter, let's build a Node.js application step by step without the command line.

Let's create the `package.json` file with application dependencies:

1. Create a folder called `chapter-07`.
2. Create a file called `package.json` within `chapter-07` and add the following code:

```json
{
  "name": "chapter-07",
  "description": "Build a real time chat application with
    Node.js and Socket.io",
  "version": "0.0.1",
  "private": true,
  "scripts": {
    "start": "node app.js"
  },
  "dependencies": {
    "body-parser": "^1.13.3",
    "cookie-parser": "^1.3.3",
    "ejs": "^2.3.1",
    "express": "^4.13.3",
    "morgan": "^1.6.1",
    "serve-favicon": "^2.3.0",
    "socket.io": "^1.4.6"
  },
  "devDependencies": {
    "gulp": "^3.9.0",
    "gulp-nodemon": "^2.0.2",
    "gulp-livereload": "^3.8.0",
    "gulp-plumber": "^1.0.0"
  }
}
```

Note that we are using the same recommended modules dependencies from the Express framework. Also, we add the task runner known as `Gulp.js`. Later in this chapter, we will explain more about **Gulp**.

3. Open terminal/shell and type the following command:

```
npm install
```

4. Create a folder called `public`.
5. Create a folder called `routes`.
6. Create a folder called `views`.

At this stage your folder must have the following structure:

```
chapter-01

    node_modules

    public

    routes

    views

    package.json
```

Adding configuration files

Dot files are very common in all web applications; these files are responsible for various tasks, including configuration of version control and text editor configuration, among many other tasks.

Let's add our first configuration file for **Bower package manager**(for more information: `http://bower.io/`):

1. Create a file called `.bowerrc` and add the following code:

```
{
    "directory": "public/components",
    "json": "bower.json"
}
```

This file tells `Bower` to install all the application components at the `public/components`; otherwise, they will be installed at the root application folder.

2. Create a file called `.editorconfig` and add the following code:

```
# http://editorconfig.org
root = true
[*]
indent_style = tab
indent_size = 4
end_of_line = lf
charset = utf-8
trim_trailing_whitespace = true
insert_final_newline = true
```

This file standardizes the type of indentation of code for the entire application. There are many editors that support this file and apply their definitions for every application.

The next configuration file is `gitignore`. As its own name indicates, it serves to tell the version control which application files should be ignored.

3. Create a file called `.gitignore` and add the following code:

```
node_modules/
public/components
.sass-cache
npm-debug.log
```

Adding task manager files

Task managers serves specific tasks in our application. In Chapter 9, *Building a Frontend Process with Node.js and NPM*, we will explore in depth their utilization in Node.js applications, but for now we focus on the file itself:

1. Create a file called `bower.json` and add the following lines of code:

```
{
  "name": "chapter-07",
  "version": "0.0.1",
  "ignore": [
    "**/.*",
    "node_modules",
    "components"
  ]
}
```

it's pretty simple code, but this file has the same importance as `package.json` for the server side. Bower will be the frontend task manager. Later in the chapter we will see how to use it. The next one is the `Gulp` file.

> You can find more information about `Gulp` file at the official website: `http://gulpjs.com/`

2. Create a file called `gulpfile.js` and add the following code (the code is fully commented and it is self-explanatory):

```
var gulp = require('gulp'),
  // Nodemon is Node.js module to reload the application when
    any file change.
  nodemon = require('gulp-nodemon'),
  plumber = require('gulp-plumber'),
  // Live reload is browser plugin to synchronize the
    application after the server side changes
    livereload = require('gulp-livereload');
      gulp.task('develop', function () {
        livereload.listen();
        nodemon({
          script: 'app.js',
          ext: 'js ejs',
          stdout: false
        }).on('readable', function () {
```

```
this.stdout.on('data', function (chunk) {
  if (/^Express server listening on port/.test(chunk))
  {
    livereload.changed(__dirname);
  }
});
this.stdout.pipe(process.stdout);
this.stderr.pipe(process.stderr);
});
});
// We can name it all gulp tasks, we have an alias as develop
 to call default task, on high scale applications we can have
 many tasks with or without alias.
gulp.task('default', [
  'develop'
]);
```

The last file is the README.md file. Usually, this file is used by GitHub, Bitbucket, and NPM to store important information regarding the project, such as the installation process, dependencies, and code examples, among other things.

3. Create a file called README.md and add the following code:

```
# Node.js chat application with Socket.io
```

Pretty simple but very useful file. This Markdown file will be rendered as a HTML file with a h1 tag with this string as a title.

> You can read more about Markdown files at this link: https://daringfire ball.net/projects/markdown/

Creating the app.js file

As we have already seen in previous chapters, the basis of all Node.js applications is the file where we set up all the dependencies and instantiate the application. In this case, we use the app.js file, but you can use any name.

Create a file called `app.js` and add the following code:

```
// Node dependencies
var express = require('express');
var path = require('path');
var favicon = require('serve-favicon');
var logger = require('morgan');
var cookieParser = require('cookie-parser');
var bodyParser = require('body-parser');
// Setup application routes
var routes = require('./routes/index');
// Create a Express application
var app = express();
// Defining the env variable process for development
var env = process.env.NODE_ENV || 'development';
  app.locals.ENV = env;
  app.locals.ENV_DEVELOPMENT = env == 'development';
// Setup view engine to use EJS (Embedded JavaScript)
  app.set('views', path.join(__dirname, 'views'));
  app.set('view engine', 'ejs');
// uncommented this line to use a favicon in your application
// app.use(favicon(__dirname + '/public/img/favicon.ico'));
  app.use(logger('dev'));
  app.use(bodyParser.json());
  app.use(bodyParser.urlencoded({
    extended: true
  }));
  app.use(cookieParser());
  app.use(express.static(path.join(__dirname, 'public')));
// Setup all routes to listen on routes file (this came from
  routes variable)
  app.use('/', routes);
// Setup a  404 error handler
  app.use(function(req, res, next) {
    var err = new Error('Not Found');
    err.status = 404;
    next(err);
  });
// Print the error stacktrace
  if (app.get('env') === 'development') {
    app.use(function(err, req, res, next) {
      res.status(err.status || 500);
      res.render('error', {
        message: err.message,
        error: err,
        title: 'error'
      });
    });
```

```
    }
// No stacktraces on production
  app.use(function(err, req, res, next) {
    res.status(err.status || 500);
    res.render('error', {
      message: err.message,
      error: {},
      title: 'error'
    });
  });
  module.exports = app;
  // Exports all the application configuration
    app.set('port', process.env.PORT || 3000);
  // Setup the server port and give a user message
  var server = app.listen(app.get('port'), function() {
    console.log('Express server listening on port ' +
      server.address().port);
  });
```

The previous code is fully commented. All the information you need to understand what is happening with the preceding code is in the comment lines; here, we have almost the same configuration as in the previous examples.

Creating the route file

Now let's create the route file.

Inside the routes folder, create a new file called index.js and add the following code:

```
// Import Express and Router
  var express = require('express');
  var router = express.Router();
// Get
  router.get('/', function(req, res) {
    res.render('index', {
      title: 'Socket.io chat application',
      lead: 'Insert your user name and start talk'
    });
  });
  module.exports = router;
```

As we are building a simple chat application, we will have just one route.

Creating the application views

Our next step is to build the application views files, so we will create new files within the `views` directory using the `.ejs` extension.

1. Create a new file called `error.ejs` and add the following code:

```
<% include header %>
  <div class="container">
    <h1><%- error.status %></h1>
    <h4><%- message %></h4>
   <p><%- error.stack %></p>
  </div>
<% include footer %>
```

2. Create a file called `footer.ejs` and add the following lines of code:

```
<script src="https://cdn.socket.io/socket.io-1.4.5.js"></script>
<script src="js/main.js"></script>
</body>
</html>
```

Note that we already included the `Socket.io` client file from a **Content Delivery Network (CDN)**. Don't worry about the `main.js` file at the end of `footer.ejs`; we will create this file in the next lines.

3. Create a file called `header.ejs` and add the following lines of code:

```
<!doctype html>
<html lang="en">
<head>
  <meta charset="UTF-8">
  <title><%- title %></title>
  <meta name="viewport" content="width=device-width,
    initial-scale=1">
  <link rel="stylesheet" href="/css/style.css">
</head>
<body>
  <div class="site-wrapper">
    <div class="site-wrapper-inner">
      <div class="cover-container">
        <div class="masthead clearfix">
          <div class="inner">
            <h3 class="masthead-brand">
              Node.js 6 Blueprints Book</h3>
```

```
            <nav class="nav nav-masthead">
              <a  class="active"  href="/">Home</a>
            </nav>
          </div>
        </div>
```

4. Create a file called index.ejs and add the following lines of code:

```
    <% include header %>
      <div class="inner cover" id="app">
        <h1 class="cover-heading"><%- title %>></h1>
        <p class="lead"><%- lead %></p>
        <div class="chat-wrapper">
          <div id="user-form" class="row">
            <div class="col-md-12">
              <form>
                <div class="input-group input-group-lg">
                  <input id="username" class="form-control"
                    type="text" placeholder="Your name or
                    nickname...">
                  <span class="input-group-btn">
                    <input type="submit" class="btn btn-success
                    btn-lg" value="Enter">
                  </span>
                </div>
              </form>
            </div>
          </div>
          <div id="message-area" class="row" style="display:none">
            <div class="col-xs-9">
              <div class="card card-inverse">
                <div class="card-header card-success">
                    Messages
                </div>
                <div class="card-block" id="chat-block">
                  <ul id="chat" class="list-unstyled">
                  </ul>
                </div>
                <div class="card-footer">
                  <form id="message-form" autocomplete="off">
                    <div class="input-group input-group-sm">
                      <input id="message" class="form-control
                      input-sm" type="text" placeholder="Type hereâ¦">
                      <span class="input-group-btn">
                      <input type="submit" class="btn btn-success
                      btn-sm" value="Send message">
                    </span>
                    </div>
```

```
                    </form>
                  </div>
                </div>
              </div>
              <div class="col-xs-3">
                <div class="card card-inverse">
                  <div class="card-header card-success"
                    id="online-users-header">
                    <span class="card-title">Users in the rooom:</span>
                  </div>
                  <div class="card-block" id="online-users-block">
                    <ul id="users"></ul>
                  </div>
                </div>
              </div>
            </div>
          </div>
          <div class="mastfoot">
            <div class="inner">
              <p>&copy; 2016 <a href="$">Node.js 6 Blueprints Book</a>,
              by <a href="https://twitter.com/newaeonweb">@newaeonweb
              </a>
              </p>
            </div>
          </div>
        </div>
      </div>
    </div>
<% include footer %>
```

Note that we are using the HTML markup from one of the examples about **Bootstrap 4**. You can see more examples here: http://v4-alpha.getbootstrap.com/examples/.

Installing frontend components with Bower

As we can see in the previous examples, we use a CDN to serve the CSS file and some JavaScript files for the example application. In this step, we will introduce a widely-used tool for dependencies management, known as **Bower,** for dealing with frontend frameworks such as the Twitter Bootstrap:

1. Open your terminal/shell and type the following command:

   ```
   npm install bower -g
   ```

   The previous command installs Bower globally on your machine.

2. Inside the root project folder, type the following command:

   ```
   bower install bootstrap#v4.0.0-alpha
   ```

The previous command will install Bootstrap inside the `public/components` folder, as we can see in the following image:

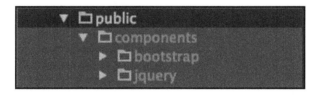

Screenshot of the components folder

Note that the previous command adds the jQuery too, because Bootstrap depends on the jQuery library. Let's add the links to `header.ejs` and `footer.ejs`:

1. Open `views/header.ejs` and add the following code:

   ```
   <link rel="stylesheet" href="components/bootstrap/dist/css
     /bootstrap.min.css">
   ```

2. Open `footer.ejs` and add the following code:

   ```
   <script src="components/jquery/dist/jquery.min.js"></script>
   <script src="components/bootstrap/dist/js/bootstrap.min.js">
   </script>
   ```

Adding some CSS

Now let's insert a few lines of CSS to stylize our example page:

1. Inside the `public/css` create a new file called `style.css`.
2. Add the following code to `style.css`:

```css
a,
a:focus,
a:hover {
  color: #fff;
}
html,
body {
  height: 100%;
  background-color: #068555;
}
body {
  color: #fff;
}
/* Extra markup and styles for table-esque vertical and
 horizontal centering */
.site-wrapper {
  display: table;
  width: 100%;
  height: 100%; /* For at least Firefox */
  min-height: 100%;
  -webkit-box-shadow: inset 0 0 5rem rgba(0,0,0,.5);
    box-shadow: inset 0 0 5rem rgba(0,0,0,.5);
}
.site-wrapper-inner {
  display: table-cell;
  vertical-align: top;
}
.cover-container {
  margin-right: auto;
  margin-left: auto;
}
.inner {
  padding: 2rem;
}
.card {
  color: #414141;
}
.card-block {
  background-color: #fff;
}
```

```css
.masthead {
  margin-bottom: 2rem;
}
.masthead-brand {
  margin-bottom: 0;
}
.nav-masthead a {
  padding: .25rem 0;
  font-weight: bold;
  color: rgba(255,255,255,.5);
  background-color: transparent;
  border-bottom: .25rem solid transparent;
}
.nav-masthead a:hover,
.nav-masthead a:focus {
  text-decoration: none;
  border-bottom-color: rgba(255,255,255,.25);
}
.nav-masthead a + a {
  margin-left: 1rem;
}
.nav-masthead .active {
  color: #fff;
  border-bottom-color: #fff;
}
#users {
  display: block;
}
@media (min-width: 48em) {
  .masthead-brand {
    float: left;
  }
  .nav-masthead {
    float: right;
  }
}
.cover {
  padding: 0 1.5rem;
}
.cover-heading, .lead {
  text-align: center;
}
.cover .btn-lg {
  padding: .75rem 1.25rem;
  font-weight: bold;
}
.mastfoot {
  color: rgba(255,255,255,.5);
```

```
  }
  @media (min-width: 40em) {
    /* Pull out the header and footer */
    .masthead {
      position: fixed;
      top: 0;
    }
    .mastfoot {
      position: fixed;
      bottom: 0;
    }
    /* Start the vertical centering */
    .site-wrapper-inner {
      vertical-align: middle;
    }
    /* Handle the widths */
    .masthead,
    .mastfoot,
    .cover-container {
      width: 100%;
      /* Must be percentage or pixels for horizontal alignment */
    }
  }
  @media (min-width: 62em) {
    .masthead,
    .mastfoot,
    .cover-container {
      width: 62rem;
    }
  }
}
```

We made some alterations in the stylesheet to get the result we wanted for the book example.

At this stage, we have the home screen.

3. Open your terminal/shell and type the following command:

```
gulp
```

4. Go to `http://localhost:3000/`, and you will see the following result:

Screenshot of home screen

Adding live reload plugin

As mentioned earlier, we will use the plugin`livereload`. This plugin is responsible for updating the browser every time we change an application file. Let's see now how to implement it in our example:

1. Remember that we created the `gulpfile.js` file at the beginning of the chapter, so we already have `livereload` task configured according to the following lines:

```
gulp.task('develop', function () {
  livereload.listen();
  nodemon({
    script: 'app.js',
    // map every file with .js, .ejs, extension and relaunch
```

```
      the application
    ext: 'js ejs',
    stdout: false
  })
  .on('readable', function () {
    this.stdout.on('data', function (chunk) {
      if (/^Express server listening on port/.test(chunk)) {
        livereload.changed(__dirname);
      }
    });
    this.stdout.pipe(process.stdout);
    this.stderr.pipe(process.stderr);
  });
});
```

> You can read more about the `gulp-livereload` plugin here: `https://gi thub.com/vohof/gulp-livereload`.

2. Open `views/header.ejs` and add the following code right after the stylesheet link:

```
<% if (ENV_DEVELOPMENT) { %>
  <script src="http://localhost:35729/livereload.js"></script>
<% } %>
```

These lines of code tell the application to inject the `livereload` plugin when we are using the development environment.

3. Now every time we change a file, we can see the following message on the terminal:

```
[11:57:09] [nodemon] restarting due to changes...
[11:57:09] [nodemon] starting `node app.js`
```

Screenshot from Terminal with a livereload message

4. But remember that we configured the `livereload` task to map only `.js` and `.ejs` files, as we can see in the following highlighted lines of code:

```
livereload.listen();
nodemon({
  script: 'app.js',
  ext: 'js ejs',
  stdout: false
})
```

To map other file formats, you must add the file extension to that line.

Checking the application folder structure

With everything in place, we now need to check the directories structure of the application. This time, your application should look like the following screenshot:

Screenshot of the application's structure

Remember that you can download the book's sample code on the Packt Publishing website (www.packtpub.com) and also on the official book's repository on GitHub.

Creating the Socket.io events

Now is the time to create the socket.io event issues in our server. The socket.io allows you to send and receive events with any type of data:

Open app.js from the root folder and add the following lines of code at the end of the file:

```
// Starting with socket.io
var io = require('socket.io').listen(server);
// Create an Array to hold users
var userList = [];
// Create an Array to hold connections
var connections = [];
// Start connection listener
io.sockets.on('connection', function (socket) {
  connections.push(socket);
  console.log("Connected:", connections.length );
  // Setup Disconnect user
  socket.on('disconnect', function (data) {
    if (socket.username) {
      userList.splice(userList.indexOf(socket.username), 1);
      updateUsernames();
    }
    connections.splice(connections.indexOf(socket), 1);
    console.log("Disconnected:" , connections.length );
  });
  // Setup new messages
  socket.on('send message', function (data) {
    io.sockets.emit('new message', { msg: data, user:
    socket.username });
  });
  // New User
  socket.on('new user', function (data, callback) {
    callback(!!data);
    socket.username = data;
    userList.push(socket.username);
    updateUsernames();
  });
  function updateUsernames() {
    io.sockets.emit('get userList', userList);
```

```
      }
  });
```

Adding socket.io behavior on the client side

As mentioned earlier, `socket.io` works with events in the previous code where we configured our server to send and receive events. Now we set our client to receive and send events. In this step, we will use the jQuery library to assist in this task, since we are already using the library in our project:

1. Inside the `public/js` folder, create a new file called `main.js`.
2. Place the following code in the `main.js` file:

```
(function() {
  // Grab all HTML elements into variables
  var socket = io.connect();
  var $messageForm = $('#message-form');
  var $message = $('#message');
  var $chat = $('#chat');
  var $messageArea = $('#message-area');
  var $userForm = $('#user-form');
  var $users = $('#users');
  var $onlineUsersHeader = $('#online-users-header');
  var $username = $('#username');
  // Form submit to send messages
  $messageForm.submit(function(e) {
    e.preventDefault();
    socket.emit('send message', $message.val());
    $message.val('');
  });
  // When a new message is sent, print username and time to
    interface
  socket.on('new message', function(data) {
    var currentHours = new Date().getHours() > 9 ? new
    Date().getHours() : ('0' + new Date().getHours())
    var currentMinutes = new Date().getMinutes() > 9 ? new
    Date().getMinutes() : ('0' + new Date().getMinutes())
    data.msg ? (
      $chat.append(`<li>[${currentHours}:${currentMinutes}]
      <strong> ${data.user}: </strong>${data.msg}</li>`) )
      : alert('Blank message not allow!');
  });
  // Form submit to username
  $userForm.submit(function(e) {
    e.preventDefault();
```

```
        socket.emit('new user', $username.val(), function(data) {
          data ? (
            $userForm.hide(),
            $messageArea.show()
          ) : alert('Ohps. What's your name!')
        });
        $username.val('');
      });
      // get all users connected on localhost:3000 and print a list
      socket.on('get userList', function(data) {
        var html = '';
        for (i = 0; i < data.length; i++) {
          html += `<li class="list-item"><strong>${data[i]}
          </strong></li>`;
        }
        $onlineUsersHeader.html(`<span class="card-title">
          Users in the room: </span><span class="label label-
          success">${data.length}</span>`);
        $users.html(html);
      });
    })();
```

Let's run the application to check what happens on the terminal.

3. Open terminal/shell on the root project and type the following command:

    `gulp`

The output on your terminal will be the following:

```
Express server listening on port 3000
GET / 200 96.303 ms - 4349
GET /css/style.css 200 23.612 ms - 2005
GET /js/main.js 200 22.388 ms - 1704
GET /components/bootstrap/dist/js/bootstrap.min.js 200 48.271 ms - 44117
GET /components/bootstrap/dist/css/bootstrap.min.css 200 61.805 ms - 88349
GET /components/jquery/dist/jquery.min.js 200 59.317 ms - 85578
GET /components/bootstrap/dist/css/bootstrap.min.css.map 200 30.781 ms - 41396
Connected: 1
```

Screenshot of the output terminal with application running

Here, we can see that we had only one connection. But if we open
`http://localhost:3000/` in a new browser window, or even in another browser, we can
see two connections, and so on.

Starting the chat application

Now we use our application in two windows simultaneously:

1. Open your terminal/shell and type the following command:

   `gulp`

2. Go to `http://localhost:3000/`, insert the name **John Doe**, and you will see
   the following result:

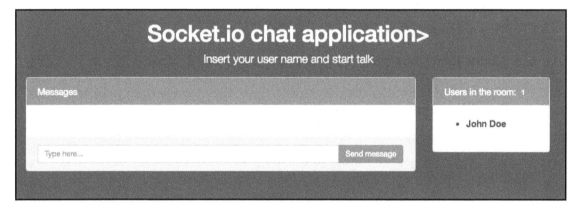

Screenshot of the John Doe user

We can see that's just one user, so now let's open another connection with the
same socket. Use a new window or another browser.

3. Go to `http://localhost:3000/` and insert the name, **Max Smith**. You should see the following result on the right-hand panel:

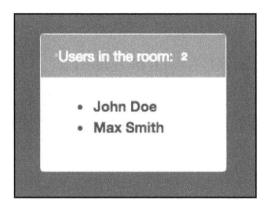

Screenshot of the users panel

Now we have two users. Let's start talking…

4. On the **John Doe** screen, type this message: **Any Body there?**

Check the **Max Smith** screen and you will see the message from **John** appear, as shown in the following image:

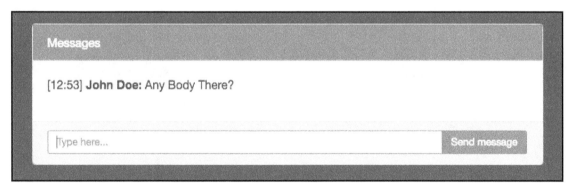

Screenshot from Max Smith screen chat

5. Go back to the John Doe screen and check the message and answer it, as we did in the following image:

Screenshot of the John Doe screen chat

Summary

In this chapter, we discussed some very important concepts of Node.js real-time applications with Node.js and Socket.io.

We have seen how to exchange messages between users in real time using a few lines of jQuery. Also, we addressed some very important topics in the development of modern web applications as frontend dependencies with Bower and the Gulp task manager using the livereload plugin.

Remember that all these tools are available in the Node.js ecosystem through your Node Package Manager (NPM).

In the next chapter, we will see how to use a Content Management System (CMS) built entirely with Node.js to build a blog application.

8

Creating a Blog with the Keystone CMS

In this chapter, we discuss the use of a CMS made entirely with Node.js, called **Keystone**.

The **KeystoneJS** describes itself as an open source platform to create database-driven websites. It already has a core engine to build web applications and a powerful blog, but it is much more than that. It is possible to build anything using the `Keystone.js` framework.

One of the main attractions of the Keystone CMS is that it uses the Express framework and Mongoose ODM, two tools that we have already used in this book.

Due to it being a very recent framework, it comes only with a simple default theme using the Bootstrap framework, but the team behind Keystone are planning to include options to customize new themes something about in the near feature.

Keystone uses the Model View Template pattern, very similar to patterns such as Model View Presentation.

In this chapter, we will see how to build a new theme using all the features of the framework and how to extend it with new features.

In this chapter, we will cover the following topics:

- Installing KeystoneJS
- The KeystoneJS structure and features
- How to customize using simple stylesheets
- Dealing with themes and how to create new themes
- Extending core functionality to create models and views.

What we are building

For this chapter, we will take as a base a simple blog. We'll see how to extend it and create new pages that can be administered through a control panel, and we will have a very similar result to the following figure:

Keystone Blog Theme home page

Installing Keystone framework

As we have done in previous chapters, we will use the official `Keystone.js` yeoman generator.

 You can find more information about the KeystoneJS at this link: `http://k`
`eystonejs.com/`.

Let's install the generator. Open your terminal/shell and type the following command:

```
npm install keystone -g
```

Creating the scaffold application

Now it is time to create a new folder and start to development our blog application:

1. Create a folder called `chapter-08`.
2. Open your terminal/shell at the `chapter-08` folder and type the following command:

```
yo keystone
```

After this command, the `keystone.js` will trigger a series of questions about the basic configurations of the application; you must answer them, as shown in the following screenshot:

```
Welcome to KeystoneJS.

? What is the name of your project? chapter-08
? Would you like to use Jade, Swig, Nunjucks, Twig or Handlebars for templates? [jade | swig | nunjucks | twig | hbs] swig
? Which CSS pre-processor would you like? [less | sass | stylus] sass
? Would you like to include a Blog? Yes
? Would you like to include an Image Gallery? Yes
? Would you like to include a Contact Form? Yes
? What would you like to call the User model? UserAdmin
? Enter an email address for the first Admin user: john@doe.com
? Enter a password for the first Admin user:
  Please use a temporary password as it will be saved in plain text and change it after the first login. 123456
? Would you like to include gulp or grunt? [gulp | grunt | none] gulp
? Would you like to create a new directory for your project? No
? ------------------------------------------------------
    KeystoneJS integrates with Mandrill (from Mailchimp) for email sending.
    Would you like to include Email configuration in your project? Yes
? ------------------------------------------------------
    Please enter your Mandrill API Key (optional).
    See http://keystonejs.com/docs/configuration/#services-mandrill for more info.

    You can skip this for now (we'll include a test key instead)

    Your Mandrill API Key:
? ------------------------------------------------------
    KeystoneJS integrates with Cloudinary for image upload, resizing and
    hosting. See http://keystonejs.com/docs/configuration/#services-cloudinary for more info.

    CloudinaryImage fields are used by the blog and gallery templates.

    You can skip this for now (we'll include demo account details)

    Please enter your Cloudinary URL:
? ------------------------------------------------------
    Finally, would you like to include extra code comments in
    your project? If you're new to Keystone, these may be helpful. Yes
```

Prompt questions from Keystone generator

3. After the end of all generator tasks, we can see the following output on our terminal window:

```
Your KeystoneJS project is ready to go!
  For help getting started, visit http://keystonejs.com/guide
  We've included a test Mandrill API Key, which will simulate
  email sending but not actually send emails. Please replace
  it with your own when you are ready.
  We've included a demo Cloudinary Account, which is reset daily.
  Please configure your own account or use the Local Image field
  instead before sending your site live.
  To start your new website, run "npm start".
```

Note that before starting the application, we need to correct two small bugs. At the time of writing, the generator has this fault; however, when the book is released this should have been fixed. If not, here's the workaround for this issue.

Fixing the lint error and admin object name

1. Open `gulpfile.js` in the rootproject folder and remove line about `lint` task:

```
watch:lint
```

2. Fixing admin user name, open the `Keystone.js` file in the root folder and replace the following code:

```
keystone.set('nav', {
  posts: ['posts', 'post-categories'],
  galleries: 'galleries',
  enquiries: 'enquiries',
  userAdmins: 'user-admins'
});
```

That's all, we already have our blog. Let's check the result.

Running the Keystone blog

1. Open terminal/shell and type the following command:

```
gulp
```

2. Go to `http://localhost:3000/`; you should see the following result:

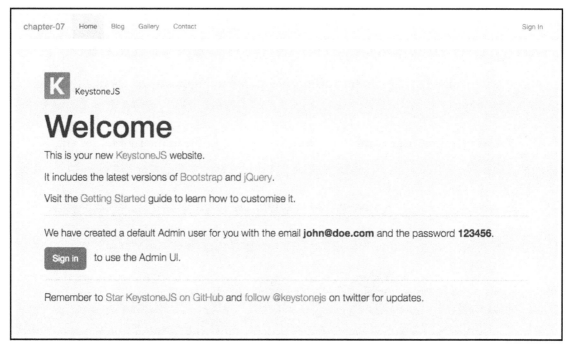

Keystone home screen

As previously commented on, the interface is very simple. It can view the default information generated by the generator, including the information about the user and password.

3. Click on the **Sign in** link in the top-right corner and fill in the `login` form with the user and password from the previous screenshot. The result will be the control panel, as shown in the following figure:

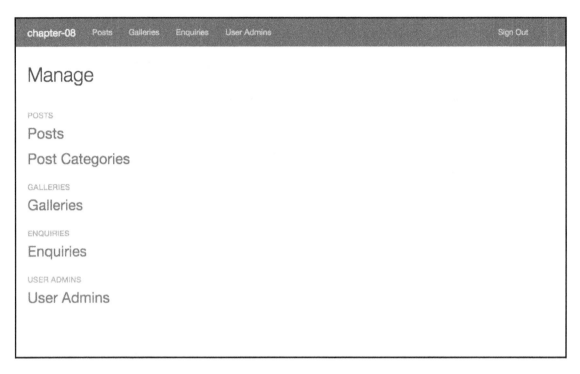

Keystone Control Panel

Each link has a form to insert data for the blog, but don't worry about this at this time; later in the chapter, we will see how to use the admin panel.

As we can see in the previous images, the layout is very simple. However, the highlight of this framework is not its visual appearance, but the power its core engine has to build robust applications.

You can read more about Keystone on the official website at: `http://keys tonejs.com/`.

Anatomy of the Keystone engine

Before we dive directly into the code, we will understand how the directories structure of Keystone works.

After starting the application, we will have the following result:

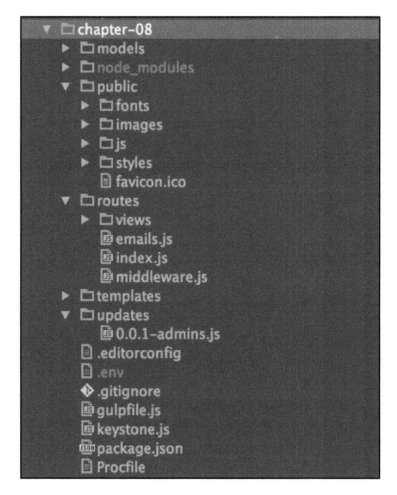

Keystone directories structure

Here's a description of what makes each directory/folder:

Folder Name	Folder Path	Description
Models	/models/	Application database Models.
Public	/public/	Images, JavaScript, Stylesheet, and fonts.
Routes	/routes/ /routes/views	View controllers (On Restful API we can use a folder called API).
Templates	/templates/ /templates/emails/ /templates/layouts/ /templates/mixins/ /templates/views	Application views templates.
updates	/updates/	Migration scripts and database population.

Also, we have in the root folder the following files:

- .editorconfig: Setting the editor's indentation
- .env: Setting Cloudnary Cloud credentials
- .gitignore: Ignore files for Git Source Control
- gulpfile.js: Application tasks
- keystone.js: Bootstrap application
- package.json: Project configurations and NPM modules
- procfile: Configurations for **Heroku** deployment

In the coming lines, we will see in depth what each of these parts performs.

 The Routes folder has some files that we will not explain right now, but don't worry about that; we will see these files in the next topics.

Changing the default bootstrap theme

We will show two ways to customize our blog: one superficial, changing only the stylesheet, and a deeper one, changing all the page's markup.

For the stylesheet changes, we are using the `http://bootswatch.com/` free Bootstrap themes.

The bootstrap framework is very flexible for this; we will use a theme called the `superhero`.

1. Go to the `http://bootswatch.com/superhero/_variables.scss` URL.
2. Copy the page content.
3. Inside `public/styles/boostrap/bootstrap`, create a new file called `_theme_variables.scss` and paste the code copied from the Bootswatch page.
4. Open `public/styles/bootstrap/_bootstrap.scss` and replace the following lines:

```
// Core variables and mixins
@import "bootstrap/_theme_variables";
@import "bootstrap/mixins";
```

   Now we will repeat *steps 1* and *2*, but now with a different URL.

5. Go to the `http://bootswatch.com/superhero/_bootswatch.scss` URL.
6. Copy the page content.
7. Create a file called `_bootswatch.scss` in: `public/styles/bootstrap` and paste the content.
8. Open `public/styles/bootstrap/_bootstrap.scss` and replace the following highlighted line:

```
// Bootswatch overhide classes
@import "bootswatch";
```

9. Done. Right now we have a different layout to the standard one adopted by `keystone.js`, so let's see the result. Open your terminal/shell and type the following command:

```
gulp
```

10. Go to URL: `http://localhost:3000/`, and you should see the following result:

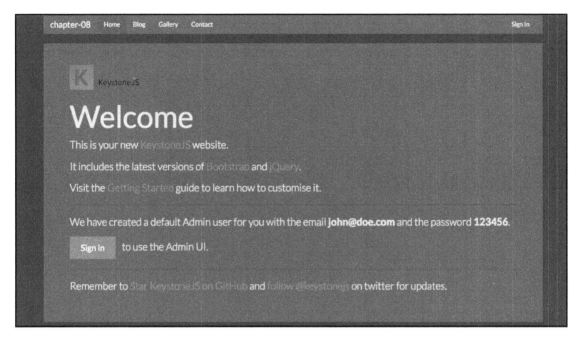

Keystone home screen

With this small change, we can already see the results achieved. However, it is a very superficial customization, since we do not change any HTML markup files.

In the preceding images, we can see that we just changed the colors of the page as it kept the markup intact, using only a bootstrap theme.

In the next example, we will see how to modify the whole structure of the application.

Modifying the KeystoneJS core template path

Now let's do a little refactoring of the templates directory.

1. Inside `templates`, create a folder called `default`.
2. Move all files in the `templates` folder to the new `default` folder.

3. Copy all the contents from the `default` folder and paste them in a new folder called `newBlog`.

The result will be the following screenshot, but we need to change the `keystone.js` file to configure the new folder:

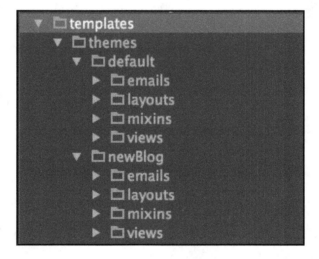

Templates folder structure

4. Open the `keystone.js` file from the `root` folder and update the following lines:

```
'views': 'templates/themes/newBlog/views',
'emails': 'templates/themes/newBlog/emails',
```

Done. We have created a folder to hold all our themes.

Building our own theme

Now we will change the theme markup. This means that we will edit all the HTML files inside the `newBlog` theme. We are using as reference and source the following free template from `https://github.com/BlackrockDigital/startbootstrap-clean-blog`. Our goal is to have a layout similar to the following screenshot:

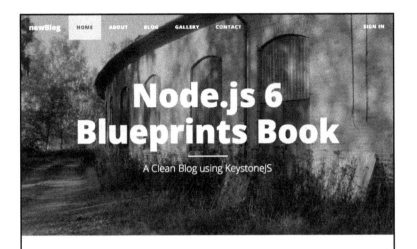

Sample Post Example With Image

Lorem ipsum dolor sit amet, consectetur adipiscing elit, sed do eiusmod tempor incididunt ut labore et dolore magna aliqua.

Posted by Admin on May 28th, 2016

Sample Post Example Without Image I

Lorem ipsum dolor sit amet, consectetur adipiscing elit, sed do eiusmod tempor incididunt ut labore et dolore magna aliqua.

Posted by Admin on May 28th, 2016

Sample Post Example Without Image II

Lorem ipsum dolor sit amet, consectetur adipiscing elit, sed do eiusmod tempor incididunt ut labore et dolore magna aliqua.

Posted by Admin on May 26th, 2016

OLDER POSTS →

Node.js 6 Blueprints book | Powered by KeystoneJS.

Keystone home screen

1. Open `templates/themes/newBlog/layouts/default.swig` and add the following code to the `<head>` tag:

```
{# Custom Fonts #}
<link href="http://maxcdn.bootstrapcdn.com/font-awesome/4.1.0
 /css/font-awesome.min.css" rel="stylesheet" type="text/css">
<link href='http://fonts.googleapis.com
 /css?family=Lora:400,700,400italic,700italic'
 rel='stylesheet' type='text/css'>
<link href='http://fonts.googleapis.com
 /css?family=Open+Sans:300italic,400italic,600italic,
 700italic,800italic,400,300,600,700,800' rel='stylesheet'
 type='text/css'>
```

2. Remove all lines between the `{# HEADER #}` and `{# JAVASCRIPT #}` comments.

Note that this action will remove all the content after the `body` tag and the JavaScript links at the bottom of the `default.swig` file.

3. Now place the following lines of code between the `{# HEADER #}` and `{# JAVASCRIPT #}` comments:

```
<div id="header">
{# Customise your sites navigation by changing the
 navLinks Array in ./routes/middleware.js
  ... or completely change this header to suit your design. #}
<!-- Navigation -->
<nav class="navbar navbar-default navbar-custom
 navbar-fixed-top">
  <div class="container-fluid">
    <!-- Brand and toggle get grouped for better mobile
    display -->
    <div class="navbar-header page-scroll">
      <button type="button" class="navbar-toggle"
      data-toggle="collapse" data-target="#bs-example-navbar-
      collapse-1">
        <span class="sr-only">Toggle navigation</span>
        <span class="icon-bar"></span>
        <span class="icon-bar"></span>
        <span class="icon-bar"></span>
      </button>
      <a class="navbar-brand" href="/">newBlog</a>
    </div>
```

```
      <!-- Collect the nav links, forms, and other content
        for toggling -->
      <div class="collapse navbar-collapse" id="bs-example
        -navbar-collapse-1">
        <ul class="nav navbar-nav navbar-left">
          {%- for link in navLinks -%}
            {%- set linkClass = '' -%}
            {%- if link.key == section -%}
              {%- set linkClass = ' class="active"' -%}
          {%- endif %}
          <li{{ linkClass | safe }}>
            <a href="{{ link.href }}">{{ link.label }}</a>
          </li>
          {%- endfor %}
          </ul>
            <ul class="nav navbar-nav navbar-right">
              {% if user -%}
                {%- if user.canAccessKeystone -%}
                  <li><a href="/keystone">Open Keystone</a>
                  </li>
                {%- endif -%}
                  <li><a href="/keystone/signout">Sign Out</a>
                  </li>
                {%- else -%}
                  <li><a href="/keystone/signin">Sign In</a>
                  </li>
                {%- endif %}
            </ul>
    </div>
    <!-- /.navbar-collapse -->
    </div>
    <!-- /.container -->
  </nav>
  <!-- Page Header -->
  <header class="intro-header">
  <div class="container">
    <div class="row">
      <div class="col-lg-8 col-lg-offset-2 col-md-10 col-
        md-offset-1">
      <div class="site-heading">
        <h1>Node.js 6 Blueprints</h1>
        <hr class="small">
        <span class="subheading">A Clean Blog using
          KeystoneJS</span>
      </div>
    </div>
  </div>
</div>
```

```
    </header>
  </div>

  {# BODY #}
  <div id="body">
  {# NOTE: There is no .container wrapping class around body
    blocks to allow more flexibility in design.
  Remember to include it in your templates when you override
    the intro and content blocks! #}
  {# The Intro block appears above flash messages (used for
   temporary information display) #}
  {%- block intro -%}{%- endblock -%}
  {# Flash messages allow you to display once-off status messages
   to users, e.g. form
  validation errors, success messages, etc. #}
  {{ FlashMessages.renderMessages(messages) }}
  {# The content block should contain the body of your templates
   content #}
  {%- block content -%}{%- endblock -%}
  </div>
```

4. Open `templates/themes/newBlog/views/blog.swig` and replace the code with the following code:

```
{% extends "../layouts/default.swig" %}

{% macro showPost(post) %}
<div class="post" data-ks-editable="editable(user, { list:
  'Post', id: post.id })">
  <div class="post-preview">
    {% if post.image.exists %}
      <img src="{{ post._.image.fit(400,300) }}" class="img
        text-center" width="100%" height="260px">
    {% endif %}
    <a href="/blog/post/{{ post.slug }}">
      <h2 class="post-title">
        {{ post.title }}
      </h2>
      <h3 class="post-subtitle">
        {{ post.content.brief | safe }}
      </h3>
    </a>
    <p class="post-meta">Posted by <a href="#">
      {% if post.author %} {{ post.author.name.first }}
      {% endif %}
    </a>
      {% if post.publishedDate %}
    on
```

```
            {{ post._.publishedDate.format("MMMM Do, YYYY") }}
            {% endif %}
            {% if post.categories and post.categories.length %}
      in
      {% for cat in post.categories %}
      <a href="/blog/{{ cat.key }}">{{ cat.name }}</a>
        {% if loop.index < post.categories.length - 1 %},
        {% endif %}
      {% endfor %}
      {% endif %}
    </p>
    {% if post.content.extended %}
    <a class="read-more" href="/blog/post/{{ post.slug }}">
      Read more...</a>
    {% endif %}
  </div>
  <hr>
  </div>
  {% endmacro %}

  {% block intro %}
    <div class="container">
    {% set title = "Blog" %}
      {% if data.category %}
        {% set title = data.category.name %}
      {% endif %}
      <h1>{{ title }}</h1>
    </div>
  {% endblock %}

  {% block content %}
  <div class="container">
    <div class="row">
      <div class="col-sm-8 col-md-9">
        {% if filters.category and not data.category %}
          <h3 class="text-muted">Invalid Category.</h3>
        {% else %}
        {% if data.posts.results.length %}
          {% if data.posts.totalPages > 1 %}
            <h4 class="text-weight-normal">Showing
              <strong>{{ data.posts.first }}</strong>
              to
              <strong>{{ data.posts.last }}</strong>
              of
              <strong>{{ data.posts.total }}</strong>
              posts.
            </h4>
          {% else %}
```

```
      <h4 class="text-weight-normal">Showing
        {{ utils.plural(data.posts.results.length, "*
        post") }}
      </h4>
   {% endif %}
   <div class="blog">
      {% for post in data.posts.results %}
        {{ showPost(post) }}
      {% endfor %}
   </div>
   {% if data.posts.totalPages > 1 %}
   <ul class="pagination">
      {% if data.posts.previous %}
      <li>
        <a href="?page={{ data.posts.previous }}">
          <span class="glyphicon glyphicon-chevron-left">
          </span>
        </a>
      </li>
      {% else %}
      <li class="disabled">
        <a href="?page=1">
          <span class="glyphicon glyphicon-chevron-left">
          </span>
        </a>
      </li>
      {% endif %}
      {% for p in data.posts.pages %}
        <li class="{% if data.posts.currentPage == p %}
          active{% endif %}">
        <a href="?page={% if p == "..." %}{% if i %}
          {{data.posts.totalPages }}{% else %}1{% endif %}
          {% else %}{{ p }}{% endif %}">{{ p }}
        </a>
        </li>
      {% endfor %}
      {% if data.posts.next %}
      <li>
        <a href="?page={{ data.posts.next }}">
          <span class="glyphicon glyphicon-chevron-right">
          </span>
        </a>
      </li>
      {% else %}
      <li class="disabled">
        <a href="?page={{ data.posts.totalPages }}">
          <span class="glyphicon glyphicon-chevron-right">
          </span>
```

```
        </a>
      </li>
      {% endif %}
    </ul>
    {% endif %}
    {% else %}
      {% if data.category %}
        <h3 class="text-muted">There are no posts in the
          category {{ data.category.name }}.
        </h3>
      {% else %}
        <h3 class="text-muted">There are no posts yet.</h3>
      {% endif %}
    {% endif %}
    {% endif %}
  </div>
  {% if data.categories.length %}
    <div class="col-sm-4 col-md-3">
      <h2>Categories</h2>
        <div class="list-group" style="margin-top: 70px;">
          <a href="/blog" class="{% if not data.category %}
            active{% endif %} list-group-item">All Categories
          </a>
          {% for cat in data.categories %}
          <a href="/blog/{{ cat.key }}" class="{% if
            data.category and data.category.id == cat.id %}
            active{% endif %} list-group-item">{{ cat.name }}
          </a>
          {% endfor %}
        </div>
    </div>
  {% endif %}
</div>
</div>
{% endblock %}
```

5. Open `templates/themes/newBlog/views/contact.swig` and replace the code with the following code:

```
{% extends "../layouts/default.swig" %}

{% block intro %}
  <div class="container">
    <h1>Contact Us</h1>
  </div>
{% endblock %}

{% block content %}
```

```
<div class="container">
  {% if enquirySubmitted %}
    <h3>Thanks for getting in touch.</h3>
{% else %}
  <div class="row control-group">
    <div class="col-lg-8 col-lg-offset-2 col-md-10 col-md-
      offset-1">
      <form method="post">
        <input type="hidden" name="action" value="contact">
          {% set className = "" %}
          {% if validationErrors.name %}
            {% set className = "has-error" %}
          {% endif %}
        <div class="form-group {{ className }} col-xs-12
          floating-label-form-group controls">
          <label>Name</label>
          <input type="text" name="name.full" value="{{
            formData['name.full'] | default('') }}" class=
            "form-control" placeholder="Name">
        </div>
        {% set className = "" %}
        {% if validationErrors.email %}
          {% set className = "has-error" %}
        {% endif %}
        <div class="form-group {{ className }} col-xs-12
          floating-label-form-group controls">
          <label>Email</label>
          <input type="email" name="email" value="{{
          formData.email | default('') }}" class=
          "form-control" placeholder="E-mail">
        </div>
          <div class="form-group col-xs-12 floating-label-
            form-group controls">
            <label>Phone</label>
            <input type="text" name="phone" value="{{
              formData.phone | default('') }}" placeholder=
              "Phone Number (Optional)" class="form-control">
          </div>
          {% set className = "" %}
          {% if validationErrors.enquiryType %}
            {% set className = "has-error" %}
          {% endif %}
          <div class="form-group {{ className }} col-xs-12
            floating-label-form-group controls">
            <span class="title-label text-muted">
            What are you contacting us about?
            </span>
            <br>
```

```
                    <select name="enquiryType" class="form-control">
                      <option value="">(select one)</option>
                      {% for type in enquiryTypes %}
                        {% set selected = "" %}
                        {% if formData.enquiryType === type.value %}
                          {% set selected = " selected" %}
                        {% endif %}
                        <option value="{{ type.value }}"{{ selected }}>
                          {{ type.label }}</option>
                      {% endfor %}
                    </select>
                  </div>
                  {% set className = "" %}
                  {% if validationErrors.message %}
                    {% set className = "has-error" %}
                  {% endif %}
                  <div class="form-group {{ className }} col-xs-12
                    floating-label-form-group controls">
                      <label>Message</label>
                      <textarea rows="5" class="form-control"
                        placeholder="Message" name="message">
                      </textarea>
                      {{ formData.message }}
                    </div>
                    <br>
                    <div class="row">
                      <div class="form-group col-xs-12">
                        <button type="submit" class="btn
                          btn-default">Send</button>
                      </div>
                    </div>
                  </form>
                </div>
              </div>
          {% endif %}
          </div>
      {% endblock %}
```

6. Open `templates/themes/newBlog/views/gallery.swig` and replace the code with the following code:

```
{% extends "../layouts/default.swig" %}

{% block intro %}
<div class="container">
  <h1>Gallery</h1>
</div>
{% endblock %}
```

```
{% block content %}
  <div class="container">
  {% if galleries.length %}
    {% for gallery in galleries %}
      <h2>{{ gallery.name }}
      {% if gallery.publishedDate %}
        <span class="pull-right text-muted">{{
          gallery._.publishedDate.format("Do MMM YYYY") }}
        </span>
  {% endif %}
      </h2>
      <div class="row">
      {% if gallery.heroImage.exists %}
        <div class="gallery-image">
          <img src="{{ gallery._.heroImage.limit(0.73,200) }}">
        </div>
        <br>
        <hr>
          <div class="row">
            <div class='list-group gallery'>
            {% for image in gallery.images %}
            <div class='col-sm-6 col-xs-6 col-md-4 col-lg-4'>
              <a class="thumbnail fancybox" rel="ligthbox"
                href="{{ image.limit(640,480) }}">
                <img class="img-responsive" alt="" src="{{
                  image.limit(300,320) }}" />
              </a>
            </div>
            {% endfor %}
          </div>
        </div>
      {% else %}
      <div class="row">
        <div class='list-group gallery'>
          {% for image in gallery.images %}
          <div class='col-sm-6 col-xs-6 col-md-4 col-lg-4'>
            <a class="thumbnail fancybox" rel="ligthbox"
              href="{{ image.limit(640,480) }}">
            <img class="img-responsive" alt="" src="{{
              image.limit(300,320) }}" />
            </a>
          </div>
          {% endfor %}
        </div>
      </div>
    {% endif %}
  </div>
  {% endfor %}
```

```
{% else %}
  <h3 class="text-muted">There are no image galleries yet.</h3>
{% endif %}
</div>
{% endblock %}
```

7. Open `templates/themes/newBlog/views/index.swig` and replace the code with the following code:

```
{% extends "../layouts/default.swig" %}

{% block content %}
  <div class="container">
    <div class="row">
      <div class="col-lg-8 col-lg-offset-2 col-md-10 col-md-
        offset-1">
      {% for post in data.posts %}
      <div class="post-preview">
        <a href="/blog/post/{{ post.slug }}">
        <h2 class="post-title">
          {{ post.title }}
        </h2>
        <h3 class="post-subtitle">
          {{ post.content.brief | safe }}
        </h3>
        </a>
        <p class="post-meta">Posted by <span class=
          "text-primary">
          {% if post.author %} {{ post.author.name.first }}
          {% endif %}
          </span> {% if post.publishedDate %}
            on
          {{ post._.publishedDate.format("MMMM Do, YYYY") }}
          {% endif %}</p>
        </div>
        <hr>
      {% endfor %}
      <!-- Pager -->
      {% if data.posts %}
      <ul class="pager">
        <li class="next">
          <a href="/blog">Older Posts &rarr;</a>
        </li>
      </ul>
      {% endif %}
    </div>
  </div>
</div>
```

```
{% endblock %}
```

Note that here, in `index.swig`, we add some lines of code to show a list of posts on the index page, so we need to change the `index.js` controller.

8. Open `routes/views/index.js` and add the following lines of code:

```
var keystone = require('keystone');

exports = module.exports = function (req, res) {
  var view = new keystone.View(req, res);
  var locals = res.locals;
    // locals.section is used to set the currently selected
    // item in the header navigation.
    locals.section = 'home';
    // Add code to show posts on index
    locals.data = {
      posts: []
    };
    view.on('init', function(next) {
      var q = keystone.list('Post').model.find()
      .where('state', 'published')
      .sort('-publishedDate')
      .populate('author')
      .limit('4');
    q.exec(function(err, results) {
      locals.data.posts = results;
      next(err);
    });
  });
  // Render the view
  view.render('index');
};
```

9. Open `templates/themes/newBlog/views/post.swig` and replace the code with the following code:

```
{% extends "../layouts/default.swig" %}

{% block content %}
<article>
  <div class="container">
    <a href="/blog">&larr; back to the blog</a>
    <div class="row">
      <div class="col-lg-8 col-lg-offset-2 col-md-10 col-md-
        offset-1">
        {% if not data.post %}
```

```
            <h2>Invalid Post.</h2>
        {% else %}
            <h1>{{ data.post.title }}</h1>
              {% if data.post.publishedDate %}
              on
        {{ data.post._.publishedDate.format("MMMM Do, YYYY") }}
        {% endif %}
        {% if data.post.categories and
          data.post.categories.length %}
        in
        {% for cat in data.post.categories %}
          <a href="/blog/{{ cat.key }}">{{ cat.name }}</a>
        {% if loop.index < data.post.categories.length - 1 %},
        {% endif %}
      {% endfor %}
    {% endif %}
    {% if data.post.author %}
      by {{ data.post.author.name.first }}
    {% endif %}
    <div class="post">
      {% if data.post.image.exists %}
        <div class="image-wrap">
          <img src="{{ data.post._.image.fit(750,450) }}"
            class="img-responsive">
        </div>
      {% endif %}
      {{ data.post.content.full | raw }}
        </div>
      {% endif %}
    </div>
  </div>
</div>
</article>
<hr>
{% endblock %}
```

With this block of code, we have finished the HTML markup changes. Now we need to apply the new stylesheet.

Changing the stylesheet

As we chose SASS to deal with stylesheets on the `keystone.js` setup, we already have everything to use the **SASS** features.

Open `public/styles/site/_variables.scss` and replace the code for the following lines of code:

```
// Override Bootstrap variables in this file, e.g.
 $font-size-base: 14px;
// Theme Variables
$brand-primary: #0085A1;
$gray-dark: lighten(black, 25%);
$gray: lighten(black, 50%);
$white-faded: fade(white, 80%);
$gray-light: #eee;
```

Remember that we used the `http://blackrockdigital.github.io/startbootstrap-clean-blog/index.html` as a reference and we just picked some blocks of code. Note that the template uses LESS instead **SASS,** but here we re-write all the code to fit SASS syntax.

For reasons of space, we do not put the entire stylesheet in this example. You can download the sample code from the Packt Publishing website (`www.packtpub.com`) or directly from the book repository on GitHub.

It is important to note that we have created the same stylesheet for our sample blog, but we convert the **LESS** syntax to **SASS**.

1. Open `public/styles/site/_layout.scss` and use the code.
2. Create a new file called `_mixins.scss` inside `public/styles/site/` and add the following lines of code:

```
// Mixins
@mixin transition-all() {
  -webkit-transition: all 0.5s;
  -moz-transition: all 0.5s;
  transition: all 0.5s;
}
@mixin background-cover() {
  -webkit-background-size: cover;
  -moz-background-size: cover;
  background-size: cover;
  -o-background-size: cover;
}
@mixin serif() {
```

```
    font-family: 'Lora', 'Times New Roman', serif;
  }
  @mixin sans-serif () {
    font-family: 'Open Sans', 'Helvetica Neue', Helvetica, Arial,
      sans-serif;
  }
```

Now we just need to edit the `public/styles/site.scss` to include the new `mixins` file.

3. Open `public/styles/site.scss` and add the following lines of code:

```
// Bootstrap
// Bootstrap can be removed entirely by deleting this line.
@import "bootstrap/bootstrap";
// The easiest way to customise Bootstrap variables while
// being able to easily override the source files with new
// versions is to override the ones you want in another file.
//
  // You can also add your own custom variables to this file for
    // use in your site stylesheets.
@import "site/variables";
// Add mixins
@import "site/mixins";
// Site Styles
// ===========
// Add your own site style includes here
@import "site/layout";
```

4. Add the `image header-bg-1290x1140.jpg` from the `sample-images` folder (you can download all the examples files from Packt Publishing or on the GitHub official book page) to the `public/images/` folder.

Adding the Gallery script

As we can see, the default `Keystone.js` theme is very simple and uses only the Bootstrap framework. Now we will use a jQuery plugin called Fancybox to apply a new style in our gallery.

> You can get more information about **Fancybox** at the official website: `http://fancybox.net/`.

1. Open `templates/themes/newBlog/layouts/default.swig` and add the following highlighted code inside the head tag:

```
{# Customise the stylesheet for your site by editing
 /public/styles/site.sass #}
<link href="/styles/site.css" rel="stylesheet">
<!-- fancyBox -->
<link rel="stylesheet" href="//cdnjs.cloudflare.com/ajax/libs
 /fancybox/2.1.5/jquery.fancybox.min.css" media="screen">
{# This file provides the default styling for the KeystoneJS
  Content Editor #}
{%- if user and user.canAccessKeystone -%}
  <link href="/keystone/styles/content/editor.min.css"
    rel="stylesheet">
{%- endif -%}
```

2. Now let's add the following highlighted lines of code to scripts at the bottom of `templates/themes/newBlog/layouts/default.swig`:

```
{# Add scripts that are globally required by your site here. #}
<script src="//cdnjs.cloudflare.com/ajax/libs/fancybox/2.1.5
   /jquery.fancybox.min.js"></script>
<script>
$(document).ready(function(){
   // Gallery
$(".fancybox").fancybox({
      openEffect: "elastic",
      closeEffect: "elastic"
});
// Floating label headings for the contact form
   $("body").on("input propertychange", ".floating-label-
      form-group", function(e) {
      $(this).toggleClass("floating-label-form-group-with-value",
        !!$(e.target).val());
      }).on("focus", ".floating-label-form-group", function() {
        $(this).addClass("floating-label-form-group-with-focus");
         }).on("blur", ".floating-label-form-group", function() {
           $(this).removeClass("floating-label-form-group-
             with-focus");
           });
});
</script>

{# Include template-specific javascript files by extending
   the js block #}
{%- block js -%}{%- endblock -%}
```

As we already use jQuery in the project, since Bootstrap depends on it, we do not need to insert it again.

3. Open your terminal/shell and type the following command:

```
gulp
```

4. Go to `http://localhost:3000/gallery`, and you can see the following result:

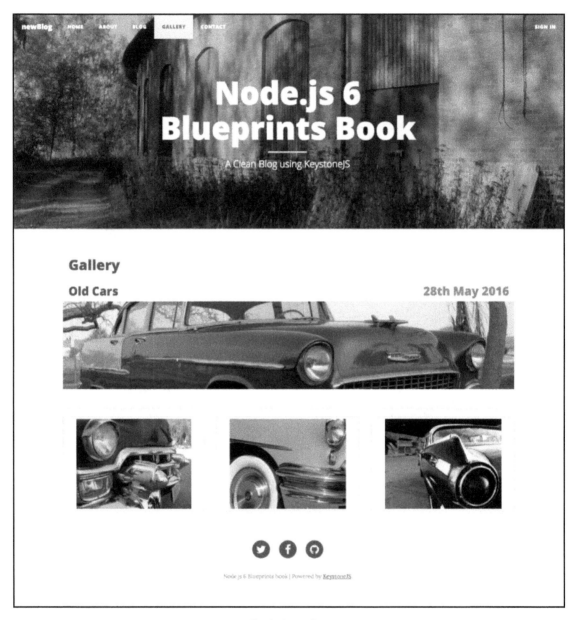

Template image gallery

Note that we already include the sample content to our blog, but don't worry about this; later in this chapter we will see how to include content.

Extending the keystone.js core

Now we have the new theme almost ready.

We will now see how we can extend the core `keystone.js` and add another page on our blog, as the previous screenshot shows, we have an **ABOUT** menu item, so let's create it:

1. Create a new file called `About.js` inside `models/folder` and add the following lines of code:

```
var keystone = require('keystone');
var Types = keystone.Field.Types;

/**
 * About Model
 * ==========
 */

var About = new keystone.List('About', {
  // Using map to show title instead ObjectID on Admin Interface
  map: { name: 'title' },
  autokey: { path: 'slug', from: 'title', unique: true },
});

About.add({
  title: { type: String, initial: true, default: '',
    required: true }, description: { type: Types.Textarea }
});

About.register();
```

2. Add the new module to admin navigation, open `keystone.js` in the root folder, and add the following highlighted lines of code:

```
// Configure the navigation bar in Keystone's Admin UI
keystone.set('nav', {
  posts: ['posts', 'post-categories'],
  galleries: 'galleries',
  enquiries: 'enquiries',
  userAdmins: 'user-admins',
  abouts: 'abouts'
});
```

Note that the word on the left will be displayed at the nav bar as an About menu item and the word on the right-hand side is the about.js collection.

3. Let's customize the column display. Add the following lines of code, before the register() function on the About.js file:

```
About.defaultColumns = 'title, description|60%';
```

4. To add the route to the about page, open routes/index.js and add the following highlighted lines of code:

```
// Setup Route Bindings
exports = module.exports = function (app) {
    // Views
    app.get('/', routes.views.index);
    app.get('/about', routes.views.about);
    app.get('/blog/:category?', routes.views.blog);
    app.get('/blog/post/:post', routes.views.post);
    app.get('/gallery', routes.views.gallery);
    app.all('/contact', routes.views.contact);

    // NOTE: To protect a route so that only admins can see it,
    use the requireUser middleware:
    // app.get('/protected', middleware.requireUser,
    routes.views.protected);
};
```

Now let's create the controller for the routes.views.blog function.

5. Create a new file called about.js inside the routes/views/ folder and add the following code:

```
var keystone = require('keystone');
exports = module.exports = function (req, res) {
  var view = new keystone.View(req, res);
  var locals = res.locals;

    // locals.section is used to set the currently selected
    // item in the header navigation.
    locals.section = 'about';
    // Add code to show posts on index
    locals.data = {
      abouts: []
    };
    view.on('init', function(next) {
      var q = keystone.list('About').model.find()
            .limit('1');
```

```
    q.exec(function(err, results) {
      locals.data.abouts = results;
        next(err);
  });
});
// Render the view
view.render('about');
};
```

6. Add the route on `routes/middleware.js`, as the following highlighted code:

```
exports.initLocals = function (req, res, next) {
  res.locals.navLinks = [
    { label: 'Home', key: 'home', href: '/' },
    { label: 'About', key: 'about', href: '/about' },
    { label: 'Blog', key: 'blog', href: '/blog' },
    { label: 'Gallery', key: 'gallery', href: '/gallery' },
    { label: 'Contact', key: 'contact', href: '/contact' },
  ];
  res.locals.user = req.user;
    next();
};
```

In this example, we see how it is possible to extend the functionality of the framework using the built-in functions.

You can read more about the **Keystone API** at this link: `https://github.com/keystonejs/keystone/wiki/Keystone-API`.

So, the final result for all these steps will be like the following screenshot:

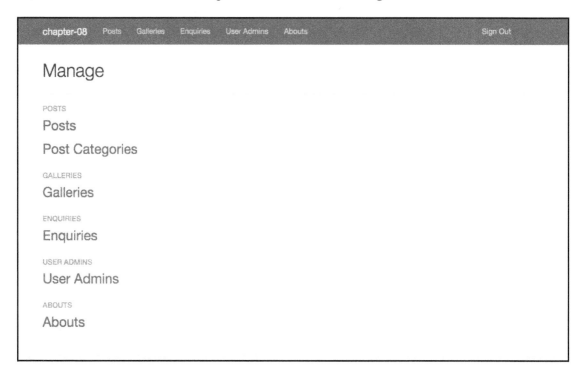

Keystone Control Panel with Abouts menu item

Note that we can see the **Abouts** menu on the previous screenshot.

Inserting content using control panel

After all these steps, we managed to create a fully customized layout for our blog; we will now enter content using the available images in the `sample-images` folder that you can find in the download of the book's source code:

1. Go to `http://localhost:3000/keystone`, use the user: `john@doe.com` and password: `123456` to access the control panel.

2. Go to `http://localhost:3000/keystone/post-categories`, click on the **Post Categories** link.

3. Click on the **Create Post Category** button, insert the Old Cars title into the input field, and click **Create** button.

4. For the book example, we will use only one category, but in a real application you can create as many as you want.

5. Go to `http://localhost:3000/keystone/posts`, click on the **Create Post** button and add the content as shown in the following screenshot:

Sample content on create post screen

6. Repeat the same process as for *step 4* for the second post entry and change the title to Sample Post Example Without Image II.

7. Repeat the same process as for *step 4* for the third post entry and change the title to Sample Post Example With Image, click on the **Upload Image** button, and use the file `sample-blog-image.png` from the `sample-images` folder.

Note that you can download the book source code and image samples at any time from the Packt Publishing website or directly from the GitHub book repository.

At the end of *step 6*, our control panel will be as in the following screenshot:

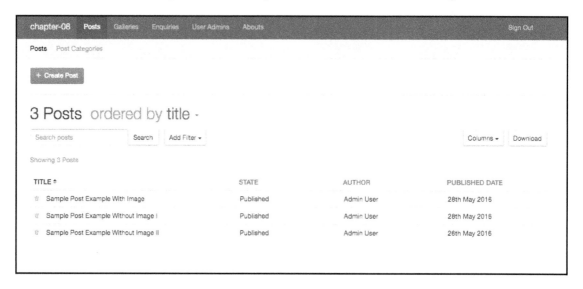

Posts Control Panel

As we can see, `Keystone.js` has a very simple and easy-to-use interface. We can extend all the features of the framework to create incredible things.

Our Posts page was as follows:

Screenshot of the Blog page

Summary

In this chapter, we discussed some very important concepts about the `Keystone` framework to create applications and websites with a database.

We saw how we can extend the framework by creating new models, views, and templates, using the internal Keystone API.

In addition, we showed two different ways to customize the CMS using only a stylesheet, as well as how to completely alter the page structure and how to insert new functionalities, such as the **Fancybox** plugin, to the Images Gallery.

In the next chapter, we will see how to use Command-line Interface (CLI) for JSLint, Concat, Minify, and other tasks, using only the Node Package Manager (NPM) to build and deploy the application.

9
Building a Frontend Process with Node.js and NPM

As we mentioned before in previous chapters, we can use the facilities from Node Package Manager (NPM) to replace Gulp and the **Grunt** task manager, which are the most popular tools for dealing with frontend dependencies. We can combine both tools, but in this chapter we will explore only NPM and some commands that will help us create our application.

We will create building tasks to lint, concatenate, and minify Javascript files, optimize images, compile SASS stylesheets, and deploy the application to a server in the cloud, by just using the command line. Furthermore, for this example we will use the Loopback.io framework to create the application example with MongoDB as the database.

In this chapter, we will cover:

- How to create an application using only the Loopback.io CLI
- How to install eslint, imagemin, and browserify
- How to create tasks to lint errors, concatenate JS files, and optimize images
- How to deal with SASS import and compile
- How to deploy an application to Heroku using the Heroku toolbelt

What we are building

For this chapter, we will build a simple gallery application, very similar to `chapter 04`, *Don't Take a Photograph, Make it â╦╦ An App for Photographers*, but this time we will using a Restful API with the Loopback.io framework. We'll see how to create building tasks using the NPM command line, and the final result will be very similar to the following screenshot:

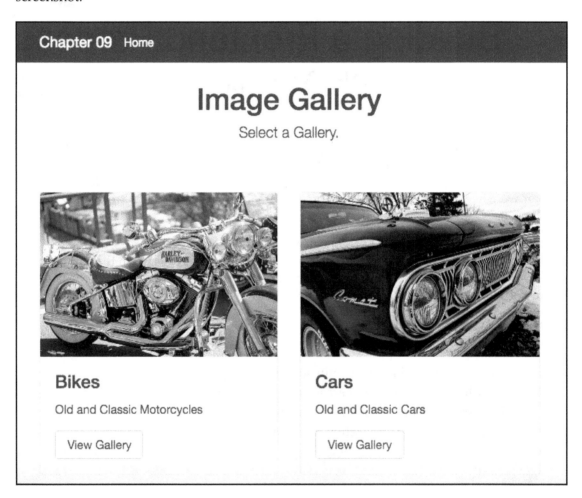

Home screen

Creating the baseline application

Although we already used the Loopback framework, we strongly recommend that you install it again, to ensure that you will have the most up-to-date version on your machine:

```
npm install -g loopback
```

In this example, we will not make many changes to the generated code, since our focus is to create building tasks, but we will use some interesting features of the Loopback framework using the command line:

1. Open terminal/shell, and type the following command:

```
slc loopback
```

2. Name the application chapter-09.
3. Choose empty-server (an empty LoopBack API, without any configured models or data source's) and press Enter.

Now we have created the application scaffold. Don't worry about the next commands suggested by the terminal output, as we will discuss these commands later in the book.

> You can read more about **Loopback CLI** at this link: https://docs.stron gloop.com/display/public/LB/Command-line+reference.

Adding a Datasource to the project

Before we create our models as we did in Chapter 06, *Building a Customer Feedback App with Restful API and Loopback.io,* this time, we will add the datasource first. This is because we are using the command line to create the entire project. This means that we don't edit any files manually.

A good practice, when we use the command line, is to create the datasource first instead of the application models. This procedure prevents the need to manually edit the files to connect models with the datasource application:

1. In terminal/shell, go to the chapter-09 folder and type the following command:

```
slc loopback:datasource
```

2. Fill in the following questions as shown in the following screenshot:

```
? Enter the data-source name: galleryDS
? Select the connector for galleryDS: MongoDB (supported by StrongLoop)
Connector-specific configuration:
? Connection String url to override other settings (eg: mongodb://username:password@hostname:port/database):
? host: localhost
? port: 27017
? user:
? password:
? database: n6b-chapter-09
? Install loopback-connector-mongodb@^1.4 Yes
```

Datasource setup

By default, we don't need to set up a user and password if we are working with MongoDB on localhost. Don't worry about this now, but later we will see how to change this configuration to deploy the application. If you want, you can add a user and password in your local environment too.

Creating application models

Now let's create the application models; for this example, we are using two models:

1. Open the terminal/shell inside the `chapter-09` folder, and type the following command:

   ```
   slc loopback:model
   ```

   Use the model name `gallery`.

2. Fill in the questions as shown in the following screenshot:

```
? Enter the model name: gallery
? Select the data-source to attach undefined to: galleryDS (mongodb)
? Select model's base class PersistedModel
? Expose gallery via the REST API? Yes
? Custom plural form (used to build REST URL): galleries
? Common model or server only? common
Let's add some gallery properties now.

Enter an empty property name when done.
? Property name: name
   invoke    loopback:property
? Property type: string
? Required? Yes
? Default value[leave blank for none]:

Let's add another gallery property.
Enter an empty property name when done.
? Property name: description
   invoke    loopback:property
? Property type: string
? Required? Yes
? Default value[leave blank for none]:
```

Gallery model setup

After the second property, press **Enter** to finish model creation.

3. Open the terminal/shell inside the chapter-09 folder, and type the following command:

```
slc loopback:model
```

Use the model name bike.

4. Fill in the questions as shown in the following screenshot:

```
? Enter the model name: bike
? Select the data-source to attach undefined to: galleryDS (mongodb)
? Select model's base class PersistedModel
? Expose bike via the REST API? Yes
? Custom plural form (used to build REST URL): bikes
? Common model or server only? common
Let's add some bike properties now.

Enter an empty property name when done.
? Property name: name
   invoke    loopback:property
? Property type: string
? Required? Yes
? Default value[leave blank for none]:

Let's add another bike property.
Enter an empty property name when done.
? Property name: model
   invoke    loopback:property
? Property type: string
? Required? Yes
? Default value[leave blank for none]:

Let's add another bike property.
Enter an empty property name when done.
? Property name: category
   invoke    loopback:property
? Property type: string
? Required? Yes
? Default value[leave blank for none]:
```

Bike model setup

After the third property, press **Enter** to finish model creation.

You can read more about model creation at this link: `https://docs.stron gloop.com/display/public/LB/Model+generator`.

Don't worry about the relationships between the models at this time, we will see this in the next step, using only the command line.

Adding relationships between application models

Let's define the relationship between our models; we will use two types of relationship, which are:

- **hasmany**: A gallery can have many bikes
- **belongsTo**: A bike can have one gallery

Remember, we are just trying to make something useful, but not complex, to illustrate the building process with NPM, follow these steps:

1. Open the terminal/shell inside the `chapter-09` folder and type the following command:

   ```
   slc loopback:relation
   ```

2. Choose the `bike` model and fill in the questions as shown:

   ```
   ? Select the model to create the relationship from: bike
   ? Relation type: belongs to
   ? Choose a model to create a relationship with: gallery
   ? Enter the property name for the relation: gallery
   ? Optionally enter a custom foreign key:
   ```

   Bike model relationship

3. Choose the `gallery` model and fill in the questions with the following information:

   ```
   ? Select the model to create the relationship from: gallery
   ? Relation type: has many
   ? Choose a model to create a relationship with: bike
   ? Enter the property name for the relation: bikes
   ? Optionally enter a custom foreign key:
   ? Require a through model? No
   ```

   Gallery model relationship

So let's check whether everything has been written properly.

4. Open the `common/models/gallery.json` file and you will see the following highlighted code:

```json
{
  "name": "gallery",
  "plural": "galleries",
  "base": "PersistedModel",
  "idInjection": true,
  "options": {
    "validateUpsert": true
  },
  "properties": {
    ...
  },
  "validations": [],
  "relations": {
    "bikes": {
      "type": "hasMany",
      "model": "bike",
      "foreignKey": ""
    }
  },
  "acls": [],
  "methods": {}
}
```

5. Open the `common/models/bike.json` file and you will see the following highlighted code:

```json
{
  "name": "bike",
  "base": "PersistedModel",
  "idInjection": true,
  "options": {
    "validateUpsert": true
  },
  "properties": {
    ...
  },
  "validations": [],
  "relations": {
    "gallery": {
      "type": "belongsTo",
      "model": "gallery",
      "foreignKey": ""
    }
```

```
    },
    "acls": [],
    "methods": {}
}
```

You can find more information about **Relation generator** at this link: `http`
`s://docs.stronggloop.com/display/public/LB/Relation+generator`.

Using only three commands, we managed to create the basis for our sample application.
The next step is to create a static website in the client's folder.

Setting up a static site

As we did in `chapter 06`, *Building a Customer Feedback App with Restful API and Loopback.io*
let's set up the client folder as a static site:

1. Rename the `server/boot/root.js` file to `server/boot/_root.js`.
2. Add the following highlighted lines to `server/middleware.json`:

```
{
  "initial:before": {
    "loopback#favicon": {}
  },
  "initial": {
    "compression": {},
    "cors": {
      "params": {
        "origin": true,
        "credentials": true,
        "maxAge": 86400
      }
    },
    "helmet#xssFilter": {},
    "helmet#frameguard": {
      "params": [
        "deny"
      ]
    },
    "helmet#hsts": {
      "params": {
        "maxAge": 0,
        "includeSubdomains": true
```

```
        }
      },
      "helmet#hidePoweredBy": {},
      "helmet#ieNoOpen": {},
      "helmet#noSniff": {},
      "helmet#noCache": {
        "enabled": false
      }
    },
    "session": {},
    "auth": {},
    "parse": {},
    "routes": {
      "loopback#rest": {
        "paths": [
          "${restApiRoot}"
        ]
      }
    },
    "files": {
      "loopback#static": {
        "params": "$!../client"
      }
    },
    "final": {
      "loopback#urlNotFound": {}
    },
    "final:after": {
      "loopback#errorHandler": {}
    }
  }
```

3. Inside the `./client` folder, create a new file called `index.html` and add the following content:

```html
<!DOCTYPE html>
<html>
  <head><title>Bikes Gallery</title></head>
  <body>
    <h1>Hello Node 6 Blueprints!</h1>
  </body>
</html>
```

Now it is time to check the previous changes and see the final result in your browser.

4. Open the terminal/shell and type the following command:

   npm start

5. Open your favorite browser and go to `http://localhost:3000/`.

   You should see the **Hello Node 6 Blueprints!** message.

We also have the Restful API at `http://localhost:3000/api/bikes` and `http://localhost:3000/api/galleries`.

Now we will see how to restructure some of the directories to prepare the application for deployment in the cloud using the NPM building tasks.

Refactoring the application folder

Our refactoring process includes two steps.

First, let's create a directory for the application source files, such as JavaScript, SCSS, and images files.

In the second step, we will create some directories within the `client` folder to receive our scripts.

Let's create the source folder for images, libs, scripts, and scss files.

Creating the images folder

In this folder, we will store the images before processing an optimization technique using `imagemin-cli`.

1. Inside the root project, create a folder called `src`.
2. Within the `src` folder, create a folder called `images`.
3. Within the `images` folder, create a folder called `gallery`.
4. Download the sample images file for `chapter 09`, *Building a Frontend Process with Node.js and NPM* from the Packt website (`www.packtpub.com`) or from the official book repository on GitHub, and paste the images into the `gallery` folder.

You can read more about imagemin cli at this link: https://github.co m/imagemin/imagemin-cli.

Creating the libraries folder

The libraries folder will store some jQuery plugins. Inside the src folder, create a folder called libs.

Creating the scripts folder

As we are using jQuery and some plugins, we will need to write some code to use the jQuery libs; we will do that using this folder:

1. Inside the src folder, create a folder called scripts.
2. Inside src/scripts folder, create a file called gallery.js and add the following code:

```
(function (){
    'use-strict'
    //jQuery fancybox activation
    $('.fancybox').fancybox({
        padding : 0,
        openEffect  : 'elastic'
    });
})();
```

In this example, we are using only a single plugin, but in large applications, it is very common to use several plugins; in this case, we would have a file for each feature.

Then, targeting a performance improvement in our application, we recommend concatenating all the scripts into a single file.

Creating the SASS folder

The SASS folder will store the `scss` files. We are using the Bootstrap framework, and for this example we will set up the Bootstrap framework using the SASS separated version; don't worry about this now, as later in the chapter we will see how to get these files:

1. Inside the `src` folder, create a folder called `scss`.
2. Inside the `scss` folder, create a folder called `vendor`.

Installing Bower

As we have seen in previous chapters, we will use Bower to manage frontend dependencies:

1. Open the terminal/shell and type the following command:

```
npm install bower -g
```

2. Create a file called `.bowerrc` and save it in the root folder.
3. Add the following content to the `.bowerrc` file:

```
{
  "directory": "src/components",
  "json": "bower.json"
}
```

4. Open terminal/shell and type the following command:

```
bower init
```

5. Fill in the questions as shown in the following screenshot:

```
? name chapter-09
? description Node 6 blueprints book, chapter 09 example
? main file server/server.js
? what types of modules does this package expose?
? keywords Npm, building, process
? authors Your email will appear here
? license MIT
? homepage
? set currently installed components as dependencies? Yes
? add commonly ignored files to ignore list? Yes
? would you like to mark this package as private which prevents it from being accidentally published to the registry? Yes

{
  name: 'chapter-09',
  description: 'Node 6 blueprints book, chapter 09 example',
  main: 'server/server.js',
  authors: [
    ' Your email will appear here
  ],
  license: 'MIT',
  keywords: [
    'Npm',
    'building',
    'process'
  ],
  moduleType: [],
  homepage: '',
  private: true,
  ignore: [
    '**/.*',
    'node_modules',
    'bower_components',
    'src/components',
    'test',
    'tests'
  ]
}
```

Bower.json setup

Installing application dependencies

In this example, we are using just one jQuery plugin plus the Bootstrap framework, so let's first install Bootstrap using the Bower CLI:

1. Open the terminal/shell and type the following command:

   ```
   bower install bootstrap#v4.0.0-alpha --save
   ```

   Just open the src/components folder to check the Bootstrap and jQuery folders.

2. Now we will install the `jQuery fancybox` plugin in the images gallery. Open the terminal/shell and type the following command:

```
bower install fancybox --save
```

So the `src` folder will have the following structure at this point:

- components/
    - bootstrap/
    - fancybox/
    - jquery/

Create the scss folder structure

Now let's set up the `scss` folder to compile the `bootstrap.scss` files:

1. Open `src/components/bootstrap` folder and copy all the contents from SCSS folder.
2. Paste the content inside the `src/scss/vendor` folder.
3. Create a file called `main.scss` inside the `src/` folder and add the following content:

```
// Project Style

// Import Botstrap
@import "vendor/bootstrap";

//
body {
  padding-top: 5rem;
}
.starter-template {
  padding: 3rem 1.5rem;
  text-align: center;
  @include clearfix
}
```

Many developers do not use the Bootstrap framework this way, some just use the `bootstrap.css` or `bootstrap.min.css` files in their projects. This is ok, but when we use the framework the way shown here, we can use all the framework's resources in our own stylesheet, so we can use all `mixins` and `variables` within our stylesheet.

For example, the highlighted code came from Bootstrap mixins and we can apply it to our own stylesheet:

```
.starter-template {
  padding: 3rem 1.5rem;
  text-align: center;
  @include clearfix
}
```

You can read more about SASS at this link: http://sass-lang.com/.

Refactoring the client folder

The client folder will have a pretty basic structure for any web application with folders to store CSS, JavaScript, and images files.

For this example, we will use the latest stable version of AngularJS to create the pages of our application:

1. Inside the client folder, create the following folders:

   - css/
   - images/gallery/
   - js/
   - js/libs/
   - js/scripts/
   - views/

After creating all these folders, the `client` directory will look like the following screenshot:

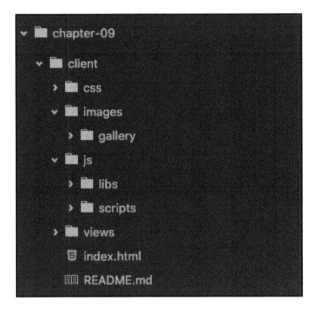

Client folder structure

Adding the application views

Now is time to create the application views folder to store all the application templates:

1. Inside the `client/src` folder, create a new file called `home.html` and add the following code:

```
<div class="col-md-6" ng-repeat="item in vm.listProducts">
  <div class="card" >
    <img class="card-img-top" ng-src="{{ item.image }}"
     alt="Card image cap" width="100%">
    <div class="card-block">
      <h4 class="card-title">{{ item.name }}</h4>
      <p class="card-text">{{ item.description }}</p>
      <a ui-sref="galleries({itemId:item.id})" class="btn
       btn-secondary">View Gallery</a>
    </div>
  </div>
</div>
</div>
```

2. Inside the `client/src` folder, create a new file called `galleries.html` and add the following code:

```html
<div class="row">
  <div class="col-md-4" ng-repeat="item in vm.listProducts">
    <div class="card" >
      <a href="{{ item.image }}" class="fancybox" rel="gallery"
       >
        <img class="card-img-top" ng-src="{{ item.image }}" alt=
        "{{ item.name }}" width="100%"/>
      </a>
      <div class="card-block">
        <h4 class="card-title">{{ item.name }}</h4>
        <p class="card-text">{{ item.model }} - {{ item.category }}
        </p>
      </div>
    </div>
  </div>
</div>
```

3. Open the `client/index.html` file and replace the code with the following content:

```html
<!DOCTYPE html>
<html ng-app="bikesGallery">
  <head><title>Bikes Gallery</title></head>
    <link rel="stylesheet" href="css/main.css">
    <link rel="stylesheet" href="components/fancybox/source
     /jquery.fancybox.css">
  <body>
    <nav class="navbar navbar-fixed-top navbar-dark bg-inverse">
      <div class="container">
        <a class="navbar-brand" href="#">Chapter 09</a>
          <ul class="nav navbar-nav">
            <li class="nav-item active"><a class="nav-link" href="/">
            Home <span class="sr-only">(current)</span></a>
            </li>
          </ul>
      </div>
    </nav>

  <div class="container">
    <div id="title">
      <div class="starter-template">
        <h1>Image Gallery</h1>
          <p class="lead">Select a Gallery.</p>
        </div>
```

```
      </div>
    <div class="" ui-view>

</div>
</div>
</div>

<!-- Scripts at bottom -->
<script src='js/libs/jquery.min.js'></script>
<script src="js/libs/angular.js"></script>
<script src="js/libs/angular-resource.js"></script>
<script src="js/libs/angular-ui-router.js"></script>
<script src="js/app.js"></script>
<script src="js/app.config.js"></script>
<script src="js/app.routes.js"></script>
<script src="js/services.js"></script>
<script src="js/controllers.js"></script>
<script src="js/libs/libs.js"></script>
<script src="js/scripts/scripts.js"></script>

</body>
</html>
```

Installing AngularJS files

Now it is time to install the AngularJS files and create the application. In this example, we will explore the AngularJS SDK from the Loopback framework later in this section; for this we choose to use AngularJS to build our frontend application:

1. Open the terminal/shell and type the following command:

   bower install angularjs#1.5.0 --save

2. Open the terminal/shell and type the following command:

   bower install angular-resource#1.5.0 --save

3. Open the terminal/shell and type the following command:

   bower install angular-ui-router --save

You can read more about AngularJS at this link: https://docs.angular js.org/api.

Creating the AngularJS application

Finally we will create the AngularJS application, so follow the next steps:

1. Inside the `client/js` folder, create a new file called `app.js` and add the following code:

```
(function(){
    'use strict';
    angular
    .module('bikesGallery', ['ui.router','lbServices']);
})();
```

Don't worry about the `lbServices` dependency at this point; later in this chapter we will see how to create this file using the AngularJS SDK tool built with the Loopback framework.

2. Inside the `client/js` folder, create a new file called `app.config.js` and add the following code:

```
(function(){
    'use strict';
    angular
     .module('bikesGallery')
     .config(configure)
     .run(runBlock);

    configure.$inject = ['$urlRouterProvider', '$httpProvider',
                         '$locationProvider'];

    function configure($urlRouterProvider, $httpProvider,
                       $locationProvider) {

      $locationProvider.hashPrefix('!');
      // This is required for Browser Sync to work poperly
      $httpProvider.defaults.withCredentials = true;
      $httpProvider.defaults.headers.common['X-Requested-With']
        = 'XMLHttpRequest';
      $urlRouterProvider
      .otherwise('/');
    }
    runBlock.$inject = ['$rootScope', '$state', '$stateParams'];
    function runBlock($rootScope, $state, $stateParams ) {
      $rootScope.$state = $state;
      $rootScope.$stateParams = $stateParams;
    }
```

```
})();
```

3. Inside the `client/js` folder, create a new file called `app.routes.js` and add the following code:

```
(function(){
  'use strict';

    angular
      .module('bikesGallery')
      .config(routes);

    routes.$inject = ['$stateProvider'];
    function routes($stateProvider) {
      $stateProvider
      .state('home', {
          url:'/',
          templateUrl: 'views/home.html',
          controller: 'HomeController',
          controllerAs: 'vm'
      })
      .state('galleries', {
          url:'/galleries/{itemId}/bikes',
          templateUrl: 'views/galleries.html',
          controller: 'GalleryController',
          controllerAs: 'vm'
      });
    }
})();
```

4. Inside the `client/js` folder, create a new file called `controllers.js` and add the following code:

```
(function(){
  'use strict';

    angular
      .module('bikesGallery')
      .controller('GalleryController', GalleryController)
      .controller('HomeController', HomeController);

    HomeController.$inject = ['Gallery'];
    function HomeController(Gallery) {
      var vm = this;
      vm.listProducts = Gallery.find();
      //console.log(vm.listProducts);
    }
```

```
GalleryController.$inject = ['Gallery', '$stateParams'];
function GalleryController(Gallery, $stateParams) {
  var vm = this;
  var itemId = $stateParams.itemId;
  //console.log(itemId);
  vm.listProducts = Gallery.bikes({
    id: itemId
  });
  //console.log(vm.listProducts);
  }
}) ();
```

Using Loopback's AngularJS SDK

We will use the built-in AngularJS SDK from the Loopback framework to automatically generate all application services:

1. Open the terminal/shell and type the following command:

    lb-ng ./server/server.js ./client/js/services.js

    The previous command will create a file called `services.js` inside the `client/js` folder with all the methods (Create, Read, Update, and Delete) and many more available in the Restful API created by the Loopback framework.

     You can check your local API by running the `npm start` command in your terminal/shell at the root project folder. The API will be available at `http://0.0.0.0:3000/explorer`.

2. The `lbServices` section has the following CRUD methods and many others:

    ```
    "create": {
      url: urlBase + "/galleries",
      method: "POST"
    },
    "upsert": {
      url: urlBase + "/galleries",
      method: "PUT"
    },
    "find": {
      isArray: true,
      url: urlBase + "/galleries",
      method: "GET"
    },
    ```

```
    "deleteById": {
      url: urlBase + "/galleries/:id",
      method: "DELETE"
    },
```

3. To use one of these methods, we just need to inject the factory into the Angular controller as the following highlighted code:

```
GalleryController.$inject = ['Gallery', '$stateParams'];
function GalleryController(Gallery, $stateParams) {
    ...
}
```

Then we can use the methods inside the controllers, as in the following example:

```
Gallery.create();
Gallery.find();
Gallery.upsert({ id: itemId });
Gallery.delete({ id: itemId });
```

This is a simple and very useful service to deal with all endpoints created in our application for all the models that we have.

The first part of the application is already almost complete, but we still need to add some content to make it more pleasant.

Let's create some content. As already mentioned earlier, you can download the entire sample code for the book from the Packt website (www.packtpub.com), or directly from the book's GitHub repository.

Adding content to the application

You can add content in two ways, the first is using the endpoints created by the application and the second is by using the migration file.

In the following lines, we will show how to use the second option; it may be a brief and interesting procedure for creating a migration file:

1. Inside the server/boot/ folder, create a file called create-sample-models.js and add the following content to create a migration file for **Gallery Model**:

```
module.exports = function(app) {
    // automigrate for models, everytime the app will running,
        db will be replaced with this data.
```

```
app.dataSources.galleryDS.automigrate('gallery', function(err)
{
  if (err) throw err;
   // Simple function to create content
  app.models.Gallery.create(
    [
      {
        "name":"Bikes",
        "image": "images/gallery/sample-moto-gallery.jpg",
        "link": "bikes.html",
        "description":"Old and Classic Motorcycles",
        "id":"5755d253b4aa192e41a6be0f"
      },{
          "name":"Cars",
          "image": "images/gallery/sample-car-gallery.jpg",
          "link": "cars.html",
          "description":"Old and Classic Cars",
          "id":"5755d261b4aa192e41a6be10"
      }
    ],
    function(err, galleries) {
      if (err) throw err;
      // Show a success msg on terminal
      console.log('Created Motorcycle Gallery Model: \n',
       galleries);
    });
  });
```

2. Inside the `server/boot/` folder, add the following content to create a `migration` file for **Bike Model**:

```
app.dataSources.galleryDS.automigrate('bike', function(err) {
  if (err) throw err;
   // Simple function to create content
  app.models.Bike.create(
    [
        {
          "name":"Harley Davidson",
          "image": "images/gallery/sample-moto1.jpg",
          "model":"Knucklehead",
          "category":"Custom Classic Vintage",
          "id":"5755d3afb4aa192e41a6be11",
          "galleryId":"5755d253b4aa192e41a6be0f"
        },{
            "name":"Harley Davidson",
            "image": "images/gallery/sample-moto2.jpg",
            "model":"Rare Classic",
```

```
        "category":"Custom Classic Vintage",
        "id":"5755d3e8b4aa192e41a6be12",
        "galleryId":"5755d253b4aa192e41a6be0f"
    },{
        "name":"Old Unknown Custom Bike",
        "image": "images/gallery/sample-moto3.jpg",
        "model":"Custom",
        "category":"Chopper",
        "id":"5755d431b4aa192e41a6be13",
        "galleryId":"5755d253b4aa192e41a6be0f"
    },{
        "name":"Shadow Macchit",
        "image": "images/gallery/sample-car1.jpg",
        "model":"Classic",
        "category":"Old Vintage",
        "id":"5755d43eb4aa192e41a6be14",
        "galleryId":"5755d261b4aa192e41a6be10"
    },{
        "name":"Buicks",
        "image": "images/gallery/sample-car2.jpg",
        "model":"Classic",
        "category":"Classic",
        "id":"5755d476b4aa192e41a6be15",
        "galleryId":"5755d261b4aa192e41a6be10"
    },{
        "name":"Ford",
        "image": "images/gallery/sample-car3.jpg",
        "model":"Corsa",
        "category":"Hatch",
        "id":"5755d485b4aa192e41a6be16",
        "galleryId":"5755d261b4aa192e41a6be10"
    }

], function(err, bikes) {
    if (err) throw err;
    // Show a success msg on terminal
    console.log('Created Bike Model: \n', bikes);
  });
});
};
```

 Don't forget to delete this file after the first deployment to **Heroku**.

Creating the Building tasks

Now is the time to create our task using only NPM.

Before we begin, it is important to keep in mind that NPM has two special commands that are invoked directly, `start` and `test`. So we will use the `run` command to run all the other tasks we create.

Our goals in this section are to:

- Copy some files from the `source` directory to the `client` directory
- Verify errors in JavaScript files
- Compile SASS files from `src/scss` and save them in the `client/css` folder
- Optimize images from `src/images/gallery` to `client/images/gallery`
- Concatenate JavaScript files from `src/scripts` to `client/js/scripts`

Installing the dependencies

To accomplish these tasks, we need to install some Command Line Interface (CLI) tools:

1. Open the terminal/shell and type the following commands:

```
npm install copy-cli --save-dev
npm install -g eslint
npm install eslint --save-dev
npm install -g node-sass
npm install browserify --save-dev
npm intall -g imagemin-cli
npm install -g imagemin
```

Our purpose in this example is to show how to use the building tools, so we will not go too deep into each of them.

But before we go any further, let's set up the JavaScript validator `eslint`.

 You can read more about `eslint` at this link: `http://eslint.org/`.

2. Inside the root project, create a file called `.eslintrc.json` and add the following code:

```
{
  "env": {
    "browser": true
  },
  "globals": {
    "angular": 1,
    "module": 1,
    "exports": 1
  },
  "extends": "eslint:recommended",
  "rules": {
    "linebreak-style": [
      "error",
      "unix"
    ],
    "no-mixed-spaces-and-tabs": 0,
    "quotes": 0,
    "semi": 0,
    "comma-dangle": 1,
    "no-console": 0
  }
}
```

You can read more about `Eslint` rules at: `http://eslint.org/docs/rules/`.

Creating the copy task

We will create each task before inserting it into our `package.json` file; this way it is easier to understand the procedure of each.

The copy tasks will be the following:

- Copy the jQuery file
- Copy the AngularJS main library
- Copy the AngularJS resources library
- Copy the AngularJS ui-router library

So we need to copy these files (jQuery and AngularJS) from the source folder to the client folder:

```
"copy-jquery": "copy ./src/components/jquery/dist/jquery.js >
  ./client/js/libs/jquery.js",
"copy-angular": "copy ./src/components/angular/angular.js >
  ./client/js/libs/angular.js",
"copy-angular-resource": "copy ./src/components/angular-resource/angular-
resource.js >
  ./client/js/libs/angular-resource.js",
"copy-angular-ui-router": "copy ./src/components/angular-ui-
router/release/angular-ui-router.js >
  ./client/js/libs/angular-ui-router.js",
```

The last copy task will execute all the other copy tasks:

```
"copy-angular-files": "npm run copy-angular && npm run copy-angular-
resource && npm run copy-angular-ui-router",
```

Don't worry about running the copy tasks at the moment; later in the chapter we will execute them one by one before deployment.

Creating the SASS task

The SASS task will be very simple, we will just compile the scss files and insert them into the client/css folder:

```
"build-css": "node-sass --include-path scss src/scss/main.scss
client/css/main.css",
```

Creating the linting task

We will use the .eslintrc.json configuration to apply to all JavaScript files in the client/js folder:

```
"lint-js": "eslint client/js/*.js --no-ignore",
```

Creating the image optimization task

Another important task in any web application is to optimize all the image files, for performance reasons:

```
"imagemin": "imagemin src/images/gallery/* --o client/images/gallery",
```

Creating the concatenate task

The concat task will concatenate all scripts files from libs and scripts:

```
"concat-js-plugins": "browserify src/libs/*.js -o client/js/libs/libs.js",
"concat-js-scripts": "browserify src/scripts/*.js -o client/js/scripts/scripts.js",
```

The last concat task executes all the other concat tasks:

```
"prepare-js": "npm run concat-js-plugins && npm run concat-js-scripts"
```

Creating the build task

The build task is just the execution of each of the previous steps in a single task:

```
"build": "npm run lint-js && npm run copy-angular-files && npm run build-css && npm run prepare-js && npm run imagemin"
```

Now let's add all the tasks to the `package.json` file. Open the `package.json` file and add the following highlighted code:

```
{
  "name": "chapter-09",
  "version": "1.0.0",
  "main": "server/server.js",
  "scripts": {
    "start": "node .",
    "pretest": "eslint .",
    "posttest": "nsp check",
    "copy-jquery": "copy ./src/components/jquery/dist/jquery.js >
      ./client/js/libs/jquery.js",
    "copy-angular": "copy ./src/components/angular/angular.js >
      ./client/js/libs/angular.js",
    "copy-angular-resource": "copy ./src/components/angular-resource
    /angular-resource.js >
      ./client/js/libs/angular-resource.js",
    "copy-angular-ui-router": "copy ./src/components/angular-ui-router
```

```
            /release/angular-ui-router.js >
              ./client/js/libs/angular-ui-router.js",
            "copy-angular-files": "npm run copy-angular && npm run copy-angular-
            resource && npm run copy-angular-ui-router",
            "build-css": "node-sass --include-path scss src/scss/main.scss
            client/css/main.css", "lint-js": "eslint client/js/*.js --no-ignore",
            "imagemin": "imagemin src/images/gallery/* --o
    client/images/gallery",
            "concat-angular-js": "browserify ./src/libs/angular.js ./src/libs/
            angular-resource.js ./src/libs/angular-ui-router.js > client/js
            /libs/libs.js", "concat-js-plugins": "browserify src/libs/*.js -o
            client/js/libs/libs.js", "concat-js-scripts": "browserify
            src/scripts/*.js -o client/js/scripts/scripts.js", "prepare-js":
            "npm run concat-js-plugins && npm run concat-js-scripts", "build":
            "npm run lint-js && npm run copy-angular-files && npm run build-css
    &&
            npm run prepare-js && npm run imagemin"
        },
        "dependencies": {
            ...
        },
        "devDependencies": {
            ...
        },
        "repository": {
            ...
        },
        "license": "MIT",
        "description": "chapter-09",
        "engines": {
          "node": "5.0.x"
        }
    }
```

Using tasks with individual commands

As we mentioned before, we can perform each of the tasks that we have created individually.

For example, to optimize the image files, we can run the `imagemin` task only. Just open the terminal/shell and type the following command:

```
npm run imagemin
```

The output on the terminal will be the following:

```
8 images minified
```

We can do the same for each task.

Deploying to Heroku Cloud

The first step to deploy our application is to create a free account on **HerokuCloud Service**:

1. Go to `https://signup.heroku.com/` and create a free account.
2. Download the **Heroku toolbelt** for your platform at `https://toolbelt.heroku.com/`.
3. Follow the installation process for your platform.

   Now you must have the `Heroku toolbelt` on your machine, to test it.

4. Open the terminal/shell and type the following command:

```
heroku --help
```

The terminal output lists all the possible things to do with **Heroku CLI**.

> The book assumes that you already have git source control installed on your machine; if you don't it have yet, check out this page: `https://git-scm.com/downloads`.

Creating a Heroku application

Now we will create an application and send it to your newly created Heroku account:

1. Create a file called `.Procfile` and save it at the root project folder.
2. Paste the following code into the `.Procfile` file:

```
web: slc run
```

3. Open the terminal/shell and type the following command:

```
git init
```

   The previous command initializes a git repository.

4. The git add command adds all files to version tracking:

```
git add
```

5. The git commit command send all files to version control on your local machine.

```
git commit -m "initial commit"
```

Now it is time to log in to your Heroku account and send all the project files to Heroku git source control.

6. Open the terminal/shell and type the following command:

```
heroku login
```

Enter your username and password.

7. Open the terminal/shell and type the following command:

```
heroku apps:create --buildpack https://github.com/strongloop
/strongloop-buildpacks.git
```

The previous command will use strongloop-buildpacks to configure and deploy a Loopback application.

Creating a deploy.sh file

Finally, we will create our deploy task using a .sh file:

1. Create a folder called bin in the root folder.
2. Inside the bin folder, create a file called deploy.sh.
3. Add the following code to the bin/deploy.sh file:

```
#!/bin/bash

set -o errexit # Exit on error

npm run build # Generate the bundled Javascript and CSS

git push heroku master # Deploy to Heroku
```

4. Add the following lines of code at the end of all tasks in the `package.json` file:

```
"scripts": {
  ...
  "deploy": "./bin/deploy.sh"
}
```

Now, every time you make a commit with some changes and type the `npm run deploy` command, the engine will start the `deploy.sh` file and upload all the committed changes to Heroku Cloud Service.

5. Open the terminal/shell and type the following command:

`npm run deploy`

6. If you are facing errors with permissions, do the following. Open the terminal/shell inside the bin folder and type the following command:

`chmod 755 deploy.sh`

By default, Heroku Cloud Service will create a URL for your application, like this:

`https://some-name-1234.herokuapp.com/.`

At the end of the output on the terminal, you will see some very similar to the following lines:

```
remote: -----> Discovering process types
remote:        Procfile declares types -> web
remote:
remote: -----> Compressing...
remote:        Done: 79.7M
remote: -----> Launching...
remote:        Released v13
remote:        https://yourURL-some-23873.herokuapp.com/
               deployed to Heroku
remote:
remote: Verifying deploy... done.
To https://git.heroku.com/yourURL-some-23873.git
```

The final result will be our sample application deployed to Heroku Cloud Service.

Just got to `https://yourURL-some-23873.herokuapp.com/` and you will see the following result:

Application on Heroku Cloud Service

When you click on the Bikes View Gallery button, you will see the bike gallery, as shown here:

Image Gallery

Select a Gallery.

Harley Davidson

Knuklehead - Custom

Classic Vintage

Harley Davidson

Rare Classic - Custom

Classic Vintage

Old Unknown Custom Bike

Custom - Chopper

Bikes gallery

Also, when you click on each bike, you will see the fancybox plugin in action.

Summary

In this chapter, we explore a little more of the Loopback framework and its command line interface.

Also, we have seen how to configure an AngularJS application using the Loopback AngularJS SDK, creating all services for each endpoint of the application.

We then explored the facilities using NPM as a single build tool.

We also addressed how to create and set up an account on Heroku, and how to automate the deployment of our application by integrating three different tools, Loopback, Git, and the Heroku toolbelt.

In the next chapter, we will see how to use the concept of containers to run a Node.js application.

10
Creating and Deploying Using Continuous Integration and Docker

In this chapter, we will explore the continuous delivery development process with Node.js applications.

In previous chapters, we saw many ways to develop applications using Node.js and frameworks such as Express and Loopback, including using different databases, such as MongoDB and MySql, and some middleware for user authentication, sessions, cookies, and many others.

In `chapter 09`, *Building a Frontend Process with Node.js and NPM*, we saw how to deploy an application using the command line and how to upload the project directly to the cloud using a few commands.

In this chapter, we will see how to integrate some more tools into our development environment to deal with unit tests and automated deployment, how to set up environment variables to protect our database credentials, and how to create a full application using the concept of Docker containers.

In this chapter, we will cover the following topics:

- How to deal with CI solutions
- How to test Node.js applications
- How to configure a MongoDB cloud instance and environment variables
- How to integrate GitHub, Heroku, and Codeship in build and test processes
- How to create Docker images and how to use Docker containers

What we are building

In this chapter, we will build an application with the Express framework using some techniques already used in previous chapters, such as user session and user authentication with email and password using the Passport middleware. We will also use MongoDB, Mongoose, and Swig templates.

The result will be the following screenshot:

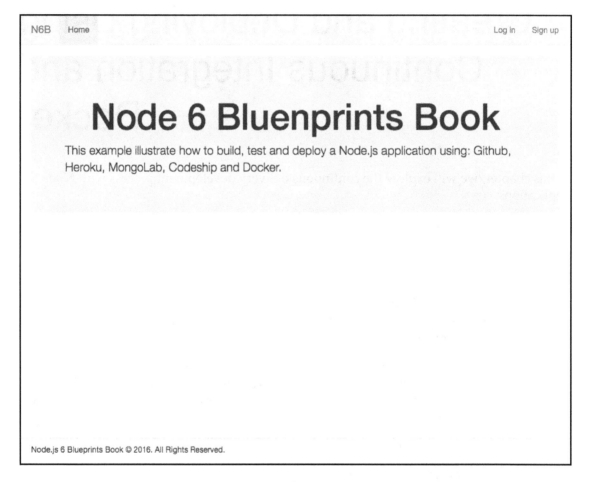

Screenshot of home screen

What Continuous Integration means

The workflow of **Continuous Integration(CI)** consists generally of four steps. We will illustrate with diagrams and a simple description of all the four stages.

The following diagram shows how CI solutions work:

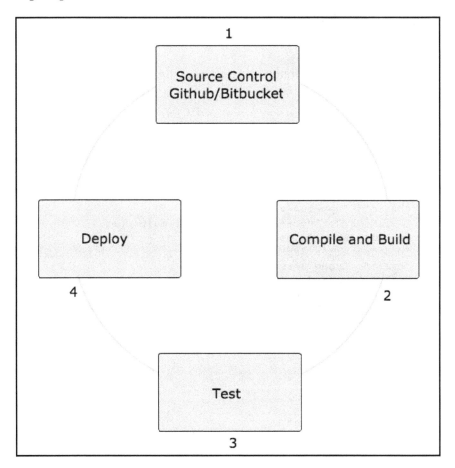

Continuous Integration process

1. Commit the code to a repository.
2. The CI interface builds the application.
3. Execute tests.
4. If all tests are successful, the code goes to deployment.

Creating the baseline application

Let's start building the application. First off, we will create an application folder and add some root files, such as .gitignore, package.json, .env, and many more.

Adding the root files

1. Create a folder called chapter-10.
2. Inside the chapter-10 folder, create a new file called package.json and add the following code:

```json
{
  "name": "chapter-10",
  "version": "1.0.0",
  "main": "server.js",
  "description": "Create an app for the cloud with Docker",
  "scripts": {
    "build": "npm-run-all build-*",
    "build-css": "node-sass public/css/main.scss >
    public/css/main.css",
    "postinstall": "npm run build",
    "start": "node server.js",
    "test": "mocha",
    "watch": "npm-run-all --parallel watch:*",
    "watch:css": "nodemon -e scss -w public/css -x npm run
    build:css"
  },
  "dependencies": {
    "async": "^1.5.2",
    "bcrypt-nodejs": "^0.0.3",
    "body-parser": "^1.15.1",
    "compression": "^1.6.2",
    "dotenv": "^2.0.0",
    "express": "^4.13.4",
    "express-flash": "0.0.2",
    "express-handlebars": "^3.0.0",
    "express-session": "^1.2.1",
    "express-validator": "^2.20.4",
    "method-override": "^2.3.5",
    "mongoose": "^4.4.8",
    "morgan": "^1.7.0",
    "node-sass": "^3.6.0",
    "nodemon": "^1.9.1",
    "npm-run-all": "^1.8.0",
```

```
        "passport": "^0.3.2",
        "passport-local": "^1.0.0",
        "swig": "^1.4.2"
    },
    "devDependencies":
        "mocha": "^2.4.5",
        "supertest": "^1.2.0"
    },
    "engines": {
        "node": "6.1.0"
    }
}
```

> Note that in devDependencies we will use some modules to write tests for our application. We will see how to do this later in the book.

3. Create a file called `.env` and add the following code:

```
SESSION_SECRET='<SESSION_SECRET>'
#MONGODB='<>'
MONGODB='<MONGODB>'
```

Don't worry about the previous code; we will replace this code using environment variables on **Heroku** and **Codeship** later in the chapter, and we will also configure this file to use Docker containers.

> For security reasons, never upload your credentials to open source repositories if you are working on a commercial project; even if you have a private repository, it is always recommended you use environment variables in production.

4. Create a file called `Profile` and add the following code:

```
web: node server.js
```

As we already saw in previous chapters, this file is responsible for making our application work on Heroku. Even though it is not mandatory, it's good practice to include it.

Also, as we are using git source control, it is good practice to include a `.gitignore` file.

5. Create a file called `.gitignore` and add the following code:

```
lib-cov
*.seed
*.log
*.csv
*.dat
*.out
*.pid
*.gz
*.swp

pids
logs
results
tmp
coverage

# API keys
.env
# Dependency directory
node_modules
bower_components
npm-debug.log
# Editors
.idea
*.iml

# OS metadata
.DS_Store
Thumbs.db
```

Note that at this point we keep the `.env` file out of the `gitignore` file; later in the book, we will un-track this file.

Creating the config folder and files

Generally, all Node.js applications uses a folder called `Config`, to store all the application configuration files. So let's create one.

1. At the root project folder, create a new folder called `config`.
2. Create a file called `passport.js` and add the following code:

```
// load passport module
var passport = require('passport');
```

```
var LocalStrategy = require('passport-local').Strategy;
// load up the user model
var User = require('../models/User');
passport.serializeUser(function(user, done) {
  // serialize the user for the session
  done(null, user.id);
});
passport.deserializeUser(function(id, done) {
  // deserialize the user
  User.findById(id, function(err, user) {
    done(err, user);
  });
});

// using local strategy
passport.use(new LocalStrategy({ usernameField: 'email' },
 function(email, password, done) {

  User.findOne({ email: email }, function(err, user) {
    if (!user) {
      // check errors and bring the messages
      return done(null, false, { msg: 'The email: ' + email +
      ' is already taken. '});
    }
    user.comparePassword(password, function(err, isMatch) {
      if (!isMatch) {
        // check errors and bring the messages
        return done(null, false, { msg:'Invalid email or
        password'});
      }
      return done(null, user);
    });
  });
}));
```

The previous code will take care of user authentication using the **Flask** middleware for error messages, as we saw in `Chapter 01`, *Building a Twitter-Like Application Using the MVC Design Pattern.*

Creating the controllers folder and files

As we are building a simple application, we will have only two controllers, one for users and another for the home page:

1. In the root project folder, create a new folder called `controllers`.

2. Create a file called `home.js` and add the following code:

```
// Render Home Page
exports.index = function(req, res) {
  res.render('home', {
    title: 'Home'
  });
};
```

Now let's add all the functions related to users, such as sign in, sign up, authorization, account, and log out. We will add each function after the previous one.

Adding modules and authentication middleware

Inside the `controllers` folder, create a new file called `user.js` and add the following code:

```
// import modules
var async = require('async');
var crypto = require('crypto');
var passport = require('passport');
var User = require('../models/User');

// authorization middleware
exports.ensureAuthenticated = function(req, res, next) {
  if (req.isAuthenticated()) {
    next();
  } else {
    res.redirect('/login');
  }
};

// logout
exports.logout = function(req, res) {
  req.logout();
  res.redirect('/');
};
```

Adding login GET and POST methods

Add the followingcode to the `controllers/user.js` file, right after the previous code:

```
// login GET
exports.loginGet = function(req, res) {
  if (req.user) {
```

```
      return res.redirect('/');
    }
    res.render('login', {
      title: 'Log in'
    });
  };

  // login POST
  exports.loginPost = function(req, res, next) {
    // validate login form fields
    req.assert('email', 'Email is not valid').isEmail();
    req.assert('email', 'Empty email not allowed').notEmpty();
    req.assert('password', 'Empty password not allowed').notEmpty();
    req.sanitize('email').normalizeEmail({ remove_dots: false });

    var errors = req.validationErrors();
    if (errors) {
      // Show errors messages for form validation
      req.flash('error', errors);
      return res.redirect('/login');
    }

    passport.authenticate('local', function(err, user, info) {
      if (!user) {
        req.flash('error', info);
        return res.redirect('/login')
      }
      req.logIn(user, function(err) {
        res.redirect('/');
      });
    })(req, res, next);
  };
```

Adding signup GET and POST methods

Add the followingcode to the `controllers/user.js` file, right after the previous code:

```
  // signup GET
  exports.signupGet = function(req, res) {
    if (req.user) {
      return res.redirect('/');
    }
    res.render('signup', {
      title: 'Sign up'
    });
  };
```

```
// signup POST
exports.signupPost = function(req, res, next) {
  // validate sign up form fields
  req.assert('name', 'Empty name not allowed').notEmpty();
  req.assert('email', 'Email is not valid').isEmail();
  req.assert('email', 'Empty email is not allowed').notEmpty();
  req.assert('password', 'Password must be at least 4 characters
    long').len(4);
  req.sanitize('email').normalizeEmail({ remove_dots: false });

  var errors = req.validationErrors();

  if (errors) {
    // Show errors messages for form validation
    req.flash('error', errors);
    return res.redirect('/signup');
  }

  // Verify user email
  User.findOne({ email: req.body.email }, function(err, user) {
    if (user) {
      // if used, show message and redirect
      req.flash('error', { msg: 'The email is already taken.' });
      return res.redirect('/signup');
    }
    // create an instance of user model with form data
    user = new User({
      name: req.body.name,
      email: req.body.email,
      password: req.body.password
    });
    // save user
    user.save(function(err) {
      req.logIn(user, function(err) {
        res.redirect('/');
      });
    });
  });
};
```

Adding account GET and UPDATE methods

Add the following code to the `controllers/user.js` file, right after the previous code:

```
// profile account page
exports.accountGet = function(req, res) {
  res.render('profile', {
    title: 'My Account'
  });
};
// update profile and change password
exports.accountPut = function(req, res, next) {
  // validate sign up form fields
  if ('password' in req.body) {
    req.assert('password', 'Password must be at least 4 characters
    long').len(4);
    req.assert('confirm', 'Passwords must match')
     .equals(req.body.password);
  }
  else {
    req.assert('email', 'Email is not valid').isEmail();
    req.assert('email', 'Empty email is not allowed').notEmpty();
    req.sanitize('email').normalizeEmail({ remove_dots: false });
  }
  var errors = req.validationErrors();

  if (errors) {
    // Show errors messages for form validation
    req.flash('error', errors);
    return res.redirect('/pages');
  }

  User.findById(req.user.id, function(err, user) {
    // if form field password change
    if ('password' in req.body) {
      user.password = req.body.password;
    }
    else {
      user.email = req.body.email;
      user.name = req.body.name;
    }
    // save user data
    user.save(function(err) {
      // if password field change
      if ('password' in req.body) {
        req.flash('success', { msg: 'Password changed.' });
      } else if (err && err.code === 11000) {
        req.flash('error', { msg: 'The email is already taken.' });
```

```
      } else {
        req.flash('success', { msg: 'Profile updated.' });
      }
      res.redirect('/account');
    });
  });
};
```

Adding account DELETE method

Add the following code to the `controllers/user.js` file, right after the previous code:

```
// profile DELETE
exports.accountDelete = function(req, res, next) {
  User.remove({ _id: req.user.id }, function(err) {
    req.logout();
    req.flash('info', { msg: 'Account deleted.' });
    res.redirect('/');
  });
};
```

Now we have finished the application controllers.

Creating the model folder and files

1. At the root project folder, create a folder called `models`.
2. Create a new file called `User.js` and add the following code:

```
// import modules
var crypto = require('crypto');
var bcrypt = require('bcrypt-nodejs');
var mongoose = require('mongoose');
// using virtual attributes
var schemaOptions = {
  timestamps: true,
  toJSON: {
    virtuals: true
  }
};

// create User schema
var userSchema = new mongoose.Schema({
  name: String,
  email: { type: String, unique: true},
```

```
    password: String,
    picture: String
}, schemaOptions);
// encrypt password
userSchema.pre('save', function(next) {
  var user = this;
  if (!user.isModified('password')) { return next(); }
  bcrypt.genSalt(10, function(err, salt) {
    bcrypt.hash(user.password, salt, null, function(err, hash) {
      user.password = hash;
      next();
    });
  });
});
// Checking equal password
userSchema.methods.comparePassword = function(password, cb) {
  bcrypt.compare(password, this.password, function(err, isMatch) {
    cb(err, isMatch);
  });
};
// using virtual attributes
userSchema.virtual('gravatar').get(function() {
  if (!this.get('email')) {
    return 'https://gravatar.com/avatar/?s=200&d=retro';
  }
  var md5 =
  crypto.createHash('md5').update(this.get('email')).digest('hex');
  return 'https://gravatar.com/avatar/' + md5 + '?s=200&d=retro';
});
var User = mongoose.model('User', userSchema);
module.exports = User;
```

Creating the public folder and files

In this example, we are using the SASS version of the Bootstrap framework, as we did in the previous chapter. But this time, we will store the source files in a different location, inside the public/css folder. Let's create the folder and files:

1. Inside the root project, create a folder called public.
2. Inside public folder we will create a folder called: css, inside css create a folder called: vendor and inside vendor, create a folder called: bootstrap.

3. Go to
   `https://github.com/twbs/bootstrap-sass/tree/master/assets/stylesheets/`
   `bootstrap`, copy all content, and paste it into the
   `public/css/vendor/bootstrap` folder.

4. Inside the `public/css/vendor` folder, create a new file called
   `_bootstrap.scss` and add the following code:

```
/*!
 * Bootstrap v3.3.6 (http://getbootstrap.com)
 * Copyright 2011-2015 Twitter, Inc.
 * Licensed under MIT (https://github.com/twbs/bootstrap/blob/
   master/LICENSE)
 */

// Core variables and mixins
@import "bootstrap/variables";
@import "bootstrap/mixins";

// Reset and dependencies
@import "bootstrap/normalize";
@import "bootstrap/print";
@import "bootstrap/glyphicons";

// Core CSS
@import "bootstrap/scaffolding";
@import "bootstrap/type";
@import "bootstrap/code";
@import "bootstrap/grid";
@import "bootstrap/tables";
@import "bootstrap/forms";
@import "bootstrap/buttons";

// Components
@import "bootstrap/component-animations";
@import "bootstrap/dropdowns";
@import "bootstrap/button-groups";
@import "bootstrap/input-groups";
@import "bootstrap/navs";
@import "bootstrap/navbar";
@import "bootstrap/breadcrumbs";
@import "bootstrap/pagination";
@import "bootstrap/pager";
@import "bootstrap/labels";
@import "bootstrap/badges";
@import "bootstrap/jumbotron";
@import "bootstrap/thumbnails";
@import "bootstrap/alerts";
```

```scss
@import "bootstrap/progress-bars";
@import "bootstrap/media";
@import "bootstrap/list-group";
@import "bootstrap/panels";
@import "bootstrap/responsive-embed";
@import "bootstrap/wells";
@import "bootstrap/close";

// Components w/ JavaScript
@import "bootstrap/modals";
@import "bootstrap/tooltip";
@import "bootstrap/popovers";
@import "bootstrap/carousel";

// Utility classes
@import "bootstrap/utilities";
@import "bootstrap/responsive-utilities";
```

Creating a custom stylesheet

Inside the `public/css/` folder, create a new file called `main.scss` and add the following
code:

```scss
// import bootstrap
@import "vendor/bootstrap";

// Structure
html {
  position: relative;
  min-height: 100%;
}

body {
  margin-bottom: 44px;
}

footer {
  position: absolute;
  width: 100%;
  height: 44px;
  padding: 10px 30px;
  bottom: 0;
  background-color: #fff;
  border-top: 1px solid #e0e0e0;
}

.login-container {
```

```
    max-width: 555px;
}

// Warning
.alert {
  border-width: 0 0 0 3px;
}

// Panels
.panel {
  border: solid 1px rgba(160, 160, 160, 0.3);
  box-shadow: 0 1px 4px 0 rgba(0, 0, 0, 0.1);
}

.panel-heading + .panel-body {
  padding-top: 0;
}

.panel-body {
  h1, h2, h3, h4, h5, h6 {
    margin-top: 0;
  }
}

.panel-title {
  font-size: 18px;
  color: #424242;
}

// Form
textarea {
  resize: none;
}

.form-control {
  height: auto;
  padding: 8px 12px;
  border: 2px solid #ebebeb;
  border-radius: 0;
  box-shadow: inset 0 1px 2px rgba(150, 160, 175, 0.1), inset 0 1px
  15px rgba(150, 160, 175, 0.05);
}

.form-group > label {
  text-transform: uppercase;
  font-size: 13px;
}
```

Don't worry about the `node-sass` building process now; we have already set up an NPM task in the `package.json` file at the beginning of this chapter.

Creating the fonts folder and adding font files

As we are using the Bootstrap framework, we need a folder to hold all the Bootstrap font files, let's create:

1. Inside the `public` folder, create a new folder called `fonts`.
2. Go to `https://github.com/twbs/bootstrap-sass/tree/master/assets/fonts/bootstrap`, copy all the content, and paste it into the `public/fonts` folder.

Creating the JavaScript folder and files

As we are using the Bootstrap framework, we need a folder to hold all the Bootstrap font files, let's create:

1. Inside the `public` folder, create a new folder `called js`.
2. Inside the `js` folder, create a new folder called `lib`.
3. Inside the `js/lib` create a new file called `bootstrap.js`.
4. Go to `https://github.com/twbs/bootstrap-sass/blob/master/assets/javascripts/bootstrap.js`, copy all the content, and paste it into the `public/js/lib/bootstrap.js` file.
5. Inside `js/lib`, create a new file called `jquery.js`.
6. Go to `https://cdnjs.cloudflare.com/ajax/libs/jquery/2.1.4/jquery.js`, copy all content, and paste it into the `public/js/lib/jquery.js` file.

Creating the views folder and files

Now we will create a very similar folder structure to that in `Chapter 01`, *Building a Twitter-Like Application Using the MVC Design Pattern*; the `views` folder will have the following directories:

```
/ layouts

/ pages

/ partials
```

Adding the layouts folder and file

Inside the `views/layouts` folder, create a new file called `main.html` and add the following code:

```
<!DOCTYPE html>
<html>
  <head>
    <meta charset="utf-8" />
    <meta http-equiv="x-ua-compatible" content="ie=edge">
    <meta name="viewport" content="width=device-width, initial-
     scale=1">
    <title>Chapter-10</title>
      <title>{{title}}</title>
        <link rel="stylesheet" href="/css/main.css">
  </head>
  <body>
    {% include "../partials/header.html" %}
      {% block content %}
      {% endblock %}
    {% include "../partials/footer.html" %}
      <script src="/js/lib/jquery.js"></script>
      <script src="/js/lib/bootstrap.js"></script>
      <script src="/js/main.js"></script>
  </body>
</html>
```

Adding the pages folder and files

It is time to create the application templates files:

1. Inside the `views/pages` folder, create a file called `home.html` and add the following code:

```
{% extends '../layouts/main.html' %}

{% block content %}
  <div class="container">
    {% if messages.success %}
      <div role="alert" class="alert alert-success">
        {% for item in messages.success %}
          <div>{{ item.msg }}</div>
        {% endfor %}
      </div>
    {% endif %}
    {% if messages.error %}
```

```
        <div role="alert" class="alert alert-danger">
          {% for item in messages.error %}
            <div>{{ item.msg }}</div>
          {% endfor %}
        </div>
      {% endif %}
      {% if messages.info %}
        <div role="alert" class="alert alert-info">
          {% for item in messages.info %}
            <div>{{ item.msg }}</div>
          {% endfor %}
        </div>
      {% endif %}
      <div class="app">
        <div class="jumbotron">
          <h1 class="text-center">Node 6 Bluenprints Book</h1>
            <p>This example illustrate how to build, test and deploy
              a Node.js application using: Github, Heroku, MOngolab,
              Codeship and Docker.
            </p>
        </div>
      </div>
  </div>
{% endblock %}
```

2. Inside the `views/pages` folder, create a file called `login.html` and add the following code:

```
{% extends '../layouts/main.html' %}

{% block content %}
  <div class="login-container container">
    <div class="panel">
      <div class="panel-body">
        {% if messages.error %}
          <div role="alert" class="alert alert-danger">
            {% for item in messages.error %}
              <div>{{ item.msg }}</div>
            {% endfor %}
          </div>
        {% endif %}
        <form method="POST">
          <legend>Welcome to login</legend>
          <div class="form-group">
            <label for="email">Email</label>
            <input type="email" name="email" id="email"
              placeholder="Email" class="form-control" autofocus>
          </div>
          <div class="form-group">
            <label for="password">Password</label>
            <input type="password" name="password" id="password"
              placeholder="Password" class="form-control">
          </div>
          <button type="submit" class="btn btn-primary btn-block">
            Sign in</button>
        </form>
      </div>
    </div>
    <p class="text-center">Don't have an account? <a href="/signup">
      <strong>Sign up</strong></a>, it's free.</p>
  </div>
{% endblock %}
```

3. Inside the `views/pages` folder, create a file called `profile.html` and add the following code:

```
{% extends '../layouts/main.html' %}

{% block content %}
  <div class="container">
    <div class="panel">
      <div class="panel-body">
        {% if messages.success %}
          <div role="alert" class="alert alert-success">
            {% for item in messages.success %}
              <div>{{ item.msg }}</div>
            {% endfor %}
          </div>
        {% endif %}
        {% if messages.error %}
          <div role="alert" class="alert alert-danger">
            {% for item in messages.error %}
              <div>{{ item.msg }}</div>
            {% endfor %}
          </div>
        {% endif %}
        <form method="POST" action="/account?_method=PUT">
          <legend>Account Details</legend>
          <div class="form-group">
            <label for="email">Email</label>
            <input type="email" name="email" id="email"
              class="form-control" value="{{user.email}}">
          </div>
          <div class="form-group">
            <label for="name">Name</label>
            <input type="text" name="name" id="name" class="form-
              control" value="{{user.name}}">
          </div>
            <br>
          <div class="form-group">
            <button type="submit" class="btn btn-primary">
              Update Profile</button>
          </div>
        </form>
      </div>
    </div>
    <div class="panel">
      <div class="panel-body">
        <form method="POST" action="/account?_method=PUT">
          <legend>Change Password</legend>
          <div class="form-group">
```

```
            <label for="password">New Password</label>
              <input type="password" name="password" id="password"
                class="form-control">
          </div>
          <div class="form-group">
            <label for="confirm">Confirm Password</label>
              <input type="password" name="confirm" id="confirm"
                class="form-control">
          </div>
          <div class="form-group">
              <button type="submit" class="btn btn-success">
              Change Password</button>
          </div>
        </form>
      </div>
    </div>
    <div class="panel">
      <div class="panel-body">
        <form method="POST" action="/account?_method=DELETE">
          <legend>Delete My Account</legend>
          <div class="form-group">
            <p class="text-muted">It is irreversible action.</p>
              <button type="submit" class="btn btn-danger">
                Delete</button>
          </div>
        </form>
      </div>
    </div>
  </div>
{% endblock %}
```

4. Inside the `views/pages` folder, create a file called `signup.html` and add the following code:

```
{% extends '../layouts/main.html' %}

{% block content %}
<div class="login-container container">
  <div class="panel">
    <div class="panel-body">
      {% if messages.error %}
        <div role="alert" class="alert alert-danger">
          {% for item in messages.error %}
            <div>{{ item.msg }}</div>
          {% endfor %}
        </div>
      {% endif %}
      <form method="POST">
```

```
<legend>Create an account</legend>
<div class="form-group">
  <label for="name">Name</label>
  <input type="text" name="name" id="name"
    placeholder="Name"
    class="form-control" autofocus>
</div>
<div class="form-group">
  <label for="email">Email</label>
  <input type="email" name="email" id="email"
    placeholder="Email" class="form-control">
</div>
<div class="form-group">
  <label for="password">Password</label>
  <input type="password" name="password" id="password"
    placeholder="Password" class="form-control">
</div>
<button type="submit" class="btn btn-primary btn-block">
  Sign up</button>
</form>
</div>
</div>
<p class="text-center"> Already have an account? <a href="/login">
  <strong>Sign in</strong></a></p>
</div>
{% endblock %}
```

Adding the partial folder and files

As we did in previous chapter, we are using the partial views concept, so let's create the `views` files:

1. Inside the `views/partials` folder, create a new file called `footer.html` and add the following code:

```
<footer>
  <div class="container">
    <p>Node.js 6 Blueprints Book Â© 2016. All Rights Reserved.</p>
  </div>
</footer>
```

2. Inside the `views/partials` folder, create a new file called `header.html` and add the following code:

```
<nav class="navbar navbar-default navbar-static-top">
  <div class="container">
```

```
              <div class="navbar-header">
                <button type="button" data-toggle="collapse"
                  data-target="#navbar" class="navbar-toggle collapsed">
                  <span class="sr-only">Toggle navigation</span>
                  <span class="icon-bar"></span>
                  <span class="icon-bar"></span>
                  <span class="icon-bar"></span>
                </button>
                <a href="/" class="navbar-brand">N6B</a>
              </div>
              <div id="navbar" class="navbar-collapse collapse">
                <ul class="nav navbar-nav">
                  <li class="{% if  title == 'Home' %}active{% endif %}">
                  <a href="/">Home</a></li>
                </ul>
              <ul class="nav navbar-nav navbar-right">
              {% if user %}
                <li class="dropdown">
                  <a href="#" data-toggle="dropdown"
                    class="navbar-avatar dropdown-toggle">
                    {% if user.picture %}
                      <img src="{{user.picture}}">
                    {% else %}
                      <img src="{{user.gravatar}}">
                    {% endif %}
                    {% if user.name %}
                      {{user.name}}
                    {% else %}
                      {{user.email}}
                    {% endif %}
                    <i class="caret"></i>
                  </a>
                  <ul class="dropdown-menu">
                    <li><a href="/account">My Account</a></li>
                    <li class="divider"></li>
                    <li><a href="/logout">Logout</a></li>
                  </ul>
                </li>
              {% else %}
                <li class="{% if  title == 'Log in' %}active{% endif %}">
                  <a href="/login">Log in</a></li>
                <li class="{% if  title == 'Sign up' %}active{% endif %}">
                  <a href="/signup">Sign up</a></li>
              {% endif %}
              </ul>
              </div>
            </div>
          </nav>
```

At this point, we have the application almost ready for deployment, but before we go further, we need to create the `test` folder and file.

Creating the test folder and test file

To run tests on Node.js applications, we need to include some dependencies/modules to help us write these tests. Fortunately, within the Node ecosystem we have many options for modules to use.

Next, we will describe how to write tests for a HTTP server using the **Supertest** module and **Mocha** test runner. The modules that we will need are inserted in our `package.json` file:

```
"devDependencies": {
    "mocha": "^2.4.5",
    "supertest": "^1.2.0"
}
```

Module	Description	More information
Mocha	Test framework	`https://mochajs.org`
Supertest	For testing HTTP servers	`https://www.npmjs.com/package/supertest`

Tests for web applications are a very complex subject and deserves a deeper approach, but we'll see how to write unit tests and how to run tests with Mocha in a Node.js application:

1. Inside the root project folder, create a new folder called `test`.
2. Inside the `test/` folder, create a new file called `app-test.js` and add the following code:

```
// import modules
var request = require('supertest');
var server = require('../server');
// Test 01
describe('GET /', function() {
  it('should render ok', function(done) {
    request(server)
    .get('/')
    // expected result
    .expect(200, done);
  });
});

// Test 02
describe('GET /bikes', function() {
  it('should not found', function(done) {
```

```
        request(server)
        .get('/bikes')
        // expected result
        .expect(404, done);
    });
});
```

The test cases are pretty simple where:

- *Test 01:*

    Checks the root URL and expect a HTTP status code of 200.

- *Test 02:*

    Expects a HTTP status code of 404.

Now let's see how to execute these tests.

 Note that you must have MongoDB up and running on your machine.

3. Replace the `.env` file at the root project folder with the following information:

```
SESSION_SECRET="3454321234"
MONGODB="localhost"
```

Note that later in the book, we will restore this file to its original state.

4. Open the terminal/shell inside the root project and type the following command:

    npm install

5. Now type the following command:

    npm test

You should see the following result on your terminal output:

```
> mocha



Express server listening on port 3000
  GET /
GET / 200 54.638 ms - -
    ✓ should render ok (151ms)

  GET /bikes
GET /bikes 404 4.402 ms - 18
    ✓ should not found


  2 passing (195ms)
```

Terminal output after tests

Note that both tests passed with a green check icon on the left-hand side of the test description.

Running the application

Now it is time to check the application:

1. Open the terminal and type the following command:

```
npm start
```

2. Go to `http://localhost:3000/signup` and create a new account with the following information:

   Name: `John Doe`

   Email: `john@doe.com`

   Password: `123456`

N6B	Home		Log in	Sign up

Create an account

NAME

Name

EMAIL

Email

PASSWORD

Password

Sign up

Already have an account? Sign in

Node.js 6 Blueprints Book © 2016. All Rights Reserved.

Signup page

After the signup process, go to `http://localhost:3000/account` and see the following screenshot, with the user information:

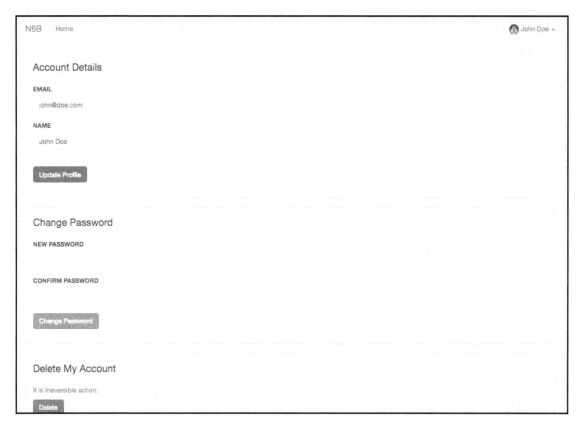

Account information

Creating a GitHub or Bitbucket free account

You can choose what service to use, as GitHub and Bitbucket do the same thing: host public and private repositories of code for collaborative software development.

The functionality of both are similar and both use git as source control. We will see how to use GitHub, but the process for Bitbucket is very similar.

> You can find more information about Bitbucket at this link: `https://bitbucket.org/`.

Creating a GitHub free account

Let's create a GitHub account:

1. Go to `https://github.com/join`, fill in the form and click the **Create an account** button.
2. Choose the **Unlimited public repositories for free** checkbox and click the **Continue** button.
3. On the third step, you must answer three questions or choose to skip this step; click the **Submit** button. From here, you can read the guide or start a project.

> Note that you need to verify your e-mail before starting a project.

4. Click the **Start a project** button and fill in the repository's name, remembering you can use this name on GitHub, but you need to choose another name for the Heroku and Codeship process. After that, you will see the following screenshot:

GitHub project

Later in the chapter, we will see how to initialize a local GIT repository and how to push the source code to GitHub repository.

Creating a Heroku free account

In the previous chapter, we deployed the application directly to Heroku using the Heroku toolbelt commands. This time, you can use the same account that we created in Chapter 09, *Building a Frontend Process with Node.js and NPM* or create a new one at https://www.heroku.com/.

Creating a MongoLab free sandbox account

MongoLab is cloud service required to use MongoDB as a service. It offers a free limited account as a sandbox, so we can use it to deploy our project:

1. Proceed to the **Sign Up** page; after that, you will receive two emails from MongoLab, one with a welcome message and another with a link to verify your account, if you don't have one yet.

   After you verify your account, you will see the following screenshot when logging in to your dashboard:

MongoLab welcome screen

2. Click on the **Create new** button.
3. Choose the **Single-node** tab.
4. From the standard line panel, choose the first checkbox for **Sandbox**.
5. Scroll down to the end of the page and insert a database name, **nb6**, and click on the C**reate new mongodb Deployment** button.

At the end of these five steps, you should see the following screen:

Database created at MongoLab

Creating a user and password for the database

It' time to create a user and password to protect our database on the cloud:

1. Click on the database name.

   You will see the following warning, suggesting you create a user and password:

Database warning: no user and password

2. Click on the **Click here** link inside the warning message.
3. Insert the following information:

   ```
   database username: nb6
   database password: node6
   ```

4. Click on the **Create User** button.

Getting the string connection

Now we have a MongoDB instance running on the MongoLab cloud service. And here's the connection string that we will use later in the chapter:

```
mongodb://<user>:<password>@ds023074.mlab.com:23074/nb6
```

You must replace the previous code with your own user and password.

Initializing a git repository and pushing to GitHub

At this time we will create our local git repository and then uploads it to account we just created on GitHub:

1. Open the terminal/shell inside the root application folder and type the following command:

   ```
   git init
   ```

2. Add a `remote repository` to project by typing the following command in the terminal/shell:

   ```
   git remote add origin https://github.com/<your github account
     name>/n6b.git
   ```

   You must use your own github username in the previous code.

3. Add all project files to source control by typing the following command in the terminal/shell:

   ```
   git add .
   ```

4. Commit the project changes by typing the following command in the terminal/shell:

   ```
   git commit -m "initial commit"
   ```

The last command is to upload all files to the GitHub repository that we created before.

5. Type the followingcommand in the terminal/shell:

```
git push -u origin master
```

Creating a Heroku application using Heroku Dashboard

This time, we will see another way to create a project using the Heroku cloud service:

1. Go to `https://dashboard.heroku.com/apps`.
2. On the Heroku dashboard, click on the **New** button, and then click on the create **new app** link.
3. Enter the following name in the app input name field: `chapter-10-yourname`
4. Click on the **Create app** button.

Linking the Heroku application to your git repository

Now we need to set up our account on Heroku to link to our github account. So let's do it the next steps:

1. On Heroku dashboard, click on the `chapter-10-yourname` project name.
2. Click on the **Settings** tab, scroll down the page to **Domains**, and copy the Heroku domain URL:

   `chapter-10-yourname.herokuapp.com`

 Note that we can't use the same name for all applications, so you need to provide your name after chapter-10.

Later we will use the app name to configure the Codeship deployment pipeline, so don't forget it.

Adding environment variables to Heroku

Now we need to create some environment variables to keep our database string safe in our public github repository:

1. On Heroku dashboard, click on the `chapter-10-yourname` project name.
2. Click on the **Settings** tab.
3. On the **Settings** tab, click on the **Reveal Config Vars** button.
4. Add your own variables, as shown in the following screenshot. On the left, add the variable name, and on the right, and add the value:

Heroku environment variables

Note that you must repeat this process on the Codeship configuration project.

Creating a Codeship free account

Codeship is a cloud service for Continuous Integration (CI) tools. It's pretty simple to create an account:

1. Go to `https://codeship.com/sessions/new` and use the **SIGN UP** button in the top-right corner. You can use your GitHub or Bitbucket account; just click your preferred button. As we are using GitHub, we will choose GitHub.
2. Click on the **AUTHORIZE APPLICATION** button.

You should see the following screen:

Codeship dashboard

The next step is to click on where you are hosting your code. In this case, we will click on the **GitHub** icon, so we will see the following screen:

Second step for Codeship configuration

3. Copy and paste the GitHub repository URL (`https://github.com/<yourusername>/n6b.git`) created in the GitHub setup process, and paste it into the **Repository Clone URL** input, as shown in the previous image.
4. Click the **Connect** button.

Now we have set up our development environment with three tools: GitHub, Codeship, and Heroku. The next step is to create setup and test commands and add a pipeline deployment to the Codeship dashboard.

Adding environment variables to Codeship

Now let's do the same as we did with the Heroku dashboard, and add the same variables to Codeship:

1. Go to `https://codeship.com/projects/` and select the `chapter-10-yourname` project.
2. Click on the **Project Settings** link in the top-right corner, as shown here:

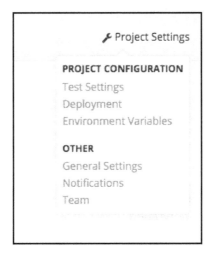

Project settings menu in the Codeship dashboard

3. Click on the **Environment Variables** link.
4. Add the Session and MongoDB variables and values, as we previously did with the configuration of the Heroku environment variables, and click the **Save configuration** button.

Creating setup and test commands in the Codeship project configuration

Now we go back to the codeship control panel, and configure the test and dploy commands for our application:

1. Paste the following code into the setup commands text area:

```
# By default we use the Node.js version set in your package.json
```

```
       or the latest
# version from the 0.10 release
#
# You can use nvm to install any Node.js (or io.js) version you
require.
# nvm install 4.0
# nvm install 0.10
npm install
npm run build
```

2. Paste the following code into the test commands text area:

   npm test

3. Click on the **Save and go to dashboard** button.

Creating the pipeline for deployment on Heroku

Well, we are almost there; now we need to create a pipeline to integrate the build with our deployment environment on Heroku:

1. Click on the **Project Settings** link in the top-right corner and then click on the **Deployment** link, as shown here:

2. At the **Enter branchname** input, type the following name: master.

3. Click on the **Save Pipeline Setting** button.
4. On the **Add new deployment pipeline** tab, choose the **Heroku** banner.

Now we will fill in the input fields as shown here:

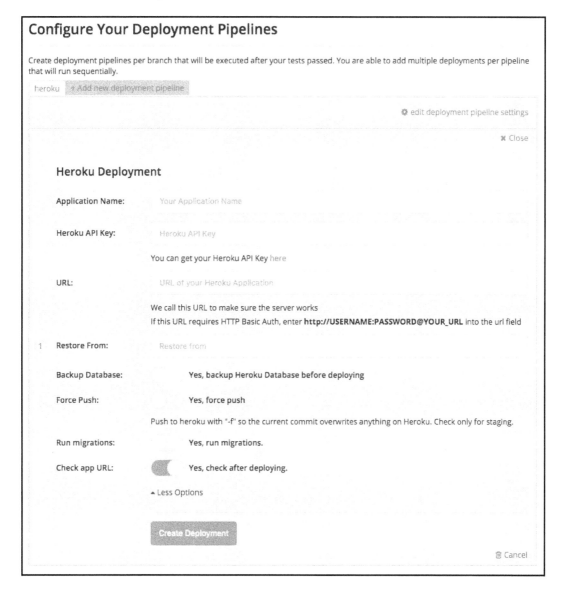

Codeship Heroku deployment configuration panel

Adding the Heroku API key to Codeship

To provide the informationrequired in the previous screenshot, we need to follow these steps:

1. Open a new browser window and go to Heroku dashboard at `https://id.heroku.com/login`.
2. Click on your **Picture** in the top-right corner, and then click on **Account Settings**.
3. Scroll down the page for API Key and click on **Show API Key**, as shown here:

Show API Key Heroku dashboard

4. Insert your password and copy the API key.
5. Go back to the Codeship browser window and paste the key into the **Heroku API key** input field.
6. Name your application: `n6b-your-own-name`.
7. Add the application URL: `http://chapter-10-your-own-name.herokuapp.com/`.
8. Click on the **Save Deployment** button.

This step completes our continuous integration. Every time we modify our code and send the changes to GitHub or Bitbucket, Codeship will run the code and the tests we set when we created the Node.js application earlier in this chapter.

At the end of testing, if everything is ok, our code is sent to Heroku and will be available at `http://chapter-10-yourname.herokuapp.com/`.

Checking the test and deploy steps on the Codeship dashboard

At this point we already have the necessary commands to set test and deploy, however we need to check that everything is correctly configured:

1. Go to `https://codeship.com/sessions/new`.
2. Log in to your account.

3. In top-left corner, click on the **Select Project** link.
4. Click on the `n6b-your-own-name` project name and you will see all your commits with **Success**, **Running**, or **Failed** flags.

When we click on one of then, we can see the following screenshot with a step-by-step process:

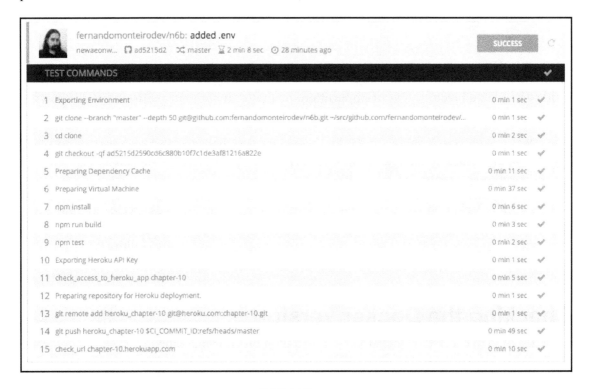

Codeship building steps

Here we have a successful build, as we can see the green check icon on the right of each step.

Note that if the testing process fails at any time, the code doesn't go to the production server, in this case Heroku.

Installing Docker and setting up the application

Before we go further, we need to understand what Docker is and the concept of containers.

 You can read more about containers at this link: `https://www.docker.com/what-docker#/VM`.

Thinking in a very simple way, Docker creates micro machines (that is, operating systems) inside an isolated box to run your application, no matter what your platform is (Windows, Linux, or OSX). Let's see what the official Docker site says:

> *"Docker containers wrap a piece of software in a complete filesystem that contains everything needed to run: code, runtime, system tools, system libraries – anything that can be installed on a server."*

So let's install Docker on your machine. A Windows machine deserves special attention, but you can find the relevant information at the following link: `https://docs.docker.com/engine/installation/windows/`. Go to `https://docs.docker.com/` and follow the instructions for your platform.

Checking the Docker version

Now it is time to check the Docker version installed on your machine:

Open the terminal/shell and type the following commands to check the version of each part:

```
docker --version
docker-compose --version
docker-machine --version
```

Creating a Docker file

To dockerize our application in a container, we need to create two files, a `Dockerfile` and a `docker-compose.yml` file, to link our application container with a MongoDb database:

1. Inside the root folder, create a new file called `Dockerfile` and add the following code:

```
FROM node:argon

# Create app directory
RUN mkdir -p /usr/src/app
WORKDIR /usr/src/app

# Install app dependencies
COPY package.json /usr/src/app/
RUN npm install
ENV PORT 3000
ENV DB_PORT_27017_TCP_ADDR db

# Bundle app source
COPY . /usr/src/app

EXPOSE 3000
CMD [ "npm", "start" ]
```

Note that the line `ENV DB_PORT_27017_TCP_ADDR` indicates the Docker container port for MongoDB; it's an environment variable.

2. Inside the root folder, create a new file called `docker-compose.yml` and add the following code:

```
app:
  build: .
  ports:
    - "3000:3000"
  links:
    - db
db:
  image: mongo
  ports:
    - "27017:27017"
```

The `db` line was set up with the `ENV DB_PORT_27017_TCP_ADDR db` name.

Before we go further, let's check out some useful Docker commands:

Command	Description
`docker ps -a`	List all containers
`docker images`	List all images
`docker rm containername`	Remove a specific container
`docker rm $(docker ps -a -q)`	Remove all containers
`docker rmi imagename`	Remove a specific image
`docker rmi $(docker images -q)`	Remove all images
`docker run containername`	Run a container
`docker stop containername`	Stop a container
`docker stop $(docker ps -a -q)`	Stop all containers

We have more commands, but during the course of the chapter we will see others.

Creating a Docker image

At this point we already have the necessary commands to set test and deploy, however we need to check that everything is correctly configured:

1. Create the Docker image for your project:

   ```
   docker build -t <your docker user name>/<projectname> .
   ```

   At the end of the output on the terminal, we can see a message similar to this: **Successfully built c3bbc61f92a6**. Now let's check the image already created.

2. Check the images by opening terminal/shell and typing the following command:

   ```
   docker images
   ```

Preparing and running the Docker image

Now let's test our Docker image. Before we proceed, we need to make a small change to our application:

1. Open the `server.js` file at the root folder and replace the following code:

```
mongoose.connect('mongodb://' + (process.env.DB_PORT_27017_TCP_ADDR
|| process.env.MONGODB) + '/<database name>');
```

2. Now open the `.env` file and replace the code with the following lines:

```
SESSION_SECRET=
   'ae37a4318f1218302e16e1516e4144df8a273798b151ca06062c142bbfcc23bc'

MONGODB='localhost:27017'
```

Step 1 and step 2 uses local credentials, different from what we do for deployment. So after configuring the environment variables on Heroku and Codeship, remove the `.env` file from GitHub tracking, but keep it on your local machine with your local credentials.

Now it is time to get a MongoDB image from Docker hub.

1. Open the terminal/shell and type the following command:

   `docker pull mongo`

   The previous command will get a new image for MongoDB. You can use the same command to get any image from Docker hub.

You can find more images at this link: `https://hub.docker.com/explore /`.

4. Start a new MongoDB container named `db` with the following command:

   `docker run -d --name db mongo`

5. Now we need to link one container to another; type the following command:

   `docker run -p 3000:3000 --link db:db <your docker user name> /<projectname>`

6. Go to `http://localhost:3000` and you will see your application running. It will look the same as it does on your machine.

Uploading the project image to your Docker hub account

Now, is time to upload your image to Docker hub, and make it available to other users.

> You can read more about **Docker hub** at this link: `https://docs.docker.com/docker-hub/`.

1. Go to `https://cloud.docker.com/` and create a free account.
2. After confirming your e-mail address, go to the `https://cloud.docker.com` sign in menu. You will see the following dashboard:

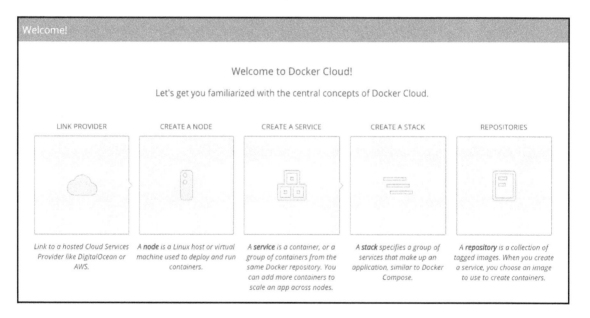

Docker hub dashboard

When you click on the **REPOSITORIES** button, you will see it is empty. So now let's push our Docker image to Docker hub.

3. Open the terminal/shell and type the following command:

```
docker login
```

Enter your credentials, the ones you created in the registration process.

4. To upload the project to Docker hub, run the following command on the terminal/shell:

```
docker push <your docker user name>/<projectname>
```

5. Go back to `https://cloud.docker.com/_/repository/list`, refresh the page, and you will see your repository published on Docker hub.

Docker is a powerful tool and must be explored further, but from this chapter we have enough knowledge to build Node.js applications with MongoDB using Docker containers, which means that you can use the container we've created on any machine. It doesn't matter what platform you use, you just need to install Docker and pull the image to your machine.

You can get any image and start to play with it on your command line.

Summary

By the end of this chapter, you should be capable of building and deploying an application using all the most modern technologies and tools that we have available at the moment to create amazing web applications.

We've explored all the resource needed to build an application using continuous delivery and Continuous Integration, combining with Git source control, GitHub, Codeship, Heroku, and Docker. We also saw how to use environment variables on both Heroku cloud services for production and Codeship for tests and continuous integration.

Index

www.ingramcontent.com/pod-product-compliance
Lightning Source LLC
Chambersburg PA
CBHW062049050326
40690CB00016B/3027